FORGED BY SPEED

FORGED BY SPEED
THE MAKING OF A MOUNTAIN BIKE WORLD CHAMPION

STEVE PEAT

WITH
TIM MARCH

Vertebrate Publishing, Sheffield
www.adventurebooks.com

FORGED BY SPEED

Steve Peat, with Tim March

First published in 2024 by Vertebrate Publishing.

VERTEBRATE PUBLISHING, Omega Court, 352 Cemetery Road, Sheffield S11 8FT, United Kingdom. *www.adventurebooks.com*

Copyright © Steve Peat 2024.

Front cover: Racing the 2010 Fort William downhill world cup as world champion.
© Sven Martin.

Photography and images © Steve Peat Collection unless otherwise credited.

Steve Peat and Tim March have asserted their rights under the Copyright, Designs and Patents Act 1988 to be identified as authors of this work.

This book is a work of non-fiction based on the life of Steve Peat. The authors have stated to the publishers that, except in such minor respects not affecting the substantial accuracy of the work, the contents of the book are true. Some names and incidental details have been changed to protect the privacy of contributors.

A CIP catalogue record for this book is available from the British Library.

ISBN: 978-1-83981-096-1 (Hardback)

ISBN: 978-1-83981-098-5 (Ebook)

ISBN: 978-1-83981-099-2 (Audiobook)

10 9 8 7 6 5 4 3 2 1

All rights reserved. No part of this work covered by the copyright herein may be reproduced or used in any form or by any means – graphic, electronic, or mechanised, including photocopying, recording, taping or information storage and retrieval systems – without the written permission of the publisher.

Every effort has been made to obtain the necessary permissions with reference to copyright material, both illustrative and quoted. We apologise for any omissions in this respect and will be pleased to make the appropriate acknowledgements in any future edition.

Vertebrate Publishing is committed to printing on paper from sustainable sources.

Printed and bound in the UK by TJ Books Limited, Padstow, Cornwall.

CONTENTS

Introduction: Blowing It	vii
1. Made in Sheffield	1
2. Trials	13
3. Fancy Riders	21
4. Red Seal Blues	31
5. Roadrunner	41
6. Coming up Fast	51
7. Fork in the Road	61
8. Lift-off	71
9. A Wide River to Cross	83
10. Amateur Dramatics	93
11. A Heart of Gold	107
12. The Mechanic	119
13. 3:55.23	127
14. Appetite for Destruction	137
15. No Cigar	149
16. The Orange Years	161
17. With or Without You	171
18. Say Hello, Wave Goodbye	181
19. Last Orders	191
20. Every King	203
Epilogue: No Final Curtain	217
Acknowledgements	223
Black & White Photographs	225

INTRODUCTION: BLOWING IT

I used to love being at the top of the hill in the minutes before a race. I'd start heading up there an hour before my start time, my bike on the outside of the gondola as we were both carried up the mountain. I'd cruise around the top, chatting to everyone. It was amazing how each of my rivals dealt with the pressure. If you're into bike racing then I recommend you go to the start gate of a downhill world cup or world championships and feel the tension rising among racers who have only three or four minutes to prove their worth and watch how they deal with that.

I had my own rituals. I'd look at the first couple of turns to see how the track was running and then thirty minutes before show time I'd start warming up on the turbo trainer, get my muscles working. I'd put tissues soaked in Olbas Oil up my nostrils to keep my airways clear. Doing the same things at the same times before each race calmed my nerves. And if that didn't work, if the nerves started to take over, I'd calm myself by visualising the track. By race day I knew every inch, every root and stone. I could see it all in my head. Five minutes before my start time I'd be off the turbo trainer and on to my downhill bike and riding around for a couple of minutes, settling in.

It was no different that late summer day in 2004 at Les Gets in the French Alps. I loved the track and the place. I'd won there before. Yet this race was different. This was the world championships. For more than a decade I'd been trying to win this title and I had a hunch this would finally be my year. In that time, I'd gone from being a lanky kid from Sheffield to the winner of two world cup series. Everything I was had come through racing. I'd travelled the world, met my wife, bought my house and found my place, all from mountain biking. Now I felt confident I would win the one prize that had escaped me.

Six or seven weeks before the race at Les Gets I'd snapped my collarbone. I'd needed surgery to fix it and followed that with experimental treatment to get me back on my bike. By the time I arrived in France it felt much improved, but in everyone else's eyes I was coming back injured. Nobody had me down as the favourite at the start of the weekend. I was the underdog and that was just how I liked it. I never wanted the pressure of being the favourite. I liked to catch my rivals unawares and take the pressure off myself. By the time I reached the gate that day, they knew I was the one to beat. I'd qualified fastest and that meant I was last down the mountain. At the bottom, French rider Fabien Barel was in the lead, in the hot seat as we say, waiting to see if I could beat him. I felt good. I felt this race was mine.

The gate sat above a steep ramp, protected from the sun by an open tent with a striped green roof. With a couple of minutes to go I took my place in its shade with my mechanic Ricky Bobby. There was a race official waiting there with the official timekeeper. I got the minute warning and another with thirty seconds to go. At that moment Ricky handed me my goggles. My feet were turning the cranks backwards, keeping my legs loose while I balanced myself on the bike with my left hand on the guardrail. Then the beeps started. I could leave any time in the next five seconds. I leant back and then fired myself forwards down the ramp and on to the mountain.

Throughout my career I always wanted to push things to the limit. Some of my fellow pros were more interested in riding for their sponsors, especially if their contract was up for renewal. Their focus was keeping the show on the road. All I wanted was to win and figured if I did the best I could then my career would last anyway. That way I could keep winning longer. When I look back on my two decades racing, my results show I was right. Despite the physical risks of downhill, despite giving it my all every time and despite how much I liked to party, I still managed to be among the most consistent riders of my generation. Pedal to the metal has its advantages.

A minute and a half into my run at Les Gets and things were going well. And if a race went well then afterwards I found my memory of it faded sooner. I can barely remember my best runs. It's the mistakes that stick out. On a great run my focus was so good that the crowds along the track disappeared. Mostly I was aware of them flicking past in my peripheral vision. At Les Gets I remember racing across some open fields before a fast left-hander to the first split that showed I was already more than a second ahead of Fabien. I didn't know that of course. He did. The TV cameras show his face suddenly become serious as he sees my time. You can see the doubt. If I kept this up, he was going to lose. I was just bombing down the mountain, laser-focused on the task at hand. As a rider I always knew when I was on a good run. And that day I was on it.

Having crossed the road I had less than a minute to go. I came down a steep grass bank gathering speed. There was a gap over a small stream and after that the track went up a bit of a rise before dropping down again to a left-hander round a huge tree and then a final jump to the finish. I'd never had a problem on this section of the course before, but I guess I came into it a little hot and a microsecond too slow on the brakes. Over the course of the weekend the track had dried out and the ground had worn, exposing the roots of the tree a bit more. My back wheel kicked up and lost traction. I leaned forward to move my weight over the front wheel, but it wasn't enough. I went into a speedway-style turning slide.

The tyres must have missed just about everything they needed to grab on to for me to save the slide I was now in. All they touched was loose dirt. I was collapsing, my lower body shoved down low trying to save this monstrous slide into the dip around the tree. My upper body was bunched over the front trying to get some grip somewhere. With both wheels still on the move and all my weight into the bike, as I came out of the dip there was nothing I could do to stop the whole bike spinning round under me. At 2 minutes and 30.7 seconds, just 200 metres and a few seconds from victory, my 2004 world championship title disappeared in a cloud of dust.

Those few seconds would play on my mind for years to come. They probably would still if things hadn't worked out for me. At thirty years old some of my competitors must have thought my chance of ever becoming world champion had gone.

But you don't give up. Not where I'm from.

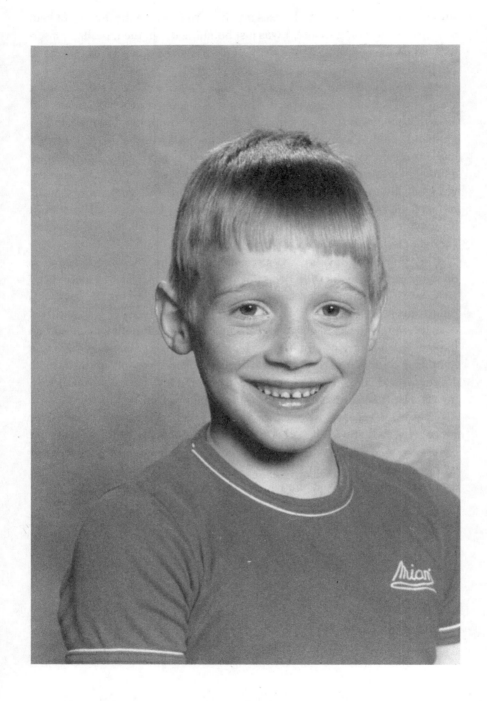

CHAPTER 1
MADE IN SHEFFIELD

Mum and me got chatting over a cuppa one afternoon round at hers. I was telling her about the book you're now reading and some things I'd like to include in it, my birth being one of them. As we sat down to natter, the silent welcome of an old friend wasn't lost on either of us: the house Mum lives in now is the same house we all lived in while I was growing up. It's the house she's lived in for the past fifty-four years of her life. Those walls and Mum's ears have probably heard just about everything that mattered to me when I was a youngster.

I was born in Chapeltown, a northern suburb of Sheffield in South Yorkshire and the best place to live in the whole wide world. My mum and dad had not been living there long. They'd moved into the town's Cowley estate four years before I arrived, after leaving Swinton, about twenty minutes away. For all you literature buffs, Mexborough, the next town east from Swinton, was where poet laureate Ted Hughes was born. Anyway, their middle son Andy arrived when they were living in 'Chap', same as me, but their firstborn, my elder brother Jonny, arrived when they lived back in their Swinton maisonette. One brother would get mad into pubs, clubs and working, the other into music.

It was music lover Andy that I was about to share a room with, being as he was the younger of the two. Though as my due date arrived things weren't right for Mum and me. There were serious complications with my delivery, which very quickly became a medical emergency. As soon as the ambulance crew reached the house and assessed Mum's condition, they got her into the ambulance in a panic and were off, all lights flashing and sirens blaring, racing full tilt to Sheffield's Northern General hospital, flat out, foot to the floor. Start as you mean to go on, I say.

Following us in his car, tailgating the ambulance, was our family doctor, who was doing well to keep up. It's a quarter of an hour's drive from our estate to the Northern during the day, but the roads were empty late at night and the ambulance was running red lights and going the wrong way round roundabouts, not stopping for anything to get us there as quick as it could. Dad was following Dr Cortley in the family's Mini Clubman, although at some distance, since he did stop at all the red lights, law-abiding citizen that he was. He clearly had a respect for our boys in blue that skipped a generation with me. In fact, Dad was so slow following the doctor that by the time Mr Cautious reached the hospital I'd been born in the back of the ambulance at the entrance. There'd been no time to get Mum into the emergency room to deliver me.

So, there I was, close to midnight on 17 June 1974, taking my first breath of beautiful Yorkshire air and snuggling up close to Mum. The panic was over. I was okay, Mum was okay too, thank God. Maybe things could have gone different, but they didn't, thanks to Mum and those first responders in the ambulance who delivered me, and the old fella for making sure he didn't tarnish the Peat family name during a medical emergency with a speeding ticket. It was the week the nation woke up to Ray Stevens' number one hit 'The Streak' and the year Leeds United were the new First Division champions thanks to the dark genius of Don Revie, my dad also hailing from Leeds. It was also the year of the three-day week, two general elections and the continuing Troubles in Northern Ireland.

My new home was a typical newish semi-detached on a suburban estate with a carport and a garage in the back garden. This garage held secrets about Dad's great passion, guarded by a force that me and my brothers would encounter regularly growing up when we fell foul of the military-like rules he imposed on us. Rules, as I soon discovered, were not something that went as well for me as they might. I'd get no encouragement from Dad regarding those secrets in the garage. Thankfully, though, I would get all the encouragement a kid could dream of from my brothers and Mum, encouragement that would give me a life I could not have even imagined in those early years of life on Woodburn Drive.

The house was (and is) right next to Chapeltown Park on Cowley Lane. Chap was a small village before the industrial age. Then it had a blast furnace and later became a coal-mining town. Smithy Wood Colliery had its own coking plant for the steel industry, and had only just closed when we moved to the town. As for living there and having places to play outside, I'd landed on my feet as a nipper. Chap was suburbia, big sprawling housing estates, one of a number of communities that looked pretty similar: Grenoside, Ecclesfield and High Green. Intermingled with the bungalows and semis are large stretches of farmland, parks and woods, as well as commercial estates built on the old industrial sites.

These woods and green fields would soon become my extended garden, a playground where my brothers took me on adventures to discover their secrets. I explored them unaccompanied from a young age, hunting for fun times with the pre-programmed single-mindedness of a heat-seeking missile. The irresistible pull of these woods would in the coming years draw me into new worlds of joy and mischief. So, despite all the troubles of that time casting a black cloud over many working-class families, I was just a brand new happy little kid with the world in front of me.

I'm sure everyone talks about the time they were born as the best, but I don't think anything could better the 1970s and early 1980s for me, despite the awful experiences my parents and families like ours were put through. Some lost their homes, their jobs, even their communities. I can't say I knew a lot about all that. I was too young in the late 1970s to be aware of the big things happening in the country. That stuff isn't important when you're six. I'm well aware of them now and like a lot of people I like to dig about in the past, finding out what those formative years were like for my parents and their three kids. Jonny would have better memories than me. In 1980 he'd have been twelve, and our Andy nine. Yet after talking to Mum, it was clearly a challenging time that affected a lot of people. Reading and watching documentaries made me realise how lucky I was to get through this period unscathed.

The UK was a very different place then than now. Fifty per cent of the country's work force belonged to a trade union. A gallon of petrol was fifty pence. A pint of milk cost four and a half pence, while a pint of beer was twenty-two pence. A single record was forty-five pence, but if you wanted a number one in the charts you'd need to sell about a million of them. Mum and Dad's three-bed house cost £3,500. I've never told them how much I paid for mine. The wages of a Premier League footballer, the First Division as it was called then, were the princely sum of 200 quid a week. The country's identity was much more defined than now but also less polarised between rich and poor. The lives of UK families were being radically transformed by consumerism; the old world was dying and a new one was struggling to be born.

My mum's dad, Grandpa Dixon, had been a colliery manager, so mining was in our family history. Once inflation took off in the early 1970s and there was a public sector wage freeze, it meant a miner's wages were worth less and less. The National Union of Mineworkers went on strike in 1972 and an overtime ban in 1973 prompted Ted Heath to declare his government's fifth state of emergency in just three and a half years. As coal stocks plummeted, he decreed the three-day working week. Pubs were shut, TV finished at 10.30 p.m. and only the hospitals and supermarkets had electricity to work through the week. Oh, and the newspapers. In 1973 the IRA had brought its bombing campaign to mainland Britain and that October the Arab oil embargo spiked petrol costs, which was rationed. Another strike in early 1974 persuaded Heath to go to the country and he lost to Harold Wilson. The miners got their pay rise.

The writing was already on the wall though. Smithy Wood wasn't the only colliery to close around that time. There were 700,000 miners in 1956 but by the early 1970s that number had more than halved to 290,000. For my parents' generation, the nation's troubles were serious. They had come of age in the 1960s, an era of optimism, growth and social mobility. Dad started working as a metallurgist in the steel industry, but when that started to collapse his job prospects looked shaky and he changed again, retraining as a service engineer. He got through a few jobs, first working for a gas welding company selling and mending gas torches and then servicing industrial kitchens where he found stable employment. With three young kids he needed the security.

We fared okay as a family. We weren't broke as both my parents were working. Neither was shy of the graft needed to keep a young family fed, warm and safe. My dad's retraining as a service engineer worked out well and Mum worked part-time, first in a DIY shop and then at a motor factor selling car parts, which meant good things for me and my brothers. Mum would take me to work with her up until I went to school in 1979, my elder brothers being at school already. I managed to keep Mum full of giggles when she was at work at the DIY shop next to the river in Chap. We'd chat and I'd bring her Victorian bottles I'd dug up out of the riverbank behind the shop where I'd be playing, whiling the hours away until we went home. I was innocent about all the world's cares and I have Mum to thank for that. What I know about that time is what was great about it.

I remember kids' TV, everything from *Swap Shop* to *Record Breakers*, although I would always sooner be outside. Sheffield's two million trees made television reception a bit tricky in those analogue days, a situation made worse by the council not allowing aerials on their properties. Dads liked to think they knew a trick or two for tuning their rented TV sets. For a while Sheffield had its own local station Sheffield Cablevision, with a kids' programme called *Hullabaloo*, a bit like *Tiswas*, except only in black and white. The music was also outstanding, everything from T-Rex to the Sex Pistols. Local heroes The Human League released their epoch-making album *Reproduction*.

According to Andy, who is the big music lover in our family, Mum and Dad would always listen to the chart show after we all came back from a motorbike trial he'd been competing in. In Dad's car there would be lots of eight-track cassettes played – Red Army Ensemble, War of the Worlds, pretty spacey weird shit that Andy and him loved, and from what I've heard he was also partial to a bit of Boney M. Mum was born in Wigan so had that Northern Soul thing too. Their marriage was Lancashire and Yorkshire, and she'd say that we all knew who won the Wars of the Roses.

An abundance of sweets was another memory. These days, health experts would look askance at how much sugar we ate as kids. On the other hand, health-wise, only one per cent of men and two per cent of women were obese. The figure now is loads higher. It's as bad for kids. By the time they leave primary school, almost a quarter of kids are obese and in deprived areas that number is higher. It's a different world to that of my childhood. The outdoor life and only three TV channels, plus no computers or mobile phones, must have had something to do with that. I'm no politician or social scientist but I do know we were all far more active then than now. I know we can't go back to those times, many wouldn't want to, but the outdoor life has served me well and maybe it could others.

There was a new energy and excitement in the country about being able to travel abroad. Yet while package holidays were all the rage, we'd take any chance we got to go camping in Britain. My birth didn't put a stop to this and from the start we'd be off round the north of the country. Most weekends as a family we were dragged along to the motorbike trials my dad was riding in with the Hillsborough Motor Cycle Club. He had always been into bikes, long before he got married. Mum would be an observer on a section at each trial and mark all the riders as they came through the challenge set them. She always made sure we'd have a bonfire and there was always something to eat in the picnic box. My brothers and me would bugger about playing in the streams, woods and bracken-covered hills, watching the hundreds of riders and their bikes taking on some really hard and technical riding. We also had our own pushbikes too and made our own obstacles to play around on.

Each year we took our annual family trip to Scotland for the Scottish Six Days Trial. This was a week-long event established in 1909 that largely took place at Fort William but was bookended with visits to Edinburgh. It's a world-class event, a bit like cycling's Tour de France in terms of its status in the trials calendar. Dad's best mate was Dave Thorpe, a Bultaco factory rider, and we were on his helpers team for years. We would go to the event every year without fail, renting a static caravan on Mrs Brown's campsite. Nana and Grandpa Dixon, Mum's parents, would rent one too. The Thorpes would be a few caravans down the line, and we'd have a great time hanging out with Dan and Sarah. Following him about for six days in the Highlands was great, watching all the amazing riders from all over the world and hanging around on our bikes, doing wheelies, jumping and skidding. It was a kid's dream. We tried our hardest to make up sections we could do on our pushbikes, imitating our trials heroes: Martin Lampkin, Dave Thorpe, Malcolm Rathmell and Tony Scarlett. This was long before a mountain bike touched down at Fort Bill, so for those that know a little of my career you can now appreciate why the place is so dear to me.

From 1977 the Scottish Six Days Trial changed slightly, dropping the connection to Edinburgh, so we were based at Fort William for the whole week. This made things a lot easier. Dad had a good level of competence on his bike and was a well-rounded rider, expert at his level, with years of experience. He was handy on a bike. I've since done the Scottish a few times myself and it's a truly brutal event. I've finished it too, I'm pleased to say, because there's many that don't. One year I had to retire with an infected elbow injury, so I know how bloody hard it is on the body.

Mum would help at events at the Hillsborough M.C.C. every weekend and in the week did the club's secretarial work and organised its annual dinner. As boys we'd be dragged everywhere Dad wanted to ride or help his mates who rode at the Scottish. We had great holidays in North Wales too. All five of us camped in a huge tent in the beautiful countryside of the Llŷn Peninsula, cooking all our food on a Calor Gas stove, spending a week on the beaches and playing silly buggers, having the time of our lives. I looked forward to those holidays every year.

Due to my high energy and penchant for being adventurous, my future of fun was pretty much mapped out already. With two older brothers, one six years older, one three years older, and both up for mischief, it was inevitable. I was outside with them a lot, which was fine by me. Every opportunity I got I spent it outdoors. But if we ever heard a high-pitched whistle, the kind that only dads can do through their front teeth, we knew we were late for tea and would have to leg it back as quick as possible so as not to piss Dad off. If we were late there would be hell to pay; being the youngest, it was less bad for me. My brothers got the worst of it. I don't think Dad had heard of nurturing kids. His approach to fatherhood was to be a stickler for rules and deliver physical punishment if they weren't followed.

When I talk to her about it now, not long after Dad passed away, Mum mentions how she and Dad were sometimes at loggerheads over how to bring us up. This created a conflict in their relationship although it never got in Mum's way of looking after me, Andy and Jonny. They weren't a united team in that respect. He was incredibly uptight and strict, while she was far more balanced and easy-going. Like me, she's a glass-half-full kind of person and that seemed to work better with us boys.

Maintaining motorbikes between weekend events takes up a lot of time, especially if you compete as a dedicated amateur or wannabe pro, which Dad was. It's a seven-days-a-week hobby; work was something that just got in the way. There's loads to do: bikes need hosing down – no jet washes then, dirty gear needs washing, boots need cleaning and polishing, and there's lots of work to be done on the bike before it's ready to be ridden at the next event. Every nut and bolt needs checking and tyres and wheels going over. It's lots of work and requires total commitment to the mundane. There are rewards too, which is why Dad loved it, and I do too.

You're probably asking yourself where he kept all this stuff: his bike, his tools and parts, all the rest of it. Where was this magical storeroom? It was of course the flat-roofed, single-skin brick structure at the side of our house: the garage. This was an Aladdin's cave of a place that hid secrets us boys wanted to know. It was for me and my brothers a place that held a lot of joy and also some conflict. Because Dad guarded this eight-foot-by-sixteen-foot Tardis with a set of strict regulations and protocols that he constantly reinforced.

It's no wonder with eight or more bikes in the garage to maintain that when he'd come home from work he would immediately disappear in there for the rest of the evening. Not before he'd had his tea though. Inside he'd while away the hours tinkering with something or other he was working on, as well as maintaining the bikes he had running, so they were at their best mechanically and safe to ride at whatever events the Hillsborough M.C.C. and other clubs he was affiliated with put on. There was somewhere to ride every weekend.

After having bikes myself and riding some competitive trials I can easily see how that garage got so full up with gear. It was wall-to-wall chaos. Mine could easily be the same. I find it no less difficult to chuck stuff away: chip off the old block in that respect. Back then he was doing everything on his own in there and he wouldn't take any help from any of his boys, which I guess suited us and allowed us to get out and do whatever we wanted.

Not all of Dad's bikes were built up. Some were being fixed; some were in the process of being put back together; some were simply being maintained. There was stuff everywhere. There were some basic engineering tools like a pillar drill, some grinding wheels bolted to a work bench, a few welding kits too, and other stuff you could use to engineer bits and bobs. There were also a couple of big toolboxes – both of which I now have in my garage – that were full to the brim with spanners, pliers and all manner of tools. It was all useful stuff you needed to have if you were going to be maintaining motorbikes and making things from metal or wood, or fixing stuff that had broken.

The hobby engineering kit he had was used to make custom bits for his trials bikes. He made some really special things to help them run better than standard. Dave Thorpe was a sponsored factory rider for Spanish manufacturers Ossa and Bultaco, and later the Bolton company CCM. He was a handy bloke to know, and Dad knew many of the other top pros as well. Dad would have got some ideas of how to tune his bike up and make trick bits from looking at their bikes and picking the mechanics' brains at events.

Along two walls of the garage was a bench whose surface was covered in engine parts, nuts, bolts, screws and other bits of motorcycle – anything from petrol tanks to mudguards and everything in between. It seemed complete chaos. Every inch of all the work surfaces and floor were piled high with motorbike bits in various states of repair. It was so bad that every time he wanted to work on a project, the garage had to be cleared of this debris so he had the space to move around. This meant our pushbikes being out in the garden irrespective of the weather, and along with them four or five of his motorbikes and other odds and sods. They at least had covers to keep them dry. That didn't change over the whole of his lifetime: more stuff going in, stuff coming out, stuff being taken apart, stuff being put back together. Patterns.

Being an engineer, Dad was really good at making stuff. He had an eye for turning what looked like a pile of junk into something useful for us kids. One year he made us all an amazing go-kart with pram wheels on the front and a rear axle from an old Mini. He kept all the motorised and non-motorised vehicles running, and anything else around the house that had a motor. We never knew what he might have in the back of his work van when he came home. It could be battered bikes found on scrap heaps, bits of old motorbikes and cars, or some other item he'd dug out of a skip. As well as being a hoarder, he was the original skip rat.

For as long as I can remember it was drilled into us that the garage was and always would be Dad's space, and no one else's. If we were to touch or use anything it would have to be put back in the exact same place it was found. The garage became a minefield of his making, and the penalty for stepping on one was usually a wallop. The fear he instilled in us and his willingness to punish held a palpable psychic power over me, Andy and Jonny. As in Super Mario Kart, we'd have an idea when Dad's bananas would show up because we had inadvertently pressed the banana button. I'm sure we all dealt with it differently, but for me it was no fun watching my brothers get clobbered for doing nothing that might warrant it. As both Andy and Jonny grew up and got their own motorbikes, they would also be in there, adding to the pressure.

Tony Peat was well known for his temper. We'd heard stories from friends of his, about him chucking rocks at his motorbike if it broke or he made a mistake riding at a trials event. We knew when he wasn't in the best of moods; it was like the weather changing. The sky got dark and dangerous very quickly. We didn't try to piss him off on purpose, we were just kids trying to keep our bikes running and we needed his tools to fix them. A puncture kit was essential to fix flatties and we needed a roof over our heads to keep us dry while we worked. Of course, in hindsight he liked to be able to find his tools when he needed them. I get that. But hey, you can't have it all can you? Anyway, that'll teach him to have three boys as kids.

Considering all the traps that had been set for us, you can appreciate why we were pretty intimidated by our forays into his domain. Remembering where stuff goes when you're a nipper isn't easy and I'm sure we left stuff all over. As kids you carry those feelings with you. If anything we used was put back out of place or couldn't be found in an instant, or we couldn't remember where we'd used it or seen it last, he would resort to the punishment he thought we needed to help us remember next time and clout us.

A clouting from the old fella was a regular occurrence. A punch wasn't uncommon I'm afraid to say. Sadly, that didn't change for a long time and my brother Jonny, being oldest, bore the brunt of it, with a great deal of bravery. And it was Jonny who eventually brought an end to it. In his teens he took some boxing lessons in the local boys' club, picking up self-defence skills to build his confidence. It obviously worked, as one day, when Dad went to thump him for some misdemeanour in the garage, Jonny, by then around sixteen years old, deftly ducked the punch and the old man's fist swung right on through and hit the wall so hard he broke his wrist and scaphoid. Served him right. It took a good six months to heal. No trials for Tony Peat for a while. That was the last time that kind of thing happened, and from then on, thanks to Jonny, we had no more physical trouble from the old man.

FORGED BY SPEED

Dad's obsession with motorbikes permeated my life and changed me for sure. When he wasn't riding his bikes or fixing them, he followed all the motorbike sports he could. In those days, the UK was a force to be reckoned with talent-wise on the two-wheel stage. The sport of BMX came to the UK from the USA in 1979 and I got a BMX bike. Speedway and scrambling were regularly broadcast on the Saturday sports show *Grandstand*. Evel Knievel came to Wembley Stadium in 1975 and in front of 90,000 fans almost jumped thirteen buses on a Harley-Davidson. It was a death trap of a bike but very fast and he bounced bikeless down the landing like a floppy puppet in his white flared one-piece leathers, coming to a halt in grinding agony from a broken pelvis with the bike in pieces.

Jumping motorcycles over long distances was a good way to make your name in the 1970s. In 1978 Eddie Kidd, Bond-movie stuntman and another rider with a dramatic personal life, came down nose first after jumping fourteen buses, these ones double-deckers, on ITV's *World of Sport* riding a modified Suzuki RM 370. Evel and Eddie, later partially paralysed in an accident, were far luckier than Robin Winter-Smith. The twenty-nine-year-old Royal Artillery motorcycle display team rider ended the UK stunt-rider decade by losing his life attempting to jump thirty Rolls-Royces on an under-geared Suzuki RM 250 motocross bike at Elstree showground. He came up short on the twenty-eighth car and collapsed into the face of the landing scaffold. American folk legend Nanci Griffith recorded a song about him.

Racing also had its daredevils and stars, not least the superstar Barry Sheene. In 1975 Barry crashed and nearly skinned himself alive testing at Daytona in the USA when his rear tyre exploded at 170 miles per hour and the wheel locked up. A few days later he was sat up in hospital, half the skin from his shoulders left on the asphalt of Daytona, smoking a fag and giving interviews to American TV journalists. A year later he was 500cc world champion. In the world of trials, Sammy Miller, Mick Andrews, Malcolm Rathmell and Martin Lampkin all won a world championship – or two. Peter Collins won his first speedway world championship in 1976 in Katowice. Sheffield Tigers Speedway was a force to be reckoned with on the national stage. Owlerton Stadium in Sheffield would be full of fans eager to get a view of four men hammering round four laps of an oval mostly sideways on bikes with no brakes. In motocross, Hampshire-born rider Graham Noyce won the world championships in 1979.

Inspired by all this, we'd spend our afternoons and evenings after school on our pushbikes up in the woods or in the parks, playing with our mates. We'd bomb every hill we could find, my brothers building jumps or making dens to hide in. I can remember hitting the infamous root jump, ski jump and horseshoe in Chap Park. We had an awesome group of mates on the Cowley estate, which I think is lost these days.

And so I made it through the chaotic 1970s unaffected by it all. Mum never let the chaos affect how she treated my brothers or me. Not once were we exposed to the worries going on inside her head. I had two brothers to play with, and Mum's friends had kids too that were good pals and still are to this day. We were always busy, either following Dad around on weekends, having the best holidays and spending weekdays doing whatever we wanted. Looking back, I don't know how it could have been better. Maybe if our dad had controlled his anger better. That would have been the icing on the cake.

CHAPTER 2
TRIALS

Thanks to Dad's love of motorbike trials and a garage full of motorbikes it was inevitable his obsession would rub off on at least one of us. By the time I was two and a half and riding a pushbike without stabilisers, Andy and Jonny were out riding bicycles all the time. In a few years they would have their own motorbikes. Growing up on the estate and having all these other kids to muck about with, it was on the cards that riding would be something I did too. Everyone learned to ride a bike back then. I don't think it's the same now; there are lots more things for kids to do and most of them involve sitting in front of a screen.

Whether I'd end up like my dad riding trials bikes was another matter. Our weekends away as a family, watching him and other riders compete, was always going to make me want to get on a motorbike at some point. I'd have to wait a long time for that to happen though. Eventually both my brothers got their own motorbikes and I ended up with their hand-me-downs. I'd always hoped that one day I'd get the chance to have a go, but I remained realistic. Dad was never the nurturing type; the weekends were about him and his sport. Although we went along with him to his events, it always felt like we were getting in his way and cramping his style. We were left to get on with filling up the day with activities we did on our own.

Although it was made crystal clear to all of us that it was his hobby and not ours, that didn't stop us from wanting to be involved in any way we could. Andy had a Yamaha TY 80 and Jonny a TY 175. I'm guessing Dad bought them both. They were really good bikes, not cheap and they could take a real thrashing, which they regularly got. Jonny competed a few times when we went to trials as a family, but he didn't pursue it. Thinking about

Dad's garage and Jonny brings back the memory of the very first time I got to ride a motorbike, out and about with Dad and Andy.

There's a great spot in Sheffield on the skyline high above the city centre. Parkwood Springs is a mile north of the city and a 15-minute drive south for us from Chap, faster with a few shortcuts. All the kids of around my age and older who had off-road motorbikes or BMXs knew about it and went there to ride. Forty years ago, we could make tracks and bomb around, have a good laugh and not worry about the police turning up to give us a bollocking. The hill itself is grand, a nigh-on 200-metre-high ridge of sandstone covering around 150 hectares of rough common land all the way from Neepsend in the south to the Herries Road pond a mile and a half north, on the eastern side of the upper Don valley.

In Tudor times, it was a wooded deer park but soon after was turned into coppice wood, for making charcoal. The whole hillside was covered in forest. Then in the 1800s all that was cleared to make way for quarrying, mining and brickmaking. Heavy industry moved in and polluted much of the area. Then the trees grew back but were once again felled during the Second World War. There's little to see of the vibrant village that used to be there. Sheffield was heavily bombed in the war and a quarter of the houses in Shirecliffe were destroyed or damaged. It took until the 1970s to clear it all for redevelopment. There are still wartime anti-aircraft gun mountings at the top of the hill.

When I first went there, the place had been largely ignored for years so we could pretty much do what we wanted. So we did. On a clear day, you can see for bloody miles from the top, all over the city and beyond. The area back then was rough and ready and a bit of an eyesore. People had been dumping stuff there, some of it toxic, and the hill had certainly seen better days. That made it perfect for getting up to mischief and having fun, and the Springs became a hive of activity for bored youths.

Its height and all the varying kinds of surface, from exposed sandstone to heath and moorland, made it perfect for all kinds of riding and it offered some really challenging terrain on which to learn good bike-riding skills. It was a place Dad would ride with his mates from the trials club; he'd been going there long before I was born. Dad was trying to teach Andy to ride the TY 80 and turn him into a budding Martin Lampkin, so it was at Parkwood Springs that Andy and I got our first taste of the joys of a two-stroke combustion engine.

Although Parkwood was well known to many, we knew quite a few spots where you could just rock up on your field bike or take a bike off a trailer and ride round some rough ground without getting any hassle from

TRIALS

the police. Riding field bikes, which are really just stripped-down road bikes, on common land was quite the norm back then. It still happens now but nowhere near as much due to more green-space protections. It's certainly not like it was when we were growing up and buggering around on our bikes. These days, finding places to ride is difficult.

With the bikes unloaded, the first thing you do with a two-stroke engine is warm it up, because after you've kick-started the thing it takes a bit of time to run at its best. So that when you turn the throttle a load of white smoke doesn't come out of the exhaust. You always know when it's good to go as the throttle has more response, the revs on the bike sound crisper and the bike pulls properly when you turn the throttle. After the oil in the clutch warms up there should be no drag when you put it in gear and the bike should stay put until you let the clutch out. When it's not warmed up there's a bit of a lag and there's no point trying to ride anything until it's running sweet. You soon get to know the different sounds the engine makes when it's running properly or not.

The only protective gear we wore would have been a helmet and wellington boots, and maybe gloves. Because he was already really handy on a bike, Dad knew what skills were important for Andy to learn first. He was getting him to do figure of eights really slowly which is a good way to learn throttle and clutch control. If you get either of those wrong you'll either stall the bike and lose balance or go too fast and not be able to control where the bike is going. Balancing and going really slowly in tight circles is hard; the bike wants to push out into larger circles. Controlling your speed is much harder than it looks. It's five times harder than trying to learn how to do a three-point turn in a car on a hill. Get one thing wrong and it all goes tits up.

It felt like Andy had been doing these drills for hours and I was getting bored and starting to nag Dad that it was my turn. Finally, the old fella looked at me.

'You have a go.'

I'd never ridden a motorbike before and I was about seven years old. Dad, I hoped, was about to impart all his years of wisdom and knowledge to me so I would ride this strange new beast safely. Unluckily for me, all he said was, 'Turn the throttle gently and let the clutch out slowly.' So, when he stuck the bike and me in front of a big pile of bricks that had been dumped on the waste ground, that's what I tried to do. Except I revved too hard, let the clutch out too fast and with the engine screaming rocket-launched myself over the pile of bricks while doing a stand-up wheelie in a glorious moment of madness before crashing in a heap on the other side.

I got up with a huge grin on my chops experiencing the greatest feeling of accomplishment. Thinking back, I do ask myself now why he made Andy ride round in figure of eights for what seemed like weeks and then told me, who was three years younger, to ride over a bloody great pile of bricks. I can't ask him now but likely my badgering must have triggered his short temper into thinking, 'Right, I'll show the little bugger.' Except, instead of putting me off, my hair-raising stunt had the opposite effect. I loved every second of it. It was a great end to a good day. The feeling I had as we drove home was amazing, me and Andy grinning at each other after our day out with Dad, looking forward to getting home to Mum and a warm bath, and telling Jonny all about it. It didn't lead to me riding motorbikes that often for a few years, but it was the beginning of it.

Parkwood Springs looks very different now than when I used to go there in the 1970s and 1980s. I can remember when I was a teenager going there with friends on our pushbikes. My mate Wayne took a mini-digger up there to build jumps for him and his mates to mess around on on their motocross bikes. In 1988, the Sheffield Ski Village opened, which started the transformation. In the 1990s I can remember pushing my first car, a Lada Riva, out on to the ski slope so I could jump over it for a bit of fun. There were also some early mountain bike races there in the late 1990s, the 'Iron Justice' dual track being one, built by local lads. Sadly, the ski village burned down and never got to re-open again. You can still see huge sections of the ski slopes slowly being consumed by vegetation.

The area is more developed now, a process that started in 2002 when Sheffield City Council launched an initiative to get local communities involved in bringing the space back into responsible public use. They have big plans for it and around £22 million in the pot. They want Parkwood Springs listed as a country park in the city, part of the ongoing plan to make Sheffield the Outdoor City. Throughout my life as a Sheffield lad I've witnessed this battered hill transformed from somewhere neglected and often abused into a really vibrant green space for the people who live around there. In 2012 I got involved in the reimagining of its use. I was asked to help design two kilometres of bike trails, perfect for riding the heath and moorland there. The route down the hill was designed specifically to protect areas of ecological importance and when it's used properly riders are alert to people who use the area for walking and running.

The ancient woodlands have recovered somewhat, thanks also to a replanting programme. Not yet to the extent they once were, but the trees are on their way back. Scraith Wood and Rawson Spring Wood form the slope on the north of the hill. Wardsend at its foot is home to a spooky

Victorian cemetery. Overgrown and untouched for years and years, undergrowth twists its way to the tops of blackened headstones that are barely visible as they fight to stay in the light. Wardsend was originally called the World's End and it marks a northerly boundary between Sheffield and the parish of Ecclesfield, which we went through to get to the Springs from our house.

I made a video for Steel City Media in 2018 called *Gamble* that was filmed at the Springs. For my part of the film, I jumped on and off two containers that I remembered from the original ski village. The containers were used to store all the ski gear when the place was still a viable business and we were going there regularly. If you look closely at some of the riding clips you'll see remnants of the old dry ski slope. I spent a lot of money there learning to snowboard when I first started racing. I lost count of the times I dragged wooden launch ramps on to the ski slope to jump off on my snowboard and occasionally the bike. I met some lifelong friends there, including Eggy.

No one can use the Springs any more like we used to, bombing around on motorbikes like me and my brothers did, and generally having a riotous time. Those days are long gone. I have such good memories about the place that I still love going there and reconnecting with that part of my childhood that brought me such fun. My tyre marks are all over the place. It's a talisman for me with a lot of history as far as Sheffield goes, the place where I first slung a leg over a motorbike, and for that alone it will be in my heart forever.

Dad died of motor neurone disease in August 2018. Tony Peat had a lot of trials bikes over the years and I'm lucky enough now to have a few of them. One is a lovely blue 1970s Bultaco Sherpa; another is his old 1960s Triumph Tiger Cub. Jonny and I have ridden the Triumph at Dad's old club, the Hillsborough M.C.C., in the Tony Peat Classic, which they put on every August in his memory. The club have done a great job establishing this special trial in his honour, acknowledgment for all the hard work he and Mum put into the club over the years. The first event was in 2019 but because of Covid there was no 2020 event. So, 2021 was only the second time I rode his bike there. I love the Cub because it still has lots of the special bits he made in that higgledy-piggledy shambles of a garage, like the exhaust brackets. It's proper mint trick stuff and when I ride it and look at them, I do think of him, the old bugger. It also amazes me the stuff I can ride over on a 1960s bike with the rear brake and gears on the wrong side of the bike – this gets scary on the downhills!

Despite the dark spells the garage cast on us, Dad did have some rituals that I really liked. These would happen as part of his regular bike mainte-

FORGED BY SPEED

nance schedule after every trial. My favourite was a grubby circular tin the size of a layer cake full of solid wax tucked away on a shelf. After he'd cleaned his bike, he'd take off the chain, degrease it with petrol to remove all the crap and then re-grease it in the tin before putting it back on the bike. It was a very simple design and is still used today. He'd pop the top off with a screwdriver to reveal a green-grey hard wax that filled it to just over half-way. He'd then roll the clean chain up like a coiled snake in his dirty hands and pop it on top of the wax. Then the old fella reached for his camping gas stove and having sparked it up waited until it was good and hot before grabbing the tin with his gloved hands and setting it on top to melt the wax. The best part was waiting for the tin to heat and the wax to liquefy. I used to love watching that. The outside edges softened first as the metal tin got hotter. Then slowly you would see the wax melt into the middle. The chain, having sat proudly on top of the goo, would start to sink slowly into the murky depths as the wax melted around the metal links.

Once it was in and fully liquefied, Dad left it for a good while to make sure the wax got thin enough to get into all the links of the chain and leave a residue of wax on every possible surface. Getting the chain out required a bit of ingenuity, and before he would drop the chain in the wax he'd slide a piece of wire or an old bent spoke through the end link so he could fish it out more easily when the process was finished. Then he'd pull the chain out and hang it up on a nail he'd banged in the wall to drip dry and wait for the wax to harden. All of the excess wax fell on a bit of old newspaper he'd spread underneath. It would leave a cooling gloopy mess, not unlike candlewax. I got such pleasure watching the drips pile on to each other, layer upon layer. I never got bored of watching it, no matter how many times he did it.

Dad had this idea that if he showed you something once, you would remember it and he would never have to show you again. That might be okay when you're older, but when you're around seven it's not helpful. Fixing punctures was my Achilles heel. We were allowed to use his puncture kit, which was like a magic box to me: a brass oblong tin with a clip on its lid, half a dozen elastic bands wrapped round it, all stained and in varying states of decay, to keep the lid on. Inside was a small square piece of folded sandpaper to rough up the tube so the glue would take, a stick of chalk and a rough surface to rub the chalk on to make a powder of it, and a tube of glue with a black-hex easy-twist head, the small aluminium body squeezed and wrinkled with the end rolled up to keep the glue at the top. Us boys of course didn't pay much heed to such details and would leave it squeezed in the middle, much to his annoyance.

TRIALS

Inside this box of delights were patches of different sizes, foil on one side, greaseproof paper on the other. Find the hole, sand the area lightly a little bigger than the patch and apply a thin layer of glue. Get the patch ready, peel off the foil and wait for the glue to go tacky. Place the patch on the tube, leave it for five minutes and peel off the paper. Take the chalk powder and sprinkle it on the patch and make sure it covers the area that has glue residue on it. That way the tube won't stick to the inside of the tyre when you inflate it. For good measure Dad made his own patches, from old inner tubes, pre-cut and ready for use. It was all in there and it took me years to learn how to put one on properly. I got so nervous when he was giving me the 'I'm-only-going-to-show-you-this-once' spiel that his words would go in one ear and out the other.

As I said, things changed after Dad broke his wrist trying to land a right hook on Jonny. I can't speak for Jonny, but I wonder if he ever forgave Dad for what happened to him growing up. That day did change things though, at least for Andy and me; growing up was now a far more pleasant and easier ride than my first decade had been. I don't think the old fella's temper got any better, but the wallops became less frequent. Now, forty years later, my toolbox is as ordered as his was. And if I borrow stuff from anyone, I always put it back as I found it and expect the same in return. The only difference being no one gets a clip if they don't. So, Dad did instil a bit of discipline in me, and I appreciate that. But I'm glad I have none of the troubles he did, where he felt the need to take his anger out on us kids. That's something I'm grateful for, and I have the rest of my family to thank for that.

CHAPTER 3
FANCY RIDERS

There comes a time in every kid's life when they see someone do a wheelie or a skid on a bike and in the blink of an eye their world changes. It may be a friend or family member. It may be Evel Knievel on a TV show or, these days, a stunt on a console game. For me, it was watching my brothers who were doing them long before I was. And, of course, Dad was doing them on his trials bike when we went to watch him ride at trials events, passing on the baton so to speak. After seeing all that, watching speedway and scrambling on the box on a Saturday afternoon, it was a given that Tony Peat's son was going to master the art of the wheelie.

One of the biggest influences on me though was neither sibling nor parent. The wheelie king of the area I lived in was a kid called Martin Stocks. He could ride around the whole perimeter of the top block on our estate on his back wheel. He was a few years older than our Jonny and could 'mono' – another name for a wheelie at the time – his road bike for miles, literally. He was my first wheelie-king-type character and I never saw anyone round our way wheelie further than him.

What is it about the wheelie that seems so alluring to kids of all ages from all over the world? Let me explain why this particular skill is worth getting lumps of grit stuck in your knees or losing the skin off your fingers. What is that feeling? To me it's as close to flying, gliding or floating along as you can get without much effort and just a tickle on the pedals to keep the front up. It's also a sense of something a bit otherworldly. If you were lucky, sometimes you could glide along without pedalling. Just you, on this tiny balance point where if you move millimetres the wrong way you'll be off or down. What a magic feeling. And let's not forget how cool it looks.

When I saw Martin Stocks or my brothers get a bike or motorbike up on the back wheel it gave me a rush. Even though I wasn't doing it myself, it was as if I was. I was imagining I was watching myself. I would get all hot and excited and my emotions would race around my head like a pinball. Bells were ringing, pings were pinging and it was like I had ants in my pants. I just had to learn to do one and couldn't stop thinking about it.

None of us knew it, but pulling stunts on bicycles has a deep history, much deeper than kids on housing estates in the 1970s could imagine. In the late nineteenth century a lot of circuses would have cyclists doing tricks, pulling bigger crowds than stunt riders get now. Really crazy stuff too, like looping the loop, bunny hops and plenty of other death-defying acts of madness. It turns out that there's a long list of shoulders all of us freestyle and sports cyclists are standing on. It was called 'fancy riding' and the characters doing it were 'fancy riders'. I didn't know it, but that's what I wanted to be.

The fancy rider credited with the first wheelie was an American called Daniel J. Canary. One stunt legend dubbed him 'the father of us all'. In 1879, still pretty much a boy, he bought a penny farthing, known also in those days as the 'ordinary', from a mate who couldn't get on with it. Dan Canary turned the ordinary into something extraordinary, pulling tricks on it that boggled his audiences. He rode his penny farthing down the steps of the Capitol in Washington DC. He rode it no handed while lifting the tiny back wheel into the air, effectively converting it into a unicycle. In 1884 one American newspaper dubbed him 'the champion of the world'.

On a stunt tour of Europe he discovered what was dubbed the 'safety' bicycle, with wheels the same size, and immediately saw the possibilities. The safety bicycle, so called because you weren't as high off the ground as you were on an ordinary, had been around for a couple of decades but had only recently become a commercial success with a properly functioning chain. Returning to the US in 1890, Don Canary travelled to Niagara Falls for a fancy riding exhibition, when he performed his most famous trick, as one newspaper put it, 'then regarded as impossible, of riding on the rear wheel, with the front wheel elevated'. In other words: the wheelie. 'Mr Canary believes he was the first rider to perform the feat.' To say he mastered this outrageous new stunt would be an understatement. In 1894, he impressed San Franciscans by riding down three flights of stairs without handlebars and pedals, balancing on just one wheel. Eat your heart out Danny MacAskill.

Today, and when I was learning to wheelie myself, we'd call what we were doing 'freestyle' rather than fancy cycling. For that we have BMX and

FANCY RIDERS

San Diego's prodigal son Bob Haro to thank. It was Haro who coined the moniker 'BMX freestyle' in the late 1970s. Bob was a bright-eyed teenage West Coast surf kid who had a nose for a good marketing slogan. He grew up surfing and skateboarding around the Carlsbad area where the word freestyle was used to describe having fun, improvising what you were doing without any constraints, without rules or regulations. In 1979 when I was learning the trade as a five-year-old Herbert on wheels, BMX was the best thing ever. That's the first bike I remember ever wanting with a real passion.

Different two-wheeled sports have different reasons for getting the front wheel up. Speedway riders wheelie out of the gate, and as the wheel hovers inches above the ground, its trajectory is controlled by the right hand on the throttle and the left hand slipping the clutch to bring the wheelie under control. The measured rage of an eighty-five-horsepower methanol-breathing single-cylinder unsuspended track bike has to be deftly manoeuvred. The bikes have so much torque that as the riders come out of the gate and ready themselves to turn left, the front wheel is still hovering a few inches in the air and the rear tyre is warping out of shape as the riders pitch themselves into turn one. Four laps later a wheelie over the finish line to celebrate a win will be something every speedway fan has seen.

Trials riders like my dad wheelied their bikes at slower speeds to pull their bikes around awkward obstacles. They perform them far closer to the balance point than a speedway rider and control their movements by huge shifts in body weight and pressure on the foot pegs to pivot the bike in a very small radius. Martin Lampkin was an early master of this technique. Their skills are mind-blowing and it's a very different use of the skill to make it work for you and improve your chances of riding a section clean. Modern riders like Toni Bou have taken it to a new level. What they can do is just unreal. Unlike speedway, there's a necessity to be able to wheelie like a pro if you want to make it to the top of the trials world.

Motocross racers use the wheelie to float over huge whoops, a series of bumps on the track, as they pull up the front to keep the back wheel on the ground pushing forward and under power. You'll rarely get to the sweet spot of the balance point, no need for that, all you're trying to do is keep the front high enough not to clip the top of the whoops in front of you. That skill means the difference between winning and losing, especially in a race where the whoops are deep and challenging. In a thirty-five-minute grand prix race, a rider with serious wheelie skills will be able to shave seconds off lap times on a sandy whooped-out track compared to someone who can't do it as well. It's a skill worth learning for all motocross racers.

The one thing all these different types of wheelies have in common is the balance point: how you get to it and how you keep the bike there. Get the balance point wrong, go too far or drop the front wheel, and you've got the wheelie wrong. In any circumstance on any two-wheeled machine, if you go past that point of no return there are only two outcomes. One is that you've managed to grab the back brake on a bicycle or your right foot on a motorcycle to bring the front down, in which case you'll be lucky and live to tell the tale unscathed. Get a wheelie wrong in the other direction and you'll be off the back of the bike flat on your arse. The fear of that happening is a highly motivating part of getting it right too.

One thing I learned during my time riding on the world cup circuit is the difference in set-up between UK and American bikes. I always have my back brake on the left, front on the right. US riders have them the other way around. Many's the time I pissed myself laughing as an American rider jumped on a UK rider's bike or vice versa and instantly went for the cool wheelie through the pits, only to lose the balance point fractionally and then out of habit reach for the wrong brake lever to pull the front down. You can imagine the fright the rider gets when the rear brake doesn't kick in and they fall flat on their back in front of a busy pit full of mechanics and spectators.

The wheelie is the bike rider's first science project. That crucial balance point is what you're trying to discover, the place you want to get to know. Pick a good spot to learn and don't go on a downhill. You'll end up going too fast and won't be able to keep up pedalling. Even doing it on the flat makes it harder when you're learning. A slight uphill gradient is good; it keeps the speed more manageable when you finally get it going. First thing is to pedal along normally, then put in a strong pedal stroke as you pull up hard on the handlebars. The front will come up and you'll immediately know if you've got anywhere near the balance point. You'll either drop the front or, if you've gone beyond, you've already jumped off the back and are now picking yourself and the bike up off the ground. It goes like that for a while, too much wheelie or too little, but the journey has begun. The aim of course is to be able to get the front wheel up and pedal along, balancing on the tipping point. To be a wheelie master you will need to learn to pedal for a distance, always under control, using the rear brake to drop the front a little while keeping a good cadence on your pedals and using a little force to push the front up again if it drops.

Wanting to go fast on a bike is very different from wanting to do tricks on one. As a young lad I was all about learning tricks, and the wheelie was the first one that needed to be mastered. I remember the first time I pulled one off. I was about four or five. There was a hill near our house where I'd been riding a fair bit with my brothers. I was on a hand-me-down bike from Andy or Jonny, probably a 'bitsa' bike: bits of this and bits of that. Set right on the corner at the top of this hill was a big kerb, which was handy as I could use its upslope to help get the front of the bike up. I can't remember exactly how it happened, but I ended up pulling this wheelie for about four or five pedals, which is not bad for someone so young. That feeling was the best thing ever; I can remember it, the real ecstasy of it. Gives me shivers even now. Once I had it mastered, I focused on how many white lines in the middle of the road I could wheelie along and wondered whether I'd ever be as good at wheelies as Martin Stocks.

In the mid-1980s, around the time I turned ten, I was out and about on my BMX with Jonny and Andy, following my brothers and their mates around. I could keep up with both of them now pretty easily, although whether that's what they wanted I don't know. I tagged along anyway. We'd make jumps and imitate tricks we'd seen in magazines or seen other kids do. Our Jonny and his mates would build jumps out of blocks and bits of wood and then ask me to test them. For some crazy reason I would, which earned me the nickname 'Kamikaze Kid' for a while.

Jonny, being six years older, was starting to leave the bike thing behind as the pubs were now calling. He was also spending more time at the boxing gym and was soon on his own programme. That didn't involve dragging me around so much. Then it was Andy I was spending most of my time with on my BMX and that wasn't far off ending too as he got more into climbing than riding a bike. Jonny soon got his own place and left home. His Mongoose Motomag was not getting a lot of action and he was growing into a young man, capable of making his own decisions about his life and how to live it. This didn't always go down well with Dad, the broken wrist being a good example and his fashion sense another.

I was never sure why Jonny got the brunt of the old man's bad temper. We were all aware that Dad was not always the most open-minded of individuals. I remember one family day trip not long after Jonny committed the ultimate sin of getting himself a very snazzy wedge haircut, which was all the rage at the time. This new look was not to Tony Peat's liking and now it was in the same car as him. It didn't take long before Dad kicked off, hurling insult after insult at Jonny about the effeminate look of his hair. Mum told the old man to pull over and stop the car. Dad reluctantly complied. She got out of the car and took us boys with her, united in our support for Jonny and his haircut. Then we walked the several miles back home.

Doing things together as a family could be magical though, especially on holiday. Two favourites were our trips to the Llŷn Peninsula in North Wales and the Isle of Arran on the west coast of Scotland. In Wales we'd always camp at the Williams farm, not far from Nefyn, on the north side of the Llŷn, known for its beautiful coastline and deserted beaches. There were no facilities at all, just a field and us, with the van, our tent, a portable toilet and our cooking gear. The beach was a quarter of a mile away down lovely winding roads flanked by slate walls. We'd have it all to ourselves for two weeks. We had a big inflatable dinghy and Dad would tie long bits of rope to each end so we'd not end up drifting out into the Irish Sea. This was long before the Llŷn was pitched as an investment opportunity for second-home owners. You can read about the locals' opinion of that in the local press.

The peninsula itself is magical. We spent our time fishing the coves for blennies and searching the coastline for washed-up wood for fires and anything else of interest. One year when I was ten we were woken in the morning by the ground shaking, an even weirder feeling on an inflatable mattress. It was an earthquake, 5.4 on the Richter scale and felt as far away as Liverpool. I felt like the world was going to eat me. Dad was trying to pull his trousers on to investigate but fell over due to the motion of the ground. As a family we loved to go mushrooming. That was a right crack and always a competition to see who got the most. Mum would then cook them up and we'd have them on toast with beans. We cooked all our meals on the gas stove, and it was easy to find adventures to occupy our enthusiasm and curiosity. Even now, with all the travelling I do, there's nothing that makes me feel the same as the sight of those lovely slate-lined lanes.

The other holiday I loved was to the Isle of Arran. Although we rented a caravan in Fort William for the Scottish trials, on Arran we camped as we did in Wales. One year we got to our usual campsite and set up in the same field we always did, putting up the tent, tightening the guy ropes, inflating mattresses and setting up the cooking area. Andy had come with his mate John to find some local climbing routes with their own tents, some distance from us. The Peat family was in contented mode but that soon changed. A storm rolled in and Andy and John returned to the family tent. The wind strengthened to eighty miles per hour and the tent's flysheet blew off in the middle of the night, flying up the field with all the poles and guy ropes attached before snagging on a fence.

Dad was leaping around in his Y-fronts, screaming orders to me, Andy and Mum, trying to save anything he could. Then the pegs holding down the tent floor started pulling out of the soaked ground. I grabbed a corner, John and Mum held the others, and we tried to manhandle the whole tent

FANCY RIDERS

base into the back of our Transit. Andy was sat inside trying to stay out of the gale and so Dad laid into him, which scared the shit out of all of us. It took ages to get the tent back into the van, one great big folded mess of canvas, water and broken wills. We all ended up in the van, soaked and cold, the wind roaring all night. You could have cut the tension with a knife. In the morning, we discovered we'd lost the van keys and John had come down with a stomach bug and was shitting and puking everywhere. Electing to bail, we reached the ferry port only to discover that sailings that day were cancelled. We spent another night in the van and Dad's temper didn't subside for a minute.

Generally speaking, I was easy to please and stayed out of the way of the old fella as best I could. I got better at that than my brothers by watching their mistakes. Anyway, I was busy out on the streets on my Piranha BMX bike. There was loads to ride close by: Chapeltown Park and the local slag heaps were easy pickings. BMX bikes don't really ever break. I got the occasional puncture but that's about all that went wrong with it. I could now fix a puncture easily, so it was dead reliable and easy to work on, even if you were young. God knows how my twelve-year-old self would manage changing a cable on a modern bike, hidden away in tubes and handlebars. Bloody nightmare.

I hung around with other riders from our estate, but when it came to going anywhere I was usually with my brothers and their mates. One favourite spot was a field behind a disused factory built for toolmakers F. Parramore & Sons. The place was guarded by security, which normally meant you'd not be allowed near the place, but the security bloke was into BMX so he let all us lads in. When I got there I couldn't believe my eyes. The local kids had built this amazing ghetto BMX track with all the disused wood they could find lying about the place. I spent a few days there riding the ramps and buggering about but it was quite a daunting place and not somewhere I'd go back to on my own.

Inside one of the old factories, the same kids had built a BMX track using huge wooden beams and two wooden tabletops. It was mind-blowingly good and great for me to experience. Only the BMXers knew about this place, which meant it was a 'Mum's the word' kind of deal to go there. I certainly never told my mum where I was. Outside in the adjacent field I'd feel a bit more comfortable and all the BMXers would have competitions to jump as many barrels as we could find that had been left there. I managed ten, which was the most anyone had jumped apparently. I'm not sure about that being right, as I was still young and the other riders were older and much better on their bikes. Still, ten barrels is a long way for any kid.

27

There was another venue with some big jumps my brothers told me about. Bolehills BMX track was in Crookes near Walkley and is now home to the Sheffield Dirt Society. High up on the east side of the Rivelin valley, riding there was quite a mission from my house. It was a fair few miles, six at least, and on a BMX that's a bloody long way, and with a huge hill at the end. Despite that, it was totally worth it, even though I didn't race or get to ride around. I just wanted to watch everyone bomb around, bang bars, jump stuff, do stunts and fall off. The BMX track is still there today. Loads of people still ride there. It's also a proper club written deep in the folklore of British BMX history with some really great riders calling it home. It's still a great place for riding but a lot different now to how it was then, built up with loving care by the locals. The jumps are way bigger than when I was a nipper.

Years later, at a mountain bike national event in Broxa Forest in the North York Moors, I would meet Bolehills BMX thrasher Will Longden. Both our families were into trials and Will was mad on cyclo-cross so we knew of each other. But it had been at Bolehills that I first heard of him. BMX never happened for me though. Not having the right kind of mates of the same age who were fully into BMX was the likely reason, that and being so young. I also think it was to do with Dad riding trials every weekend. If I was going to take BMX seriously I'd have needed a lift to races. And I knew that would never happen. There are clips online of me riding at Bolehills years later on my mountain bike. They're a reminder of what a crack we all had there over the years. I can't ever remember having a burning desire to focus on BMX at all. It certainly gave me skills that translated into the mountain bike. But it was just something that was fun to do and not take too seriously. And at both of those I was expert.

CHAPTER 4
RED SEAL BLUES

I wasn't born with a work ethic; I was just born busy. I like to be busy doing things I like. Even doing things I don't like doing is better than not being busy. When I was young I didn't like to be sat around if there was an option of doing something physical instead. I didn't watch much TV as a kid. I was only really interested in two programmes, *The A-Team* and *The Dukes of Hazzard*. That was it. They were my Saturday evening shows and nothing else on TV was interesting enough for me not to be outside making my own fun and – it has to be said – mischief. As a teenager I watched even less TV and consequently the shenanigans increased. When I think back now to when I was younger some of that drive and energy was put to use to earn me a few bob, but also got me into trouble with the powers that be.

I went to Ecclesfield School, halfway between Chapeltown and Ecclesfield, when I was thirteen, the age you left middle school and went off to be readied for the world of work. As far as schools go it was okay, a typical comprehensive. I wasn't really interested in going there other than to meet mates and have a laugh. As soon as the bell went I couldn't wait to leave. The last hour was the worst, watching the clock on the wall as the minutes crawled past. It was like the hour hand was stuck in glue. Thanks to the timetable, I knew in advance just how mind-numbingly boring the next five years of my life would be. It was an uncomfortable experience knowing that for six hours of each day, five days a week, all I would think about was not being there and dreaming about getting up to no good. At least being there with friends made it bearable.

Design and technology was my favourite lesson. At least we made stuff. Frustratingly, it was only once a week. There was another lesson that

FORGED BY SPEED

involved us all learning to ride these little Honda C90 motorbikes outside. I have no idea how that came about or why they thought it important, but it was brilliant. Everything else was as boring as fuck though. Later on, I found one teacher running an after-school club that caught my attention, but we'll get to that in a bit.

Thanks to my efforts in the classroom I became well known to the teachers for all the wrong reasons. It was only my native wit, irresistible charm and good looks that stopped me from getting into even more trouble. Teachers frowned upon me sleeping in lessons; Heaven forbid you got caught napping while learning about crop rotation in the thirteenth century. Mum and Dad enjoyed the annual treat of reading my school report and the wisdom contained therein. They read like most reports do for a certain class of pupil: physically active, easily distracted, mischief-making kids destined for a job on the tools or in a factory. 'Steven lacks attention, could try harder, likes to be the class clown.'

Today, for example, I am sitting mid-morning in a double lesson of nearly two hours with my head on my desk. I'm exhausted and already for the third time today I've nodded off. I can faintly hear shouting. This is something that will continue throughout my time at school. It's not just because I'm bored. I'm not upset or angry. I'm not raging against the system. I'm just knackered. I've been up since 3 a.m. doing a milk round to earn a bit of cash so I can save up and buy myself some clothes and a pushbike. I'll probably have a nap in the afternoon too, and during break a sneaky fag with my mates behind the school gym well out of sight of the teachers.

A few mates had paper rounds after school. I did three and the milk round as well. Jonny had done the round before me, working with a lad called Ian Rhodes. Now Jonny had gone off to work and it was my turn. Ian's dad used to do the round before Jonny worked for Ian, but sadly he was killed when his horse kicked him in the chest while he was trying to get it in a horsebox. Ian then took over the business. Cowley Manor Farm, where Ian got his milk delivered, was near the entrance to our estate, a lovely old building of traditional stone and leaded windows. Ian rented part of it for his huge refrigerated unit where he kept the milk before we delivered it.

I would meet him there every morning at 3.30 a.m. six days a week. On Thursday evening and Saturday morning I collected the money too. The job was hard work but I didn't mind getting up early. Ian was a laugh and we got on pretty well. I also needed to work, as did Jonny. Dad didn't give us any pocket money and I liked to have my own cash to buy things. When Jonny turned sixteen, Ian got him bladdered one Saturday afternoon at the

32

pub. Or at least, Jonny had got bladdered with a lot of encouragement from Ian. Jonny woke up still pissed, crashed out on a beanbag, then stood up and pissed all over it. My ten-year-old self was looking at Mum wondering what was wrong with Jonny. It's fair to say Mum and Dad were a little wary of Ian after that. Now here I was working for the same fella that led poor Jonny astray on his birthday.

In case you've never been to Sheffield, the weather is not known to be wholly agreeable and more likely cold and wet. Winters are nasty but it toughens you up a fair bit. Getting wet and freezing your arse off on a regular basis is something you get used to pretty quickly living up this way. It wasn't ideal for an outdoor job, but it wasn't something I ever worried about. It did me okay regarding my bike riding since bad weather never bothered me a bit and there's plenty of it on the world cup circuit.

As for the milk round, I always set the alarm for 3 a.m., getting dressed downstairs so as not to wake Andy as we still shared a bedroom, much to his annoyance. After a short walk down the road to meet Ian, we were both off in his old Leyland Sherpa. Sometimes, though not too often, I slept through the alarm, usually because I was totally exhausted from five hours' sleep the night before. On those days, Ian would throw stones up at my bedroom window at 3.30 a.m. to wake me up and then for the next three hours take the piss out of me and ask if he woke Andy up as well. I can't ever remember Ian being cross with me. I'm grateful for that, but I did a good job and that's what matters.

Despite knowing loads of people on the estate on a first name basis, collecting the money wasn't as easy as delivering the milk. There was an old dear up at Burncross whose house I hated visiting. Ian thought it hilarious to make me go in and get the money she owed. As soon as the handle turned and the door cracked open the smell hit me. Following her through the house towards the kitchen, I'd glance into the sitting room where piled up in the fireplace was a two-foot-high mountain of shit-covered toilet tissue ready to be used to start the fire. Sometimes I couldn't cope with the smell and could feel vomit rising up through my chest to my throat. By this time, I'd legged it out of the house without the money and straight into Ian, who took great pleasure in my revulsion. Then he'd go inside to get the cash, apparently immune to the stench.

Working for Ian I made forty quid a week, with a bit extra chucked in for Saturday mornings or collecting on a Thursday night. With the money I was also making from my paper rounds, I was saving quite a bit of cash. Ian was a good boss and we kept things interesting to pass the time. Each morning was high energy. There was nothing better than jumping out of the moving

FORGED BY SPEED

wagon, running across people's gardens, hopping hedges and jumping walls, with six bottles in my hand, delivering to people's doorsteps and then sprinting to jump back in while Ian was still on the move. It was all part of the fun.

I got it wrong a few times, and knocked myself out once as I cocked up my timing and head-butted the van's sliding door. Another time I didn't see a lamp post as I was about to jump out and smashed six full bottles on it, covering me from head to toe in milk and glass shards. Still, I loved running between houses, being as efficient as possible getting milk to people for their early morning brews. Shaving seconds off where I could. We were finished by 7 a.m. every day, like clockwork. I'd get off back home, wash the milk off my hands and clothes and if it was raining and I was soaking I'd have a shower and get my school clothes on. Then I'd have breakfast and get off to school where, at some point, I'd probably fall asleep.

I also liked the paper round, which I did on my Piranha BMX, a bike Mum and Dad bought me. The newspaper shop was Copley's on Chapeltown roundabout, not far from my house, sadly now gone. Me and mates from school used to nick a few sweets and crisps there on our lunchtime jaunts, which I do feel a bit of remorse for now. To be fair I'd try to nick crisps and sweets as I was always hungry and had a sweet tooth. Around the same time, I got caught in a newsagent's in Fir Vale and legged it from the fella as he said he was going to call the police. Halfway down the road I felt a terrible pang of guilt as my mates were still there, so I went back and handed myself in to the owner. He let us go with a telling-off because I went back. He said he thought that was a good thing to do. I still carried on nicking sweets and crisps sometimes though.

I did two evening rounds for Copley's that paid three quid a night and one at the weekend that paid a couple of quid. Between the milk round, the paper rounds and larking about after school, I was getting very little sleep. I wasn't going to bed until 10 or 11 p.m., and I was up at 3 a.m. and running round like a blue-arsed fly all day and night. After I finished the paper rounds, I'd be out with my brothers on my BMX bike, riding around with mates, hanging out on park benches, eating sweets and crisps and talking crap. At one point towards the end of school I was working in a pizza shop in Chap, so along with the milk and paper rounds I was also chucking dough about at night and getting three or four hours' sleep at best. The pizza shop was fun though and I had my own little hustle going on there. Mates would come in and get cash deals with some going in the till and the rest being spent in the pub.

As I got closer to leaving school I was having too much fun on weekday evenings so I dropped the paper rounds and dedicated my time to staying out later. No wonder I was knackered, but I was happy. Working the milk and paper rounds meant I could afford to buy Skyway Tuff wheels for my BMX bike. Andy got ACS Z-Rims for his. We thought we were so cool bombing around on them. The wheels probably cost me more than the bike cost Mum and Dad. Having my own money was good. It meant I could buy my own clothes, jeans and tops I liked. I liked wearing good stuff.

Having settled in at school and got to know a group of friends, it was hardly surprising that we started to experiment. We were occasionally smoking cigs in break and hanging around together after school too. Smoking cigs was seen then as a rite of passage. That didn't last long, only around a year of me buying Embassy Filters because they were quite small and I could finish them quick. I hated smoking but liked how it looked.

Through one friend in particular I was introduced to stuff called squidgy black or, to give it the name I remember when we had to buy some, 'red seal'. At first, this was only a now-and-again thing, but Friday nights were never the same again. I'd given up my paper round and was now waiting for the man, as Lou Reed put it, only we weren't in Harlem at Lexington and 125th Street, we were on the 75 bus to Burngreave in north-east Sheffield and it wasn't heroin we were waiting for, it was hash, and the man wasn't some fella in a brownstone in New York but one of my schoolmates, Scott. It was anything but glamorous, but it was exciting, and what was originally just a Friday thing soon turned into an occasional weekday thing too for a few of us who liked getting stoned and having a laugh.

I was never brave enough to go and score the drugs. Scott was the only one of us who had the balls to do that. The Burngreave and Pitsmoor areas of Sheffield were notorious for being pretty lawless places. For kids our age, a visit there was not for the faint of heart. The area was run-down with little shops and alleys and cut-throughs. It was lively though, despite the lawlessness, and there were really good underground clubs, pubs and bars run out of sight for the best part in cellars, back rooms and empty buildings. The clubs attracted good crowds, much to the annoyance of Sheffield's finest, who raided such places frequently.

It was also common knowledge that things could get dodgy, with gangs running the area. There was the occasional murder when things got too hot between certain families and factions. Mum and Dad wouldn't go near the place and neither of them had any idea that we were popping down there after school to score hash. We felt we were going into the danger zone. Had we been older we probably would have ended up there in the early hours to keep the party going, but were just a bunch of green teenagers trying to score some squidgy black. And none of us liked the blues.

Despite always getting off the bus together and saying we'd go up to Catherine Street with Scott to score some red seal, we never did. Scott always had to go on his own. We'd wait somewhere else, sticking out like sore thumbs. He wasn't scared at all. In fact, he liked going there, a story that doesn't have a happy ending, as we shall see. I'd have money from my milk round and the rest of the lads chipped in a quid or two to make up a fiver's worth, the smallest amount we could buy but more than enough for a few spliffs. For mates who didn't have part-time jobs, it was dinner money they'd saved in the week.

All manner of drugs were available on Catherine Street and we knew how the system worked, where to go, who to give the money to and where to wait. It was easy to get ripped off if you didn't have your street head on. That's why we sent our mate down there, as he always came back with the goods. Mostly. One time Scott came back with a wrap but as soon as he opened it we could see it was road tar. He was so gutted he'd been ripped off. We all liked red-seal squidgy, which looking back now was probably the cheapest stuff we could get. The notorious Catherine Arms was knocked down a while ago now after losing its licence and the place is still pretty run-down, but every time I go past there on the way to town it always brings a huge grin to my chops.

———

Given the number of weekends I spent away with the family growing up, following Dad around watching trials, it was inevitable that I'd show an interest at some point. The first time I heard a two-stroke engine was in my pram. The penny took a long time to drop though. For years I still saw it very much as Dad's thing, and he very much kept it his thing; they were his bikes, it was his garage, his weekends, his trials, his sport.

At home though we had the Yamaha TY 175, a great little two-stroke trials bike, easy to ride, great fun and virtually bulletproof, a hand-me-down from my brothers that I rode whenever I wanted. Pretending to be a trials rider, I'd now make up some difficult sections to ride on slag heaps round our way. Riding with my mates we'd take goes on it and see if we could make it round without 'dabbing', a trials word for putting your foot down. As fun as that was, a lot of the time I'd just rag it around and not bother to ride so slowly. I liked hammering it and had some mint times on it. Then it broke down. I spent weeks trying to fix it myself but couldn't get it going. So as a last resort I asked Dad for some help.

'No, fix it yourself or don't ride it,' came the reply.

So, there it sat, alongside any dreams I had to be the next Tony Scarlett, next to my dusty old BMX. My interest in trials faded along with my hope of Dad fixing it so I could ride it again. I wasn't stupid with bikes, I knew how to fix them usually, but this time I couldn't and he just wouldn't help me no matter how much I asked. So, I gave up on it, resigned to taking another route to wherever it was I was going. Without me even knowing about it, another door had closed, turning me around and back on myself. What would be next?

At home things carried on as normal, although fate was conspiring to shape my future and change was in the air. Jonny had left home and Andy was now off climbing gritstone in the Peak District. I was hanging around shops and park benches with mates, distracted by more mind-altering hobbies. What's more, I had a new pastime to occupy me: football.

Aged fourteen, I played football for a year as a right back for a team called the Huddersfield 85s. I've no idea why it was called that. On Sundays, when Mum and Dad went off to motorbike trials and I didn't fancy going any more, Dad would drop me off first thing at my schoolmate Martin Gibson's house. He was one of the lads in the 85s and Martin's dad Mick was the team's manager. He was a nice bloke. Martin's mum and dad, and his brothers Nick and Paul, would take him and me to the match and back and I'd have some food there too. Mum and Dad would then pick me up on their way home from the trial. I loved playing for the 85s, never missed a match and we played every Sunday. I liked getting stuck in and running my arse off.

Eventually, I was offered a trial for Sheffield Boys Academy. Mick took a shine to me because I didn't mind grafting all game and I took great relish in playing well when it was muddy and wet. He knew how to get the best out of me. That determination was what got me the trial when they scouted me, I suppose. I was dead excited. I can't pretend I was a fount of knowledge about football teams and all that; couldn't tell you which team I supported even, but I loved playing the game. The trials were held over a two-week period. I'm not sure how much I told Mum and Dad about it beforehand but when it started they would have known. The first week sailed by and I loved it, did all my drills and thought I was doing pretty well. Everyone seemed happy with my performance.

I soon found out that Dad had other plans for me. Despite the fact the football trials had started he expected me to go up with him and Mum to

Fort William for the annual holiday, to watch their mate Dave Thorpe ride the Scottish Six Days and help out fuelling as we usually did. I didn't want to go this time. I had a week left to prove myself and get on the academy. Dad made sure I had no choice in the matter. So off I went to Scotland for the week.

When I came back and saw the boys' academy coach, he said going away hadn't helped my case. From what he saw in the first week, he said there had been a really good chance they would have chosen me. When I'd gone off without much of an explanation, he doubted my commitment and because of that they weren't going to take it any further with me. That was that. Mum says she's glad I didn't become one of those show-off footballers with too much money. Personally, I'd have quite liked the money, but like the BMX and the budding trials career, football wasn't going to be the fire that lit the fuse in the Kamikaze Kid.

So, I didn't get to find out if I was good enough for the club, and after that my interest in footy went down a few notches. Despite still playing well for the 85s, I never got offered that opportunity again. I was pissed off at the time, but I didn't dwell on it. I simply got bumped like a ball in a pinball machine on to the next flip. I still had all my mates and was about to meet someone who would help me change the focus of my interest. In the meantime, life went on as usual. School, part-time jobs, underage drinking, weekend parties and all the other great stuff there is to do if you don't mind putting some graft in to find it.

Most people who follow mountain biking know I enjoy a drink or two. While racing, win or lose I'd get pissed that evening to celebrate or drown my sorrows. There was a drink for every occasion. Then I'd move on and not dwell on things. So, as I raced into my teens, still on full throttle and with no intention of slowing up, I was going to end up spending time in pubs. My brothers had done the same, Jonny especially. Living in Chap there were plenty of pubs to enjoy. If you were crafty, there were a few I could get into while still at school. Lucky for me I was tall. When I was too young for pubs, the off-licence was our port of call. I knew a couple I'd always get served in so my mates and me never went without booze. I was also getting over Ecclesfield way, another of my favourite haunts, just down the road past school.

I have always loved being out with my mates. Those friendships were what I really lived for, still do. I was out for a good time and not bothered about waking up feeling groggy after a night on the gas. I had no problems keeping my part-time jobs going and spent the money on having a good time. I already knew all about the drugs that were available from the lads

RED SEAL BLUES

I was hanging around with and of course I was into my squidgy resin. In Chap there were also kids into sniffing glue and inhaling solvents. They were like a zombie crew. The bushes along the riverbanks around the places I'd hang out were full of discarded cans and polythene bags.

The solvents that kids were inhaling were mostly deodorants, perfumes or butane gas, and doing it at school out of the sight of teachers was common. Pouring a load of Evo-Stik in a bag and huffing on it for an evening wasn't anything I did or was interested in doing. The kids I saw do it always acted so weird and that was not anywhere I went or wanted to go. It was a lot different to having a few beers, a spliff and hammering around some lanes on my bike.

The good time vibes of squidgy black, mushrooms when we could get them, speed and alcohol were my co-conspirators. When I began racing, drug-testing protocols during the season inhibited that side of my life quite a bit. That may have been why I drank a lot more, as booze wasn't on the World Anti-Doping Agency's list of prohibited substances, not when I was racing. Now you can't drink before a drug test. If that rule had been around when I was hammering down mountains for a living, there's a few practice sessions and races I'd have been sent home from.

Looking back over my teenage years, I sometimes ponder the things I did and the decisions I made, but I don't have any regrets. As an adolescent, my life was just about as fun as it could have been, plus one. Just about everything I did was based around an unconscious league table of excitement. I was too young to really know what I was doing and I had no plan. I can see how certain random things that happened led me down a path, but I was completely oblivious to it at the time. I didn't take things at school too seriously and treated it as a recruitment camp for the new friends I'd make and who I'd knock about with. A few of those lads have ended up as life-long pals.

Now I'm older my tastes are less varied and my drink tab has shrunk. Nonetheless, I still enjoy a good piss-up and laugh with my mates. I'm lucky to have friends who I can still do that with, pals who will match me drink for drink and still be up early in the morning ready for work and a hard day's graft. I like those kinds of friends, hard-working, hard-playing and the salt of the earth as far as I'm concerned.

CHAPTER 5
ROADRUNNER

It's 1989. I'm a six-foot-plus, gangly and hyperactive fifteen-year-old. The BMX bike, the TY 175 and my footy boots are abandoned, leftovers from pastimes I don't have much time for or any interest in pursuing. I now spend most of my waking hours looking for outlets for my energy, some creative, some destructive, both equally as much fun as the other. Oblivious to what's round the corner, I continue at full throttle, addicted to fun and motoring towards nothing in particular. Life's okay. I'm enjoying myself and am blissfully unaware of my capacity to enlarge the person I've become – and I have no inclination to do so either.

But things are about to change quickly on that front. I'm about to be introduced to something that's going to get under my skin and into my blood. I'm about to catch a new, shiny and incurable virus called mountain biking. I'm going to catch it from my school friend Steve Merrill. Shortly I'll give you a little background on how Steve became one of my great friends and how his interest in a form of cycling I'd never heard about before would spark a wildfire in me, a fire that's never gone out. First, though, we need a little history about how mountain biking was born and how it came to settle on these shores in the late 1980s.

More than 8,000 miles away from my little life on our estate in Chapeltown, an exciting, gravity-focused bike scene was growing amongst some teenage kids living in Larkspur, California, just across the Golden Gate Bridge north of San Francisco. I'm sure there were scenes like this in other countries, but this is the one that made it to my house via Steve Merrill. These Larkspur riders were known to locals as the Canyon Gang, among other names. They were a freewheeling bunch, riding boxcars all over the western United States, living the hobo life. They also had a passion for cycling and would ride their beater pushbikes down the never-ending trails spread across the girth of Marin County's Mount Tamalpais, known to locals as Mount Tam. The Canyon Gang and others were America's pioneers of the new sport of mountain biking.

Their origins on Mount Tam go back to the late 1960s and early 1970s. The ten or so turned-on, tuned-in and dropped-out Canyon Gang heads all met while still at middle school. This crew were doing something similar with bikes as all us kids in the UK were doing. California mountain bike legend Joe Breeze recalls seeing them as a youngster. 'Self-described adrenalin junkies, they became obsessed with riding down the slopes of Tam. They chose cast-off balloon-tire bikes from prior decades, for their plenitude and stoutness. Through trial and error, they figured out what worked best and pieced together solid, soulful machines that inspired others to join on. Their passion popularised biking among their peers at a time when bikes were otherwise not a part of the landscape.'

Thinking about it, that wasn't so different to what me, my dad and brothers were doing, searching the dump and making up 'bitsa' bikes from old frames and parts to build something rideable and then going and destroying them in a day or two ragging them round, and thrashing down slag heaps and the crazy hills and woods of north Sheffield until they literally fell apart. Then we'd be back to the dump. Or at least Dad would, if he hadn't found anything in a skip.

In no way can the Canyon Gang and their unique brand of rescued bikes from the dumpsters of America be regarded as the definitive start of off-road cycling. That would be near impossible to date. Bikes have been ridden off-road since they were invented at least two centuries ago. But mountain biking, at least as far as the name goes, can be traced back pretty accurately to this corner of the West Coast. The name was in essence a commercial choice. Once industry pioneers decided that what they were up to would be called mountain biking, it shook off its other names and seemed to explode in popularity. The name made it so much easier to market as far as the media were concerned. The die was cast.

For the pastime to grow as quickly as it did in the mid to late 1980s required a lot of manufacturing support but mountain biking was attractive. It was seen as something adults did and since a lot of bike companies hadn't been quick enough in keeping up with youth trends like BMX, mountain biking seemed a more stable platform for the big bike brands to get a decent return on investment. So they were fully on board. It had however taken a while for that touch paper to be lit globally and we have to look back further than the 1970s for the start of that.

In 1953, a guy called John Finley Scott made a bike with flat handlebars and derailleur gears from a Schwinn World Diamond frame that had caught the attention of many cyclists. John named it a 'Woodsie' bike. In the UK that sort of bike was called a tracker and the kids who rode them were 'skid kids', speedway fans haring around bombed-out towns in the late 1940s making tracks over rubble and jumping over gaping chasms left by the Luftwaffe. They had 'cow horn' bars and big wheels so the riding position was sit up and beg, perfect for off-road fun. They also broke a lot. But despite cow-horns being popular, flat handlebars were better as they didn't move in the stem when you landed from a jump. Stems were pretty useless then and the leverage from wide cow-horns meant your bars moved all over the place.

Adapting bikes in this way was called 'repacking' in California for a reason. Mount Tam and Marin County sit perfectly positioned with the Pacific Ocean to the west amid roughly 525 square miles of prime off-road bicycle-riding terrain. Those square miles are full of fire roads and singletrack starting at an elevation of about 785 metres, the height of Mount Tam, and running to over 2,000 metres. It's a mountain biker's paradise. It's certainly more than the 150-metre elevation of Chapeltown woods and the slag heaps in Smithy Wood here in Sheff. The Canyon Gang would race down the fire roads of Marin's hills, sometimes taking a good five minutes to get to the bottom at high average speeds, using the coaster brake to slow down for the switchback turns on the fire roads. This made the bike hubs really hot and the brakes eventually stopped working. Then the wheel would jam and stop rotating. So at the end of a run, depending on how hot things had got, they'd have to take the hub apart and repack it with grease before they could go again. It was a right pain compared to a freewheel-equipped rear hub and rim brakes. They only used coaster brakes because that's what was available at the dump. Beggars can't be choosers.

The Canyon Gang had a lot going their way, although clearly not the quality of their bikes. Their vision and appetite for mischief and adventure helped, along with a bike-friendly climate. Then there was the elevation Mother Nature had provided. So, they were doing the right thing in the right place at the right time with the right people hearing about it. We didn't have the weather and nor did we have the expanse of terrain that would be anything like as perfect for the fire to take hold here. That crew had everything on their doorstep bar the name. The off-road riding at the time was known by various names, but it was 'mountain biking' that finally stuck

FORGED BY SPEED

after a concerted effort by those investing in the movement deciding on a simple-to-understand name that would make it easier to take to the mass market. And once that name arrived, mountain biking spread like Californian honey on hot buttered toast.

Even so, the UK has always had a huge passion for all sorts of cycling. Cycle speedway was a really big deal from the late 1940s, with thousands of spectators turning up to watch races. In the mid 1980s, Jim Varnish, father of Olympic track star Jess Varnish, was a real superstar in the cycle speedway world. Track racing was ever present. The legendary Herne Hill Velodrome in London hosted cycling in the 1948 Olympics. Cyclo-cross was and is popular in the winter months, and road riding and time trialling drew strong fields and spectators.

In 1955, Liverpool's Bill Paul formed the legendary Rough Stuff Fellowship at the Black Swan pub in Leominster with other cyclists interested in riding off road, although mostly on drop-handlebar bikes with the obligatory steel toe clips, essentially touring bikes. Nowadays that kind of riding would be called bikepacking or gravel riding. Those folks were quite a distance from the vibe in California. They were more likely to be smoking tobacco in their pipes than the Acapulco Gold popular with the counterculture heads up in Marin County. The closest parallel in the UK we had with the Canyon Gang would be the hill bombers riding track bikes on the edge of towns.

When BMX hit the shores of the UK in 1979 there was reluctance from some in the industry, like Raleigh, to get behind it. Halfords jumped right in though, and it took off like a mad one thanks to visionaries like legendary Tour de France commentator and Moulton-loving trike racer David Duffield. (As the Halfords marketing man, he gave the band Queen fifty bikes to shoot the promo for their single 'Bicycle Race'.) Pioneers like Duffield meant the sport got established very quickly in the UK. Kids were excited about riding bikes and what you could do on them.

I met Steve at school and we became good pals. There was one thing though that I didn't know about him. He had a mountain bike. Meeting him out of school one night I saw him riding this weird-looking bicycle. It was white with big, wide, knobbly tyres on wide-ish 26-inch rims. The cranks had three chainrings, not two like a road bike. One was tiny, called a granny ring. Brakes were cantilever, like the ones I'd seen on cyclo-cross bikes. The handlebars were one piece, called bullmoose bars, and the brake levers were almost as big as the ones I had on my motorbike. It was made by a company called Ridgeback. I'd never heard of mountain bikes at that point, let alone ridden one. I asked Steve if I could have a go.

44

I couldn't wait to get on it and it took all of five minutes to know that this was the best thing I'd ever ridden. It was love at first ride. From the moment I slung my skinny leg over the bike and popped a wheelie in the smallest ring at the slowest speed, I was hooked. It was definitely a eureka moment. I was a mountain biker. I knew it. I'd found my thing.

Everything clicked. I could ride this thing for miles. I didn't need my dad to take me anywhere now. And being about six feet tall, going far on a BMX was less than ideal. I loved all the different ratios of gears, plenty of scope for riding on all kinds of terrain as the area where I lived was all hills. This thing was perfect. Getting into Sheff and over to Ecclesfield would be easy. All these lights were going on in my head in a stream of awakening. It felt like my world had just got way bigger. I knew right then I was going to get a mountain bike. My brain went into overdrive and my vision for what was possible for me, on my own with no need for outside help, went stratospheric.

I was still doing my milk round and that was how I was going to pay for it. I'd save as much as I needed and buy a mint bike. Pretty soon I was buying *Mountain Biking UK* magazine every month. I remember one edition with Sheffield lad David Baker on the front cover along with Matlock's Tim Gould. I was really psyched to see fellas on there I'd recently heard about from around my neck of the woods. The mag was full of stuff that looked fun to do and had a vibe I could relate to: upbeat and going somewhere. I'd already saved a fair bit of cash from working in the pizza place to add to the money I'd made from my milk round. I needed some more though, and I wasn't asking Dad. So, while I was saving, I did some research.

The bike I had my eyes set on and lusted after was a white and pink Muddy Fox Roadrunner. I'd seen the ads in *Mountain Biking UK* for it, and colour-wise, 1980s-speaking, it was perfect. I went along to local bike shop JE James with the ad in *Mountain Biking UK*, deposit in hand, and laid the readies down for my all-white-with-a-splash-of-pink thrashing. JE James had to order it, since they didn't have my size in stock. In hindsight the geometry was like a 1970s Raleigh Superbe but the tubing was chromoly and the wheels were Japanese made. The parts on it were good quality. I loved it. Did I say I loved it? I still have it – it hangs in pride of place in my man shed.

As for my relationship with Steve and how that went, Chapeltown would see a few black eyes from the pair of us. He was cock of the school while still in the fourth year, with a full year above him. And I would be a close second. We were inseparable after school too, drinking QC sherry and Thunderbird Blue while riding our MTBs around on an evening. At weekends we might step up to Thunderbird Red. He was best man at my wedding, so I guess that's all you need to know about our friendship.

I'd ride with whoever was interested. I'd go on my own if no one wanted to come. I'd go miles on my Roadrunner. Then, for almost the first time ever, something amazing happened at school. Our science teacher at Ecclesfield, Mr Milson, started an after-school club for mountain bikers. Of course, Steve and I joined up. We'd spend hours after school at nearby Windmill Hill Primary School, doing laps of the school and the sports fields. It was where I met Daz Westby, who couldn't half rail a corner on his Raleigh Maverick. For ages at school that's all I did. Flying round every night, bombing all over the place. Starting at Steve's house two miles from ours, I would burn home as fast as I could. In two years, the Muddy Fox was trashed, beaten to death, and I was about to be thrown into the open jaws of the big wide world. No more milk rounds. No more paper rounds. No more pizza. No more family holidays. I signed up for the Youth Training Scheme.

Margaret Thatcher's government had introduced the YTS in 1983 to address the large numbers of unskilled unemployed in the country. For the rest of the decade, young people could go on a six- or twelve-month placement, later rising to two years, that offered thirteen weeks of training at colleges and work experience. While you were on it you couldn't claim the dole, and the wages were a pittance. Most regarded the YTS as a crafty way of concealing high unemployment rates among school leavers. It wasn't like a proper apprenticeship. It was mostly a rite of passage for working-class youths, one step up from the dole queue.

My first full-time job on the YTS was for construction company Henry Boot. I'd do a forty-hour week for forty pounds a week. I'd chosen it as I fancied being a plumber, but I was living for the evenings and the weekends on my bike. I was drinking locally, on Thursday, Friday, Saturday and Sunday nights when the pubs were busy and great fun. Both of my brothers drank in the same pubs and there would always be someone you knew to share a laugh with. I have always liked the feeling I get from booze, since those early days as a fifteen-year-old getting a buzz from a crate of Diamond White with my mates in Charlton Brook Park.

My love for alcohol hasn't waned, although my consumption of it has. I used to love a great night out with the lads. I'd sneak back into our house and the comforts of my own bed late at night still drunk as a skunk with Mum and Dad fast asleep. But I'd still be up first thing in the morning, headache and all, and no one the wiser. Or at least, no one was mentioning it. Now I'd stopped going on family holidays, when Mum and Dad went away we'd have parties at the house. Those weeks they were away were a riot. We took full advantage of the old fella not being around and partied as hard as we could. Tidying up the mess to make it look as if nothing happened was the only downside, but we did that okay too, although the house still stank of booze and fags when they came back. They knew what we'd been doing but nothing was said.

Scott, my go-to guy for squidgy black and all things I ingested that weren't legal, was still a really good friend. He'd arrived at Ecclesfield when we were about thirteen after his school was closed down. Scott lived in Ecclesfield village and hung around with a load of kids who spent their time round the shops and on the bench after school, making a nuisance of themselves. There were also quite a few older lads around him who I didn't know so well.

In the early 1990s I'd ride down to Ecclesfield on the Roadrunner in time-trial mode, cutting through gennels and parks to meet Scott and his mates. Scott and I were also friendly enough to go 50-50 on an old bashed-up field bike that we could ride on the slag heaps after school. One day we were out riding it, no helmet or protective gear, bashing the crap out of our little track on a piece of common ground, when my dad walked right past us. Bear in mind the old fella was someone who took bike riding seriously and that included the wearing of the necessary safety gear. Dad looked straight at us, walked on and didn't say a word. When I went home I thought I was in for a right bollocking, but he said nothing. I still don't know if he knew it was me or not with Scott. Got away with that one.

Scott was easy to like. Everyone loved him. There was no side to him, so for me he was a perfect collaborator in making everything we did as fun as possible. Over the years I got to know him well. I knew his mum and step-dad. They were mint: sound folk. I got on well with his older sister as well. He didn't have a bike, so my connection to him was different than with some of my other mates who rode. We were drawn together due to our interest in off-the-bike activities. He drove a Micra but I never thought to ask him if he'd passed his test. It was with Scott that my inquisitive nature was put to the test with substances most know to leave well alone. Try telling that to a fifteen-year-old me though and you'll not get far. I was up for it all.

One day I was in Ecclesfield to hang out like normal and sit at the shops, drink cans and generally mess about. Scott and another lad asked me if I wanted to try something a bit harder. I knew a few of them had been experimenting for a while, so I said, yeah, why not, let's see what it's all about. I won't go into all the details, but off we went to the land of honey dreams and velvet bed sheets, except that's not really what happened for me. Then we headed to the Fighting Cock and made our way straight to the pool table in the back.

For me, going to the pub is about having a laugh with mates and a few beers, the usual frolics. This time, though, me and the usually fun lads I was with were all sat there quiet as mice in a raucous scene full of people getting pissed and having a great time. There we were, saying nowt to each other, heads down and monging out. I hated it. Some of those lads carried on with it, but I didn't. One time after too many bevvies I agreed to have another go but this time I threw up in someone's fishpond on the way home. That was the last time. It didn't affect my friendship with Scott but I started to see less of him and I was pretty certain why that was. There was no stopping the power of that terrible stuff. It ripped through Ecclesfield and the surrounding areas.

One night a few months later, I'd gone out on my bike for a long one. After blasting round the streets all night I fancied a cuppa and ended up calling round at a mate's house and found Scott with him, hanging out. I was pleased to see him and like you do when you haven't seen someone you like for a while, we started gassing, filling in the gaps and telling stories. After we'd been chatting a bit, catching up on what we'd both been doing, my eyes started to wander to the table and I realised what they'd been up to just before I'd arrived. My heart sank. I knew that as soon as needles were involved, things weren't good.

Deep in my gut, the gut that never lies, I knew it was time for me to go. I shouted at them, 'What the fuck are you doing? You can't be doing that. You're going to kill yourselves.' Yet loads of other mates in the area were graduating to needles. I got to see less and less of them and years later would hear the horror stories of how bad things had got. How many we had lost and the lives and families it had ripped apart. I think I dodged a bullet thanks to mountain biking.

I rode off into the cold night alone, no warm cup of tea to keep me going until I made it home, just the cold spectre of the death of a friendship. My mind was rattling at full speed. *It's fucked up. You can't do that. You're gonna kill yourselves.* Then I thought about the weekend and borrowing the works' van, about the race I'd just entered. I started looking forward to meeting all these new people who were into bikes. I remember clear as day thinking to myself how I was glad I had that to focus on. Who knows what would have happened if I'd not met Steve Merrill and his mountain bike.

I thought about the times I'd spent out with my brothers on our BMXs, digging jumps when I was little, racing around, learning all the skills they were teaching me, riding motorbikes. I barely understood it then, but all that was giving me some balance and focus in my life. It was filling my time with good experiences. Despite Dad being awkward and combustible, making life difficult, times outside the house, with Mum and my brothers, were really good. There's a big difference for me between doing drugs and having fun riding my bike.

Tears filled my eyes. I kept pedalling, kept burning, lungs aflame, for hours, until there was nothing left to burn. Then I went home to the warm security of my bed. I had gone one way, and Scott another, the fork in the road split us in two.

I don't think I saw him for about a year. Then he turned up at my house trying to sell me some drills he'd nicked. I knew why he was selling them. I felt helpless. He couldn't and wouldn't be helped. His family must have been distraught, seeing this vibrant, funny kid take a turn into a darker world. Drugs and booze were fun but now I had this new feeling connected to the bike. I couldn't really describe what that feeling was, but it was present enough in me that I knew to say no to something that was going to destroy that.

If we were a chain before that moment, Scott and I were now a broken link. And that hurt.

CHAPTER 6
COMING UP FAST

A few years have flown by and school is a distant memory. The fast laps with my old teacher Mr Milson and my schoolmates are embedded in my legs and life is moving more at my pace. I've a new job, money in my pocket, places to go and new stuff to do. I'm an apprentice plumber, work is going well and my boss is into mountain biking. So, between jobs we drop into bike shops to see what they've got and what bits are better than the ones we're currently using. JE James and Langsett Cycles become regular ports in a storm if the weather's crap or we finish early. I'm looking for a replacement for my battered Muddy Fox. I have my eyes on a new bike, a Rocky Mountain, but it's a bit out of my price range at around £300. I've only got a couple of hundred saved. The boss comes to my rescue.

When I was an apprentice plumber, my boss, Steve Coleman, was a lovely fella; I worked hard for him and in return he lent me the balance on the Rocky. I bought this bike from Langsett Cycles, a Sheffield institution now sadly defunct. As with the Roadrunner, the Rocky Mountain had to be ordered in as they had none in stock. Andy who served me went on to run the business and was as passionate about bikes as Langsetts were about supporting the local scene. Langsetts closing fairly recently was a sad day.

Getting the Rocky Mountain opened new horizons. Technology had moved on a bit from my Muddy Fox; brakes, gears and general performance were all much better. I approached just about every ride as a top-speed mission. You can't beat the sensation of a lungful of cold air first thing in the morning as the sun comes up. I would go out with the aim of achieving the finely tuned rhythm of a sewing machine at full tilt. I was the needle and thread working with precision and dexterity, with mind, body and spirit in harmony. Even on mornings after I'd been on the piss, nothing would stop me. In my reckoning, until you've come back from a ride so numb from cold that your fingers need to be uncurled from the grips and an assistant is required to undo shoelaces and zips, you can't call yourself a serious cyclist. Those days become either your friend or your enemy.

Without paying much attention to training or coming close to anything like an organised ride, since catching the mountain bike bug I've become really fit. It's two miles to Wharncliffe Woods and I'm already doing three laps of a nine-mile loop, three times a week – a loop that is technically challenging and fun, and usually after a hard day's work too. Despite the hideous burning sensation pushing hard creates in my lungs and stick-thin legs, I absolutely love bombing around ticking off the miles. I like the pain; I get a kick out of it and don't really notice it enough for it to bother me. I enjoy the feeling of pushing through the worst of it, getting to the limit as I sprint out of the saddle and accelerate up hills. It feeds something deep inside me. It's addictive. Anyway, once you're fit the hills don't last that long.

I'm still investing in the local pub life, getting in late, up early, drinking a lot of lager, the weekend starting on Thursday night, arsing about with mates in Chapeltown. My usual crew has a very different social circle to me that involves everything that riding my bike does not, a contrast I really like. They can never understand how I can bob out on my bike for a quick thirty-five-miler before I meet them in a wooden shelter at Chap roundabout called the 'old man's hut' for beers or a Thunderbird to get the night started. I am also keen on keeping up with the latest fashion, buying branded hoodies, Chipie or Replay jeans, Adidas or Puma trainers. But I always save a bit too.

Right now riding is about fun and getting from A to B as fast as I can. Doesn't matter whether it's to a mate's house, the chip shop, the loop in the woods, the pub or anywhere else, I'm always on the gas. Unlike when I was younger, when that energy would fade out quicker, I can now keep it going for a fair while. Long outings on knobbly, slow-arse tyres are a regular occurrence. It's like Jimmy Page playing the guitar for hours live on stage with Led Zeppelin. He's not focused on his sore fingertips running up the strings or the pain in his tendons. He's just lost in the music. Rolling round at full tilt is the same for me. The song remains the same: fast forward, flat out.

The skills I learned earlier, as a kid, were on bikes that offered me no technical advantage on the terrain I am riding now. In fact, there were more things going wrong than going right. But they were simple enough bikes to fix. That was their appeal over the complicated two-stroke motorbikes my dad had. Learning how to maintain them needed far more hours than I was willing to put in. I learned all the new skills I needed the old-school way, in theory and then in practice. Watching others do stuff, fixing punctures, cleaning the chain, fixing broken links, keeping my crank arms tight, this was my other apprenticeship and I loved it. Simple maintenance suits me better. I am rider, trainer and mechanic, green as grass and happy as a pig in the proverbial.

I'm also just about to get my feet wet by joining a club called the Beighton All Terrain Squad, or BATS (see what they did there?). We ride at Rother Valley Country Park. They have weekday club rides and go cross-country racing. I'm as keen as ever to get as much riding in as I can so I go on as many rides as possible. Meeting new people to ride with is good and there are some fit buggers in the group I train with, none of them going as fast down hills as I do though. It's soon apparent that this is being noticed when a few of the club members mention that the fastest fella in the group is now me. This little piece of news gives me confidence as I still feel there's a long way to go before I'm really good on my bike.

I keep the club rides up, along with all the other bombing around I'm doing in the week, which in road-riding talk is described as getting miles in your legs. I have no idea if any of this is serious training or not, I'm just doing what I fancy and having a laugh, even if that is freezing my bollocks off on winter rides and coming back soaked to the skin. We've been used to that in our house for decades thanks to Dad's trials riding. This is nothing new. I really love getting out there and the weather is almost irrelevant.

For those of you who aren't so familiar with mountain biking in the early 1990s, I should explain a bit more about what the technology was like at the time I'm starting to get serious. If you walk into the North West Mountain Bike Centre in Manchester and speak to the owner, my old factory mechanic and friend Andy Kyffin, he can sell you a specific bike in your size for all manner of mountain biking specialities: downhill, eMTB, cross-country, enduro, slopestyle and a few other options to boot, with suspension ranging from 60 to 200 millimetres, enough to make your ride super plush. The suspension now has many different settings for individual weight, with preload, rebound and compression damping, and lockout options available. These are technical terms that an experienced mountain biker would under-stand but not necessarily a beginner or novice looking to buy a new bike. The technology these days can seem intimidating. Go to a good bike shop is my advice!

My knackered Muddy Fox, with its bright pink pads, and the Rocky

FORGED BY SPEED

Mountain I'd just bought, were the opposite of the bikes now on Andy's shop floor. They were really just street bikes with tweaks. The early 1990s mountain bike was simplicity itself, a machine designed to be cycling's equivalent of the Swiss army knife: good at lots of things but not great at any of them, although they did excel as off-road mile eaters. My bikes had well-made wheels from Japan, a chromoly frame and fork, Japanese groupset and gears, and lightweight, skin-wall knobbly tyres that at the time were state of the art, even if that art wasn't pretty and the bikes fell apart when I pushed them hard. The options I had for any kind of customisation to improve the bike's durability and handling characteristics were limited. The design of the frame and fork dictated what parts and tyre sizes could be used. Downhill bikes today have every bell and whistle you can imagine and are amazing out of the box.

At the end of the 1980s, and for a few years after, there was no such thing as suspension on mountain bikes. It would come but it took a while. All mountain bikes then had rigid forks and the frames were hardtails, meaning they had no rear suspension either. Riding one of these bikes fast over rough ground meant I got a battering. The only way of absorbing the bumps I was hitting at high speed was to stand up and use my long legs, arms and any other part of my body to absorb how the bike was moving underneath me. The tyres would give a small measure of absorption, but at most a few centimetres.

There were derailleur gears, similar to a road bike, but more of them to climb steep hills. This was made easier still by having three chainrings on the cranks. The smallest is called a granny ring, though that seems harsh on gnarly grannies, which everyone used to climb technical inclines that would have been impossible otherwise. Getting bounced around also created the annoying problem of dropped chains, or chain suck as it's usually called. That's where the chain bounces up and down so much it comes off the chainrings or sprockets. It didn't get sorted out for a while, so there was a lot of getting off the bike and putting the chain back on. That was normal for years on my first couple of bikes.

Another problem was vibration from the ground at high speed over rough ground. Imagine your eyeballs vibrating in their sockets so hard you can't see. Wearing protective glasses helped keep things clear but it didn't stop your eyeballs rattling round. Everything was a blur. Then, depending on the length of the descent, comes grip, specifically the grip of the hands on the bars. Every small change in the terrain under the wheels and narrow tyres was transferred up the rigid forks to the bars and through the hands, which were gripping tight, but not too tight or you'd get arm pump. I don't

54

COMING UP FAST

want arm pump. Gripping too hard creates a pump in the forearm muscles as they go into oxygen deficit. This is a downhiller's worst nightmare as it means losing feeling in the hands and fingers. A lot of new riders get arm pump as it takes a while to learn how to hold the bars properly. Everything goes numb from the elbows down. No control of the bike comes next and holding on and being in control is impossible. You can't grab the brakes or, worse still, you over-brake and can't let go. Sometimes if you're lucky there's a flat part of the track to shake out the arms, but usually by then you're in survival mode.

Wharncliffe Woods is nothing like the smooth open Marin County fire roads of northern California where the klunkers were ridden early on. The trails I rode and still ride today are highly technical, nasty, soggy, stone- and root-encrusted downhill singletrack lines. I rode those tracks through the woods as often as I could. These loops were long and challenging, half cross-country and half really fast downhill trails, and were difficult to navigate.

At the start, I was using the same bike for both cross-country and downhill and the higher seat height impacted my attempts at going as fast as possible on downhill terrain. The optimum seat height I used back then was based on height, inside-leg measurement, and arm and torso length. If you came to mountain biking from a road-racing background where custom bike fit already had a foothold, and you were used to riding in clips, transitioning to cross-country on a mountain bike wasn't too hard. The optimum seat height for cross-country was way too high for downhill though, so at times when I started riding I was working round that problem, as were all the other riders.

It worked well enough on the flat and rooty singletrack stuff, but as soon as I started to go fast downhill over technical terrain, with drops, jumps and other sketchy obstacles, the seat was in the way to an annoying degree. It would catch me on the inside of my legs or hit me up the bum, sending me forwards. It was dangerous ergonomically when you were riding the hardest stuff. Your body was in completely the wrong position. The narrow bars we used didn't help either. It's easy to see why there were plenty of crashes.

I loved the challenge of getting faster each time I went out. As I was initially focused on cross-country riding, I rode from the get-go clipped to the pedals, keeping my feet fixed in the right place for maximum efficiency. Toe clips, a basket you stuck your foot in and cinched with a strap, were less refined than the now familiar clipless pedals racers use but were okay for mountain biking since they had room enough to ride in a more robust shoe

FORGED BY SPEED

with tread on the bottom, handy if I needed to get off the bike and run with it up a hill. They could also be a pain in the arse when I needed to put my foot down to steady myself.

So, there wasn't really an option of putting my foot down anywhere without it being a nuisance, but that drawback actually honed my skills. My balance and ability to stay upright at high speed on highly technical terrain was born out of not wanting to make any mistakes on my line selection. Having to take a foot out of the clips if I got off-line would usually end up with me looking down to try to get my foot back in and going arse over tit with just Lycra and polystyrene to protect me. Upright and clipped in was best for me. There was less to think about. I chomped up the miles relentlessly every week like a sleep-deprived Pac-Man on speed.

To stop myself I was relying on caliper brakes, not discs like we have now. Caliper brakes work by applying pressure to the rim of the wheel. They weren't so bad on cross-country courses but downhill they were useless in the wet. Disc brakes are a far better option for the high speeds downhill riders reach. They also keep working when you buckle a wheel, unlike caliper brakes which catch the rim as soon as it deforms. Then it's like riding with your brakes on. Disc brake tech has also come a long way. When they were first introduced, they overheated a lot and the oil would bubble, rendering them useless. That was terrifying bombing down the side of a mountain at fifty miles per hour. You'd go to grab the brake levers but they'd pull all the way into the handlebars and nothing would happen.

Those early challenges took a while to get used to but there weren't any alternatives. I still laugh at all the old photos and footage of me racing with my tall seat and narrow bars. What was I thinking? Riding a modern downhill bike is so much easier, the front wheel tracking at speed stays glued to the ground on turns littered with roots and rocks and undulations in the terrain. A rigid bike does none of those things, there's no luxury, but it's how I learned my licks.

In those early days I would pick my way through the gnarly stuff with good 'body English'. That's a term used in motocross and trials riding meaning to counterweight the bike with body weight movements that maintain forwards motion and control of the bike. All those years watching trials helped me there. I didn't ride the trials bikes obsessively like Dad and his friends, but I'd watched all those amazing Scottish Six Days winners on our annual holidays in Fort William. Subconsciously, I took in a lot of the skills and body movements that made them world champions. That, on reflection, was another vital layer of the foundations I was building on my journey to becoming a world-class downhill mountain biker.

56

COMING UP FAST

In those early years, all that mattered was staying upright and because of the lack of suspension I had to have the skill and precision of a surgeon cutting into the flesh of a patient. One wrong move and it was all over. I'd be on my arse. That precision transferred perfectly to my races on modern bikes. I could see lines on mountainsides that other riders could not because I had spent my early years making my way down British hillsides keeping my momentum and raw speed as high as I possibly could. That was an advantage I learned that not everyone had. It also brought together two essential qualities: fitness and skill. I was as fit as a butcher's dog and learning the skills to match.

If I hadn't developed those early skills while clipped into a rigid frame, I wouldn't have had the career I did. Maintaining a world ranking for over twenty years wasn't easy, and without those early years it wouldn't have happened at all. In a way it was like the difference between bare-knuckle boxing and boxing with gloves on. With gloves on you can miss a shot and the glove will absorb the shock and your fingers won't notice the impact as much. Do that with a bare fist and you break your fingers. Riding clipped in meant no mistakes. The focus was to make sure every line I took was the one I wanted to be on, no sloppy shit-or-bust riding for me, not my style at all. I nurtured a style of riding based on total focus and obsessive precision. I grew up asking no quarter of the terrain I rode on because I knew I'd get none in return. There was no forgiving at the speeds I was riding. *Follow that if you can*, I used to think to myself as I hammered down mountain after mountain.

The suspension on the bike I ride now allows me to float over obstacles. I can hit huge stones, rock slabs, exposed roots and banks at speeds that would have been impossible on my old bikes. I've been lucky to ride the best bikes in the world during my career and I'm aware of the journey those bikes have taken to get as good as they are now. Developing and pushing the boundaries of what the bikes are capable of has been my job. And each year they get easier to ride, if not as simple to use. One thing's for sure: this sport doesn't stand still.

Lucky for me, those formative years I spent riding with no suspension, hammering through my first races as well as loops in the trails and woods, gave me a steely skillset robust enough to allow me to fulfil my potential. Just as a blacksmith at the forge works iron with fire, life on the edge of the Peak District and the early years on the race scene did the same for me. It beat me into shape, into a tool that would be strong and fit for purpose. I was making myself, I guess, driven by an energy that seemed to have no limit. It's very different for young riders following in my footsteps, with

57

bikes so much easier to ride. Groomed bike parks and lift-assisted runs have replaced the raw tech and fire roads I rode on. The skills I learned then are not as important now. Modern technology enables them to do things on their bikes that weren't possible when I started.

So that is how my mountain biking story really began: right at the foot of the metaphorical mountain. Looking back, it's strange to think I was drawn to a sport most would avoid like the plague. The dangers of racing downhill are many: racers have died pursuing this pastime, had injuries that cut careers short, been paralysed. It's not something I ever thought about. It comes with the territory and I accepted it. But what one person may see as utter madness, I saw as my natural calling. It was all I ever wanted to do. The fact you could die riding was so far down my list of worries it was out of sight.

It wasn't just me that was learning this trade. The sport itself was growing madly and changing fast. The mountain bike scene around that time was still at the grass-roots level. Courses in Britain were not yet as technically challenging or as fast as those I experienced when I started travelling abroad to world cups three or four years later. The bikes initially attracted those folks who loved going out in the woods. This new kind of rider wasn't interested in chugging miles and miles on a racing bike but wanted to get off road and away from the dangers of busy roads, where they could safely have some fun.

The bike that was most popular with British mountain bikers wasn't a mountain bike at all, it was a city bike called the Muddy Fox Courier. The Courier outsold the mountain bike I had. At a single two-day bike exhibition they sold 30,000 of them. London was awash with Couriers. Mountain biking had become a lifestyle and Muddy Fox had become the fashion leader. It had evolved from a load of dudes channelling a Big Lebowski vibe on the mountainsides in California to a new group of riders wanting to be that dude Greg LeMond racing across France for three weeks. Things were changing and I was right in the thick of it.

There were other aspects that appealed, meeting like-minded folks being chief among them. It was like being in a gang. That's how I still feel about it now. Whenever I'm out and about, if I bump into someone else on a mountain bike, I'm always up for a chat. I love the social side of it almost as much as the riding. The world cups themselves are like a travelling circus where everyone knows each other and looks out for one other, and I really connect with that aspect of mountain biking.

In the early days there was little structure to the mountain bike phenomenon in the UK. In fact, that was its appeal to many. The pioneers steered clear of the corporate tendrils of British Cycling. Early mountain bike riders and event participants wanted nothing to do with an association that was road and track focused. Not only that, mountain biking was kind of frowned upon by many roadies as a bit of a joke sport, the same attitude that greeted BMX when it landed here in 1979. The 'serious' cyclist's disdain for a cycling sport done for fun by kids was obvious.

Max Glaskin and Jeremy Torr launched the first national mountain bike series with a looser, more hip gathering of people who had an outlier mentality. Nothing too organised. A good example of just how loose was the event rulebook, which had only one rule: don't cheat. Within a few years over 500 people participated at each race. As mountain bike sales overtook those of traditional road bikes in the USA and later here in the UK, it wasn't long before commercial interests started to change things. The larger brands figured out you could sponsor a few ex-roadies and cyclo-cross pros to race against the green mountain bikers. They found it pretty easy to clean up race-wise when they dipped their toes in the scene; they had already been riding for years, were incredibly fit and could handle the bikes well on rough ground.

When the first Carlsberg-sponsored national championships were run in Aviemore in 1989, the line-up was a who's who of UK cyclo-cross talent versus the current US mountain bike world champion Mike Kloser. Over 400 riders entered the race on a course that was sixty kilometres long. That day Mike beat all the British cyclo-crossers and roadies, his long-distance experience coming in handy as he bested Chris Young by only a minute over a brutal course that featured some hardcore hills and river crossings. Sally Hibberd won the women's race. Sally is still riding and still teaching people to ride through her business Get in Gear, which she has run since retiring from racing. Chris is still racing cyclo-cross, still involved in the Yorkshire bike scene, still fit, still fast and still winning. If you're interested in seeing what bikes were like back then, footage of the race is up on YouTube.

Gary Fisher had coined the phrase 'mountain bike' in 1979. Thanks to the 'repack' crew and Fisher's 'sizzle on a steak' marketing, the touchpaper had been lit on downhill cycling across the globe. Television interest and new cycling magazines had lit a bushfire that couldn't be put out. Suddenly there were lots of opportunities for sponsorship and support for good riders. I didn't have a bloody clue about any of this when I started, but I couldn't have got into the sport at a better time. Having been an avid reader of *Mountain Biking UK* early on, I was about to come full circle as they made me an offer I couldn't refuse.

CHAPTER 7
FORK IN THE ROAD

Having negotiated the metaphorical fork in the road away from the actual spoon and a world of petty theft and hard drugs, my direction was set. My side of the street was sunnier: a life of laughs, drinks, fun and an eight-hour working day became, and remains, a large part of my life. Despite my hedonistic indulgences, life was heading in a more life-affirming direction. Although I took aspects of that old lifestyle along with me, it was far less destructive than it might have been had I not had a hobby I loved. In fact, I was becoming more creative and coming out of my shell a bit. The fact that I'd wake up some mornings feeling absolutely on my arse was neither here nor there; a thirty-five-mile trek round the woods on the bike would soon put me right.

I became a mountain biker but also a weekend warrior, as it's commonly known in the trade. I was getting the miles in, probably training as much as roadies do, eating like a horse, hammering club rides and trying to kick the arse of anyone who thought they were faster than me. I was working hard in the week, training hard in the evenings, riding hard around the woods near home and then racing hard at the weekend. Because of the progress I was making, I got some help with a discount on parts and getting to races from my local bike shop, Langsett Cycles. Having seen some potential, they took me under their wing. Without my knowledge, they bent the ear of a few of their bike brands' marketing managers. My boss also lent me the works van, which was a massive help considering I couldn't yet afford a car. The peer group I was hanging around with was complimenting me on my ability to endure pain and go fast downhill. I was getting noticed and I quite liked the feeling.

I was also making new friends. The people I was meeting on the weekends knew how to have a good time. As for me, I wasn't yet comfortable in the company of strangers, nor was I the chattiest of blokes, but I had a good gang of mates I felt at home with and loved that I could have a great time with them on race weekends. The definition of shyness is 'the feeling of being nervous or embarrassed about meeting and speaking to other people', especially in new situations or among strangers. Despite what you may see on films or read about me in magazines, that describes my day-to-day life, even now.

At this stage I'd come a fair way from the painfully shy kid I was in my younger days. I was coming out of myself a bit, without needing a few beers first, although the vibe at mountain bike events in those days was as if rave culture had found a niche in the cycling scene, so the post-race parties were great fun. Soon I was making friends farther afield too. Shrewsbury homeboy, full-time hedonist and part-time acid house raver Andrew Titley was one. He became one of my best mates and I'd end up spending lots of time with him, and Shirley and Steve, his mum and dad. They became like family to me, and although I don't see as much of them these days, it still feels the same. Local Sheffield thrasher Will Longden was another good mate. I still get to see Will at the races today. We made a bond while racing bikes that will last forever.

When I was younger, I was knocking around with my brothers. Now we'd all grown up things had changed a bit. I was still sharing a bedroom with Andy, who had not only discovered rock climbing but raving too and so was out doing his thing with his mates. I'd managed to fall out with Andy though. We had a proper barney that resulted in him smashing a mirror over my futon bed. I took revenge on Andy's hi-fi system, which I obliterated with one punch. He then chased me round the house all day. Didn't catch me though. I don't think he's forgiven me, even now. Luckily, older brother Jonny was there to stop me getting battered with a broom.

Those early rides with our crew in Sheff were such good fun. For the most part it was Will, and roadie pal Chris Horsfield who loved a bit of cross-country biking. We went everywhere together when I was in Chap, and along with a solid foundation fitness-wise we formed lifelong friendships. Will was living in a house with Helen Mortimer, Bobby Blake and some others who were all into mountain bikes. Will, me and a few others would either be hammering laps regularly at Bolehills BMX track or doing our legendary weekly 'round the block' thirty-five-mile lap that took us through all the villages and up Rivelin Valley Road, down into Derbyshire past Ladybower and over Surprise View and back.

Mum and Dad were still doing their thing on the weekends. The holidays to Wales and Scotland carried on unbroken for them both until his death. Yet for me, going to watch Dad on the weekends was now a distant speck in the rear-view mirror. I was 100 per cent committed to my own missions. I was racing on my own terms, and he took no interest in what I was up to, although I have a sneaky feeling he wanted me to do well. He'd never have said that out loud though. Mum was interested in what I was doing and was as supportive as she'd always been. Like a lot of late teenage kids, I wasn't at home much, save to eat and change clothes.

My first race was at Rother Valley, put on by BATS. I entered the novice cross-country race and beat everyone by miles. That was me hooked. I'd be racing mountain bikes for the rest of my life. I'm not sure I liked the winning because of beating other people. I liked it for challenging myself and going as hard as I could. There were times when I enjoyed beating certain people, though, as you'll see.

Once I'd got a few races under my belt and figured out how they worked, it was pretty easy to make progress as long as I put the work in during the week. So the results started coming and racing every weekend became a regular thing. If I was racing, I'd usually be able to get the Friday afternoon off work to get ready for the weekend. If the race was local, I could have a little lie-in. Further afield and I'd be up at whatever time was necessary to arrive at the race early so I could relax a bit. If it was a long distance, then I'd leave on the Friday night.

There was something about the preparation for a race that I found calming and satisfying. I'd go through a checklist. Did I have the right map? Was I familiar with the track and its challenges? What tyres would I need? Was it going to rain? I would always stock up on some beers the day before and stick a sixteen-pack in the van or car. Living in the middle of the country put me on the doorstep of the Peak District and only an hour and a half away from the Yorkshire Dales, with the Forest of Bowland and the Shropshire Hills a half hour further on. There were loads of races I could go to without having to travel the length of the country. I struck lucky in terms of where I lived.

I'd find out about an event from the club or read about what was on in a magazine. Races then were pretty basic. They all started early in the morning so we'd set off to find whatever field we'd have to park the car in. If I wasn't in the boss's van, then it was Will's Ford Escort, or later his Mondeo estate. If the distance required it, I would stretch out in the works van to save on accommodation, or else I'd camp or crash wherever I could. I was once lent the family estate but made the mistake of wearing a new pair

FORGED BY SPEED

of chunky Caterpillar work boots. With my best mate Steve Merrill in the car, I ragged it round a corner, lost control of the back end and while trying to get my newly booted feet to work the pedals, fishtailed my way into a brick wall. I whacked the car so hard it bent the chassis and concertinaed the driver and passenger seats together.

With the car now stuck on the wall and the recovery vehicle on its way, I ran multiple scenarios in my head, all of which ended with Dad going ballistic when he found out I'd totalled his ride. It was one of the few times his reaction surprised me. When I finally told him what had happened, the only thing he said was to ask if I was okay. That was the last time I was allowed the car though. After I turned pro in 1995, I saved up enough cash to buy the Lada. I liked the shape of it, a box on wheels with one careful lady owner. It was cheap as chips and all I could afford, a perfect beater to be stickered up, ridden over and bashed in.

Trying to find the venue with morning-after eyes involved searching for a roadside luminous orange cardboard arrow with the name of the race or club on it, hammered on to a small stake and stuck in the ground. This was exactly the same set-up as the trials I'd gone to with Dad, so I knew the score. Cycle sport in the UK for the most part has always been run by volunteers, so it was always an all-hands-on-deck event, marking the course out, marshalling, signing on, lap-scoring and the like. I'd find the registration area, usually a tent with a fold-up table in the corner of a field, where I'd pay my race fee, sign on to the correct category, exchange pleasantries with the crew running things and get given a programme with race times on it, along with a race plate with a number on it to put on the bike. One of the best parts about turning up for a race was bumping into the other riders I'd met before, chatting with them about what they'd been up to, where they'd been riding and what new bits they had on their bikes. At the start though I was still pretty self-contained so avoided talking to anyone I didn't know.

Checking the course out came next, a slow ride round the loop to see what lay in store. This helped loads, saving precious seconds if I found lines that others couldn't see, or on technical parts of the track where some riders wouldn't be as confident or as fast as me. My years of watching trials sections and the best way through them were a big help for this. Checking for places to rest or overtake was useful too, and the more I raced the better I got at this. Then there was the bike stuff to think about: did I have the right tyres on and was the pressure right? Where on the course might I get a puncture? All this became second nature to me.

Races were divided into different classes of rider: novice, intermediate, sport and expert. These classes were divided by the skills of the riders and

64

the number of laps they'd have to race. If the experts did five laps, sport would do four and so on. It was basic but the races were always well attended. I won my first sport category cross-country race and felt pretty chuffed with myself. That would be the way for me for a while, winning sport races.

In the late 1980s and early 1990s there weren't many downhill races. At some events I raced there would only be a cross-country course and no downhill. At others there could be a cross-country race one day, downhill the next, with a few dual slaloms chucked in for a slam fest. Finding good events was easy and every weekend I was either racing my bike or snowboarding at Sheffield Ski Village.

Although my downhill speed was a real advantage on the more undulating and challenging cross-country courses, I was really yearning to do more downhill. Most of the downhill courses weren't as hard or as technical as anything I was riding back home in the woods. The cross-country races were usually about two hours' long and hard graft. I liked doing them. Early on I made the same mistakes loads of other riders made, sometimes pushing too hard and having nothing left at the end. Anyone who has 'bonked', cycling or running slang for being hypoglycaemic, will know what that feels like: a racing heart, dizziness, nausea, cold sweats, a loss of control and no power left to turn the cranks.

Then there are the mechanicals, which are a different kettle of fish. It can take an age to fix a puncture or broken chain. These experiences help you to become race smart. Practising is fine, but nothing can replicate what happens when the gun goes and hundreds of riders head off into the unknown. At this stage I was a bit like a bull in a china shop: full of beans, rough round the edges, crashing as much as not. For reasons that are obvious to other riders, I was picking up a few nicknames: Pinball, Kamikaze, Sketch. None of them stuck, thankfully.

When I first started racing downhill world cups in 1994, the course would take around six minutes and require a ton of pedalling. These days they're around three to five minutes and the polar opposite of a cross-country race with far less pedalling than early downhill races and an incredibly high intensity of effort, both physical and mental. I would regularly hit ninety or ninety-five per cent of my maximum heart rate when I raced downhill. In cross-country it's different, you can't keep that level of intensity up for so long. One of the main factors that changed the length of downhill races over the years was how the bikes themselves improved. In the past, the courses were double the length and nowhere near as technical, partly because bikes in those days couldn't take much of a beating. In the very beginning the tracks weren't anywhere near as technical as they are now.

The first mountain bike world championships organised by the Union Cycliste Internationale (UCI), the world governing body for sports cycling, took place in September 1990 at the Purgatory ski resort in Durango, Colorado. There had been races described as world champs before, but they didn't have the approval of the UCI. There were other disciplines during the event, but only two counted for the medals – cross-country and downhill. The men's downhill race was won by Greg Herbold, with Mike Kloser second. The cross-country gold went to Ned Overend with a bronze for Matlock legend Tim Gould.

That race was just three years before I won my first Northeast Mountain Bike Association (NEMBA) downhill race, and the British Mountain Bike Federation (BMBF) sport category national title in 1993 after winning all thirteen of the cross-country races. I also won the BMBF downhill series too in 1993, which is how I got selected for the world championships. I preferred the two-event weekends, racing cross-country one day and downhill the next. These are two very different disciplines but a few of us liked to do them both. If I did well at one it would inspire me to hammer it again on day two. In fact, in 1991, the same year I won my first race, Michigan-born mountain bike legend John Tomac medalled in both disciplines at the second world championships in Il Ciocco, Italy – a feat no one has ever repeated – with gold in the cross-country and silver in the downhill. Tomac level I was not; or, at least, not yet.

At the level I was then competing at, the other racers were improving and I was really enjoying beating them. And when I was beaten, it made me even more determined to do better. There were cross-country riders who were way faster than me and some really quick lads going downhill too. But I had the bit between my teeth by then and every week I ticked off another race I could feel myself becoming fitter and faster, and a bit more savvy. I was also crashing my brains out regularly, albeit with no lasting damage to the body yet, and being young I healed up pretty quickly and put the knocks behind me.

As far as protective gear went, we were still in the dark ages. A polystyrene helmet perched on top of my head and Lycra shorts and a jersey were no match for rocks, branches, roots and loose stones. When I crashed it was usually at high speed, resulting in lost layers of skin and deep haematomas that took a while to reveal their purple and black secrets, not to mention an array of cuts differing in depth and length that needed attention. Put some Speedos and trainers on, jump on a bike, ride down the road at

FORK IN THE ROAD

forty miles per hour and jump off in Superman style and you'll get the idea. It's no fun and it hurts, although strangely, each time it happened to me it had no effect whatsoever on my desire to get back on and keep hammering. It would take a while though before the huge swathes of scabs that stuck to the bed sheets disappeared and I could walk again without being in pain.

A series that was really popular when I started was the Penshurst Off-Road Cycling (PORC) series. Penshurst was a great little bike park in Kent, although the land has now been sold, and back then there were good prizes to be won, like a £500 pair of forks or other gear donated to the organisers. I'd sell it all when I got home. As petrol was still reasonably cheap and I'd split the cost two or three ways, it was a profitable weekend as long as I didn't crash, which I did more often than not early on. I was always fast between crashes though. PORC downhill courses were good fun but not so challenging, and the courses were short too. Each run was over in about a minute, just a bit longer than a BMX race. Penshurst was also where I first met my pal Titley, and Collins Boy.

It's only in the last few years, as I've had the chance to look back on my career, that I've understood how my passion for mountain bike racing brought me out of myself. When I look back at who I was then, I see a glass-half-full type of kid, full of fun but with a few issues too. I had my love of bike riding and my success helped fill up the glass another quarter. But it wasn't until I started to get some good results and make some sound friends that I really started to come out of my shell a bit more.

Being brought up in a house where the spectre of physical violence was present meant that when it came to mixing with others I didn't have much confidence in myself. I knew I was shy because I'd encountered mates and friends at school who I thought were way more confident than I was. To all intents and purposes, I was a latchkey kid but not because my parents didn't care about where I was. My brothers both had those same freedoms.

I didn't want to be in the house when the old fella was there and possibly in a bad mood. And sharing a bedroom with my brother was difficult because I couldn't escape to it when I wanted to be on my own. He was a few years older than me and in my eyes he commanded the space, so the only choices were downstairs with the parents and the tension, or up with my brother who would be playing records. Outdoors was a way to avoid that.

So, I'd go out and spend hours and hours on my own riding about in my own world. That's okay as a coping strategy. It's probably better than most and certainly better than hard drugs. But I never got to experience what it felt like to be nurtured by my dad, the hugs, that intimacy you see some

67

FORGED BY SPEED

kids have. The proposition of 'my way or the highway' did not fill me with confidence or joy, and boy did I want to be happy. As I said, this only became apparent later in life. I wasn't self-reflective at all when I was in my twenties. I was much too busy having fun.

These days, I'm so used to the way I'm made that I can override the voices in my head that will produce a million reasons as to why something I'm doing might go wrong. In the past sometimes that got the better of me. Not so much now though. Although the voices are still there, experience has taught me to not listen to them but to go with the flow and see what happens. Even with close friends it can take me a while to relax and feel comfortable and connected to others. I'm not a go-to-see-a-therapist bloke. (Unless it would make me faster on the bike. Then I'd go.) But nowadays it's pretty much well understood that troubles at home can cause social anxieties. I've certainly got mine and I manage them as best I can. I'm very lucky to have two great kids and an understanding and supportive wife who I love dearly. They are my rocks when I start to roll.

Haro Winter Series Round 2: Clipstone Forest

(93)

Steven Peat was like a bat out of the woods trying to catch the leading Junior, but he was also busy holding off Matthew Barrett.

At last! a chance to ride a local mountain bike race! As Darcey has reverted to an almost wholly nocturnal lifestyle, my recent competitive outings have been in local cyclo-cross races. Their proximity to home and short duration (one hour) make them manageable on six hours of broken sleep! Even the dreadful weather couldn't dampen my enthusiasm.

The Clipstone Forest course was used for last summer's NPS 2. Tree-felling meant a slight change of the course, but despite the fog/mist/overnight downpours the organiser came up with a five mile, all ridable circuit. It was basically flat, with a steady climb away from the start/finish each lap. As brave souls who risked a pre-race lap of the course returned I could see that today was going to be no picnic. The mud-covered bikes and riders reminded me what winter MTBing is all about – jet washers and washing machines!

Undaunted, I set off for a quick recce of the loop. Muddy sections which weaved through the woods were linked with faster fire road stretches which gave me a chance to use the big ring. The muddy tracks were destined to get even muddier by the end of the day's racing, making forward rather than sideways movement a real effort. I made my way back to the car and sat inside with the heater on as Jamie cleaned and re-lubed my bike (he enjoys it really).

Peewees
The race action kicked off with the pint-sized Peewee boys tackling a shortened course, while proud mums and dads cheered them on their way. Top dog on the damp day was Scott Hall, who showed a dirty pair of heels to his closest rivals, Lee Claydon and Paul Pitchford.

Sprogs
Next up were the slightly bigger Sprogs. They shared the same shortened course and the same vociferous support for their race. The riders' skill and enthusiasm were great – if they're this good now, what will they be like when they're 20? The fastest Sprog on the day was Matthew Walker, who got the better of Gavin Hardwick and Adam Licence to take the chequered flag first.

Junior Men
With a Junior race you know you're guaranteed certain things: a big field, smart bikes, very fast racing, the odd enormous under-18, and even more parental support than the Peewees and Sprogs. Sure enough, I managed to tick off all five in my Observer's

MOUNTAIN BIKING UK JANUARY 1993

EARLY DAYS!!

CHAPTER 8
LIFT-OFF

The world of mountain biking moved swiftly on from those pioneering downhill races of the late 1980s. Affiliation to world and national governing bodies attracted the interest of mainstream media outlets. New sports do not come along very often, and mountain biking's sudden popularity meant a lot of energy and cash were chucked at it during its feverish and chaotic early years. Racing was now on Eurosport, which covered the world championships for cross-country, downhill and dual slalom. For a few years Grundig sponsored the world cup races and those were on terrestrial TV as well as being featured in the press. The national series of races in the UK also had big sponsors in 7 Up and Volvic.

There was always excitement in the dual slalom thanks to its knockout format and the abundance of crashes, mostly stupid T-bones at corners. It was more like a destruction derby than a bike race. I'm not sure how interesting cross-country was for Joe Public. I loved racing cross-country but back then it was about as exciting to watch as waiting for a bus on a wet November morning. Now the courses have changed and the UCI has made some really good changes to the format. They've brought the overall length of the race down from three hours to one and a half. So now it's a full-on, high-tempo race that's way better for the fans. Downhill was always a bit different. There was a time to beat, the runs were short and there wasn't the worry of being knocked off your bike by another rider, although there was still the chance of a mega-crash to keep the armchair energy-drink fans happy.

I arrived pretty much at the beginning of this period, which helped me a lot. Those innocent, pioneering years were ending, and divisions began to

FORGED BY SPEED

arise. Downhill is highly specialised now. Back then it wasn't, hence my ability, at least for a few years, to compete on a rigid bike. But when outside money comes in things change and decisions have to be made. As downhill became more popular, the tracks got better, and by 'better' I mean more challenging and technically demanding. This evolution was starting to dictate where I would have to direct my energy if I wanted to be a pro. It soon became nigh on impossible for me to compete at the top level in downhill without having a more specialised bike. I hadn't yet thought about how much faster I could go on a fully suspended bike. I was still pretty naive and happy with what I was doing. The speeds I was able to maintain back then were incredibly high, and despite the bikes getting better they were still pretty shit and broke a lot. It was easy to destroy a set of wheels and a mech in an afternoon.

British magazines were now reporting regularly on races all over the globe with a special focus on UK riders and how we were faring against the world's best. *Cycling Weekly* printed all the mountain bike race results, and by 1993, aged nineteen, I was appearing sporadically. I still have press cuttings in folders that I kept every year since I started racing. *Mountain Biking UK* was selling about 70,000 copies a month and it was for me a sort of bible. The bike tests were filled with images of skids and jumps, usually with a rider ducking down behind the bars to make it look way harder than it was. I'd drool over the mail order ads for kit I wanted. It was cheesy at times, but at its heart was a group of people passionate about bike riding. I need to thank *Mountain Biking UK* for putting me in the mag on a regular basis. I never refused an offer of being in there.

Each month *Mountain Biking UK* featured riders at the top of their game on the domestic downhill scene, and at the start of the 1990s the go-to face for the magazine was Jason McRoy. Hailing from the north-east of England, Jason was three years older than me. His dad Jim took photos for the magazines, which obviously gave Jason exposure. Jim interviewed me for the January 1994 issue of *Mountain Biking UK* where he called me the Pinball Wizard. The nickname stuck for a while, just like Shaggy, which *Mountain Biking UK* also gave me.

Jason became the face of UK downhill. He was fit and getting results, had good skills and looked great on the bike. And as his career took off, the magazine sponsored him too. Without really being aware of it, I was following what Jason did. He had it all at that time – the looks, the motorbike, the sponsors and the money. I guess it would have been hard to have had a better role model. I looked up to him, checking myself against his results and successes: luckily not forever though.

72

LIFT-OFF

I was aware I was a bit behind him in terms of all-round skills. I also knew I was as fit in my lungs as him thanks to the cross-country I'd done. I'm not sure how many people know that Jason was born with a hole in his heart, but it didn't seem to hold him back or affect his fitness. Jason had spent way more time in the gym than me and time at a velodrome; he was built like a butcher's dog. But if I was behind Jason in terms of power, I think my tolerance of pain and suffering was greater. I was willing to put myself through anything to go faster, not afraid to half kill myself doing it either. Although I was still a little rough round the edges, I was making good progress. I remember winning £500 in the dual eliminator at the Malverns Classic, a Mecca for mountain bikers every year, so I knew I'd been seen kicking ass by Jason and the rest of my peers. They knew I was coming.

I was also making some good connections in the trade. One of the real characters in mountain biking at that time was an older rider, occasional surfer and useful-product mastermind Pete 'Mr Crud' Tomkins. Pete was on the mountain bike scene a little earlier than me but was twenty years older than us kids. He'd given up his decorating job to develop an idea he had for a mountain biking product, his famous Crud Catcher mudguard. Despite having no previous experience, he had some fresh marketing ideas that were ahead of their time. I soon met the brains behind the brand and we became friends. His Crud Catcher was an injection-moulded oblong of plastic that attached to the downtube of the frame, cost pennies to make and sold like hot cakes. Everyone I knew had one. I think an issue of *Mountain Biking UK* had one free on the cover. The product evolved over time, and judging by the fact that Pete now spends most days surfing and cycling, it proved to be the gift that kept on giving.

Soon after, Pete brought out the DCD – 'Dave's Chain Device' – which kept your chain from slapping around and coming off, and by 1994 his company was really flying. He was good at marketing and asked *Mountain Biking UK* to fund a video he wanted to make that would promote his products and the riders using them. The magazine would give the video away free with their magazine. The film was called *Dirt* and was around half an hour long, filled with the kind of riding that looked like fun: loads of wheelies, not much emphasis on race gear or helmets, just young lads hammering around fields and sand dunes and shale hills at Sandsend near Whitby. Pete did all the filming and gave it a high-energy soundtrack that made you want to get out and ride. It was a massive hit. The video featured Jason McRoy, Rob Warner, Scott Dommett and Dave Hemming. Jason looked

FORGED BY SPEED

amazing in it, hammering downhill, pulling tricks and pedalling hell for leather. People still talk about that film thirty years on.

In the early 1990s, Jason and Rob were the only UK riders as good as the rest of the world's downhill elite men. They were fast becoming household names in UK mountain biking and were getting paid for it. It was a natural progression for them both to race in Europe; they were easily up to the task and deserved a crack at it. In 1992, Jason travelled to Norway to race in the downhill world cup at Lillehammer where he threw a chain and lost his pedals a few times, mechanicals being all too common back then. The spring retention systems in clipless pedals then were pretty poor. When you really pushed hard on them your feet came out, usually at the worst possible time. (Jason's did, mine did, but Rob's didn't because he always raced on flat pedals.) The Lillehammer result wasn't great for Jason, but I could see he was fast against riders who were world class. He had what it took. He also raced the 1992 world championships in Bromont, Canada, gaining more valuable experience.

The following year, 1993, Jason earned a permanent place in mountain bike history, travelling to Mammoth Mountain, California, to race in the Reebok-sponsored Kamikaze dual eliminator where he made the podium. Jim McRoy is the hero in this story for me. He saw an opportunity for Jason in America and maxed out his credit card to fund the travel, money well spent in my eyes. The phrase 'hit the ground running' is overused, but Jason did that and more, paving the way for me and other UK downhillers to become a force to be reckoned with on the world stage. The course at the Kamikaze is wide-open fire roads on loose shale. It's a race where speeds exceed sixty miles per hour and the bike drifts all over the place. Jason just thrived on that sort of terrain. The elevation and track meant a 600-metre drop off the side of the mountain if you got it wrong, but he raced his arse off, coming second to Myles Rockwell. He actually beat Myles in one of the two final races but lost on aggregate time.

For any UK MTB fan it was like hearing that England had won football's world cup. For everyone else it was a question of, 'Who the fuck is that? Sign him up quick!' He had really given Myles a run for his money as they battled neck and neck in the final. As soon as he got that result, bike brand Specialized came knocking on his door and in 1994 he left his previous sponsor, the *Mountain Biking UK* team, and moved to Specialized for big money. As soon as Jason got that deal, I saw the path to bigger things. Seeing what Jason had achieved meant there was now a marker, a possibility that this could be done, of getting to the top and being a contender.

Up until then I hadn't been focused on my future. I was more interested

74

LIFT-OFF

in living my life day by day: get the miles in, get up to the woods, get down to the Sheffield Ski Village, then get to the pub. As far as riding went, I was hopeful in a naive way but I mostly felt it was easier to go with the flow and say yes to everything that was offered to me, even if sometimes I should have said no. I didn't yet have the confidence to rock the boat too much. I didn't want to jeopardise what I had, even though that wasn't a lot.

The one thread that kept pulling at me was all the tracks in Europe where I wanted to go snowboarding in winter. It was exciting watching bikes race down these mountain resorts in summer on TV. I don't mind admitting now that I wished it were me. I wouldn't have admitted it then. I'd got used to disappointments; early life taught me that. I'd learned from those experiences that I couldn't count on anything I had no control over and there was little on offer unless I made it happen myself. So I just did what I wanted to do and rode the wave I was on without thinking about where the next one would come from. I wasn't where Jason was in terms of my game. But I knew that if I kept on track with my training and put the hours in, I'd hopefully get there. I knew there were opportunities that might take me across the sea one day. Maybe it would be with a US bike brand like Jason?

Jason and I first raced each other in 1993. This was before the *Mountain Biking UK* and Specialized deals, when his sponsors were Hardisty Cycles, independent bike shops from up his way, and Nike, and he was riding a fully suspended GT. I initially thought suspension was a bit overrated, so it took me a little longer to switch from the Kona I was then riding to something more like a proper downhill bike. I think me coming from a cross-country background had something to do with that as suspension slowed me down when I pedalled and the bike bobbed all over the place, which was a bloody awful feeling. Each pedal stroke seemed to suck energy from my legs.

Langsetts were really good to me. Dave and Andy were the main guys there. Even though I was at the bottom rung of the ladder I still felt looked after by them and they really did want the best for me, even if sometimes I wasn't that good at listening. I was green as grass and didn't know a lot about a little. They put in a good word for me with John 'JP' Saville at Kona. JP was a decent fella and had his finger on the pulse. He knew the mountain bike game well enough for me to trust him and he did what he said he would do. And Kona made some great bikes. I loved the Explosif I rode for the first couple of years on the circuit. I was also impossible to miss in the Langsett Lycra of bright yellow jersey and blue shorts on the green and orange Kona. The bits JP sent me always made the bike better, which was

75

FORGED BY SPEED

good for my confidence. He was also pointing me in the right direction with where I should race. That guidance would help me develop, getting me to tracks that were challenging against riders who were better than me, that would push me to go faster. I was soaking it all up and loving every minute of it.

The wins I was getting felt good and I'd flog whatever I'd been given as prizes to my mates when I got home. When I started racing the nationals in 1992, I was eighteen and, to all intents and purposes, an apprentice. By the end of 1993 there seemed to be a growing interest in my results and in me as a character. While Jason and Rob were getting their feet wet abroad from around 1992, I was battling with the rest of the UK guys and getting closer to those two when they were back on home soil. My confidence was growing along with my skills.

In those two or three years, bike tech moved along at breakneck speed. Suspension appeared, first with forks, which were like scaled-down motocross forks with much less travel. It was great having suspension, but they also flexed all over the place, which wasn't so good. Not being pummelled by vibrations coming through the bars at over fifty miles per hour was nice. I got less arm pump now, could go even faster and could actually see where I was headed – always a plus. Brakes were still iffy though, until Hope Tech released their first disc brake in 1991, which changed the game considerably. Clipless pedals were getting more refined, although it was still too easy to come unclipped and spend too long trying to get a foot back on the pedal. In my last year riding for them, Kona had me riding a fully suspended bike, which was okay but not the best bike out there.

Kona had started putting me in their ads in 1993 after only a year with them – I was pretty stoked that people were into my riding and were pleased with how well I'd done. I also started appearing in the press. The first image of me in a magazine was from a race that US brand Haro sponsored at the end of 1992 in Clipstone Forest. I am on my cross-country bike, splattered with mud wearing a pair of black woollen mitts and giving a thumbs-up to the photographer. I was still riding the rigid Rocky Mountain Hammer and wearing my black and yellow BATS race jersey and black winter leggings. The photo appeared in the January 1993 issue of *Mountain Biking UK*. I still have the clipping in a file and under it in silver marker pen I've written, 'Early Days!!' Although I've got clippings of all my appearances in magazines for every year I raced, I wish I'd also diarised those first years. I didn't take pen to paper properly until about 1994 to log my training. After that I then kept it up through my racing years. It's one of the

76

reasons this book exists at all – if it had been down to my memory, I left a lot of that in the bars!

As a kid who'd been largely ignored at school for his average academic achievements, this media attention felt like putting on a new pair of perfectly fitted shoes with a cushion sole. I remember thinking, *I could get used to this*. For a few riders, success and media exposure would set us up well enough financially that we'd not have to worry too much about getting proper jobs if it all went tits up. Thankfully, it never did.

Getting a race image into the magazines was a massive boost for me; to be recognised for doing well was amazing. But riders also appeared in feature articles too. *Mountain Biking UK* was pretty good at this. The magazine's captain was Tym Manley, with an editorial crew of John Stevenson and Justin Loretz. They did an awful lot to promote their version of what they wanted mountain biking to look like. Riders like me, Rob and Will were in it all the time. The big benefit came if your sponsor paid you every time you appeared in a magazine, what's called a photo contingency. Appearing in *Mountain Biking UK* was a licence to print money for me, since I've had a few photo contingencies. Having been adopted by the *Mountain Biking UK* team, I lost count of the number of trips I took down to Bath and their grand offices on Monmouth Street. I've been on the front cover so many times I can't remember them all. Steve Behr, the amazing bike photographer, was also really supportive in those early years when he was working for *MTB Pro* and *Mountain Biking UK*.

Every winter when the UK looked a bit dreary *Mountain Biking UK* would send us some place bright and sunny. We would fly somewhere like Spain and do ten to fifteen different shoots which they could then roll out over the coming months. As you can imagine, those trips could be carnage. Hire cars broken and destroyed, exploding paint and WD40 cans that set apartments alight, hotel rooms beaten up, the usual young lad kind of behaviour when someone else is picking up the bill. We would provide pages of coverage throughout the coming months and that in turn kept our sponsors happy.

Those first couple of years when I was just learning my chops, I didn't really know what a proper sponsorship deal was or who to ask about it. That was also true for setting up my bike and pretty much everything else to do with mountain bike racing. I was glad to go to races in the Langsetts van because it was such a laugh with the lads and some of us rode with each other during the week. All our bikes were pretty similar and no one really had any advantage over each other on the technology front.

Will's bike always looked the best. He worked as a pattern maker in the week on quite a good wage compared to my YTS money. Then he'd spend it all on some bike bling he had had his eye on in Langsetts. My reluctance to use the suspension that JP Saville would offer me probably cost me results, but it really didn't mither me much. A love of speed, a high level of fitness and the absence of mechanical failure were the deciding factors on who did well race-wise then. Chains dropping and flat tyres were the most typical mechanicals. Mistakes I made on the courses were usually due in some part to the ridiculous riding position. The bars were too low, too narrow and too far forward. The seat post was too high in the air. None of this was good for riding fast, technical, off-road terrain. I couldn't get far enough over the back of the bike or I'd hit my groin on the seat and catch my thighs on it. This made moving the bike around underneath me really hard. But I persevered and adapted. It wouldn't be long before stems got shorter, bars got wider and higher, and the seat post went down.

British accessory brands were appearing, and Hope Tech, a company up in the Lancashire town of Barnoldswick, had really pulled out the stops to develop a disc brake system. Another significant evolution was more controversial. Road riders had been using traditional toe-clips and then clip-in pedals for decades. I used the old toe-clips when I first started in junior cross-country. The toe-clip went over your foot and fastened round your midfoot with a strap, called a toe-strap. Once the foot was in place and the strap was tightened, that was it; you couldn't get it out unless the strap was loosened. That was fine for riding roads because you never had to take your foot off the pedal. For off-road and cyclo-cross, you had to ride with looser straps.

By 1984, Tour de France winners Bernard Hinault and Greg LeMond were using a new system that involved no straps or clips, a cycling spin-off from French skiing brand Look, which manufactured ski bindings. The Look pedals worked similarly to their ski bindings with a cleat attached to the sole of the shoe. This clipped into a spring-loaded binding on the pedal that held the cleat in place at two contact points. It was a one-sided arrangement, so if your foot came unclipped you had to spin the pedal back on to the right side before you could clip back in. That was a pain. They were a lot better than the old system though, and soon almost everyone was using them, on and off road.

My first mountain bikes all had toe-clips that were nylon and I'd just ride around in trainers. If my foot came out it was a pain in the arse to get it back in because the clips were heavy and the pedals would flip upside down. Then I'd have to look down, not ideal when I was hammering technical singletrack. Worse, they also snagged anything in their way, like

78

LIFT-OFF

exposed roots and rocks. The new 'clipless' pedals stopped all that, and by the time I was racing I was already used to riding everywhere over everything with them on my bike. They were the go-to for cross-country racing. The pedal companies developed the initial idea and double-sided pedals were soon on the market for mountain biking. If your foot came off for any reason it was easy to stamp it back on and keep going at full whack. They were perfect for my style of riding, although loose springs were still an issue. Occasionally I'd lose a pedal, but in my opinion it was still a better solution to riding flat pedals, which were also popular.

My passion for cross-country meant clipping in was essential. I grew up riding clipped in and I think it helped me develop skills that not all of my rivals had when it came to racing downhill. If your only focus is on gravity riding or racing, there are choices cross-country riders don't have, like the choice to clip in or not. There are lots of riders who don't run clips. I'd spend every minute I could at trials keeping my feet up and emulating the riders on my Piranha BMX. That said, Rob grew up riding trials bikes and he has never clipped in. Perhaps he was just more used to moving his trials boot around without taking it from the pegs. I only played on my BMX and didn't get serious about anything until I started racing cross-country.

During my career as a pro, one of my toughest competitors was the Aussie Sam Hill. Sam is a two-time world cup downhill champion and five-time world champion, twice in the junior category and three times in the senior. Sam rides on flats and likes to ride differently; he hangs it out and rides with his feet off the pedals on some corners. In contrast, I rarely take my feet off on a run at all. The challenges of both styles of riding have their own merits and drawbacks. One of the big problems you face riding over nasty terrain downhill at forty miles per hour is keeping your feet on the pedals in a position that's ideal for pedalling. If they are in the wrong position, it's easy to lose time taking them off or trying to move them to a better one. Clipped in that's not an issue. Yet if you need to take your feet out it has to be a calculated move. Sometimes I'll make a mistake and it's impossible to get my foot out of the pedals in time to save myself. By then I'll be on my arse. However, as I've been using them my whole career this rarely happens and I can get in and out pretty quickly.

Flat-pedal riders rely on small spikes on their pedals and soft-soled shoes to grip them. They don't have the same problem of releasing their feet, but they do have to angle their heels down to keep pressure on the pedal and maintain a good foot position. I don't like that. I want to be riding in the middle of the bike a bit more so when I do have to pedal I'm further forwards than they are. It's true they can lift their feet off and on the pedal as they like to steady themselves or dab in a corner to maintain speed, but getting it back in the perfect position isn't always easy. Then the pedalling efficiency problem raises its head again.

There are supporters for both sides, though most people who race downhill now clip in. I guess many, like me, grew up doing it. Sam is one of the exceptions, as is Rob. Looking at Sam's many wins it's difficult to argue that he'd have won more by clipping in, and vice versa for me. Since he retired from downhill, Sam has won three enduro world series titles on flats, upending any theories about what's right or wrong. What clipping in did for me was to make me confident in my ability to push, even though I didn't have a safety net if things went tits up. I got so used to them and rode so close to the limit that I don't feel there are any drawbacks, only positives. Getting in and out quickly became second nature. I've never had to face the problem of switching from flats to clips, which can take an age to manage; I just ride like I'm on flats and take my feet off if I need to.

If you wanted to settle it by world cup wins and world championships, it would be no contest: clips lead that score by a country mile, even more so now on the world cup scene. However, during my first ten years things weren't so clear-cut. Even now the issue can elicit passionate debate. I do feel that when Five Ten showed up to the party with their Stealth rubber soles, Sam and the other flat-pedal guys suddenly got something that made them more consistent as the grip they had on their pedal pins improved massively. If you were a flat-pedal guy on the fence because your results were suffering, you suddenly had a reason to stay on flats.

CHAPTER 9
A WIDE RIVER TO CROSS

In 1993, I won the BMBF national downhill series title by two points riding my Langsett Kona. The title came at the end of a yearlong battle with all the seniors, and I clinched it by a hair's breadth from fellow northerner Richard Thackray. To top it off, Sky Sports televised the last round at Shropshire's Eastridge Woods. Mum, Dad and my mates back home would be able to see me win my first title. This was a big deal, at least for me. The series winner at Eastridge was decided on the best results from three races. I was the most consistent rider in the series but, annoyingly, not the fastest in the last round. That was Andrew Titley, who was still a junior. Ian Collins also won seniors and I got second, which secured points for the overall (and put three mates on the podium).

I'd travelled down to Titley's on the Friday and we'd gone out in town that night for a few beers. Eastridge is in Titley's backyard, so I expected him to do well on the course. He was racing in the juniors though and at nineteen I was racing seniors. As it turned out, Titley beat all of us by a country mile on his Dave Mellor Cycles sponsored Ridgeback, posting the depressingly great time of three minutes and eight seconds, despite coming unclipped at the bottom after hitting a hole. He landed hard on his undercarriage, nearly castrating himself on the top tube. I came down in three minutes and seventeen seconds. This was a bit of a wake-up call for me. I remember thinking when I found out his time, *I can't believe Titley beat me!* It's not a good look for a junior to beat a senior. I know: I was only nineteen. Maybe I was riding a bit too cautiously with the thought of winning the overall event making me a bit tight. But still. Nine seconds is too much to

FORGED BY SPEED

get beaten by, especially when it's Titley. It wouldn't be the last time we had a seriously close battle.

It was a good series, with varied tracks and loads of fun. I got to race all the riders in the UK that would be my competition and peers in the years to come: Titley, Rob Warner, Jason McRoy, Will Longden, Matt Farmer, the whole shebang. For a relative newbie on the scene, I thought I'd ridden well and was chuffed to do well on the Kona, which I was still running rigid in a cross-country kind of set-up. A fair few bikes were now running suspension front and rear, but I was still hell bent on racing the Kona as it was and how I liked it. I was racing cross-country on it too, since the bike was good for that. I was still not 100 per cent focused on downhill and wouldn't be until the end of 1994, so 1993 was a ride-everything year. I was still mad on cross-country and really wanted to do well. I hadn't felt the need to choose between the two disciplines, but in hindsight the way I set up the Kona was clearly a bit of a disadvantage for downhill.

During that season Jason and Rob were abroad for a few races and I was yet to meet either of them personally. When they came back to race in the UK, they were fast and really hard to beat, but I could get close to them, *really* close, and that gave me a lot of confidence. Rob was good on the technical parts of courses. That came from his trials background. Jason had skills from his BMX racing and was more experienced than Rob or me. They both had advantages in their riding styles that I lacked. To be a contender at world level I knew I'd have to be the complete package. The experience they were getting racing on the world circuit definitely helped them develop as riders. That made me more determined to try to beat them and get a deal that would allow me to travel abroad too. I was well happy with my results, even though I hadn't won an elite race yet. I'd raced enough to know it would come at some point. At the start of 1993, which was my second season racing, I didn't think I'd do as well as I did come the year's end. So, yes, I was more than happy with those two national titles, one for sport class cross-country and one for senior downhill. In my eyes I'd overperformed and surprised myself. Even though at the end of the year they moved me into expert class cross-country, and I won a NEMBA and came third at the national championships in the Malverns.

Those results got me noticed. It would be nigh on impossible not to include me on the British Cycling team if and when they sent more riders abroad. While my riding early on sometimes appeared reckless to those watching me race – I lurched between winning and crashing, which wasn't helping my reputation – British Cycling probably didn't know anything about my willpower and work ethic. Despite my growing pains, I was

84

getting more in tune with my abilities and the limits of my bike. I got more experienced at pushing hard and riding on the edge, finding out how far I could go, but by going too far: I didn't mind beating myself up. I liked that in a weird way. It made me even more determined to come back stronger if I had a setback. As my confidence grew, my results and consistency improved.

I was pretty chuffed with myself, given I had only been competing for eighteen months and not even that seriously, all while holding down a full-time job and a couple of part-time jobs. I was going to make a name for myself in mountain biking, I could feel it. People also liked me, which was a bit of a shock. So I was pleased but not surprised when I got the phone call from British Cycling to say I'd been picked along with a bunch of other riders to represent Great Britain at the world championships at the end of 1993. The race was being held at the ski resort of Métabief in France, north of Lausanne and close to the Swiss border. It's an amazing location and was one of the first ski resorts to open for bikes. The world stage had become a reality and I was revved up to be going.

Compared to how I felt as a kid, with not a great deal of self-confidence, doing well on my bike had helped me a lot emotionally. I was good at something that I could control. That's why I was excited when I was offered the place on the British team. It was validation that I was on the right track. And I couldn't wait to travel abroad to represent my country. In previous years being in close proximity to larger groups of people was a challenge for me. I preferred a bit of space. That's why hours spent alone on my bike learning and training were easy.

We travelled down to Métabief by coach. Tim Flooks was team manager and I got on well with him. We're still friends. He had a great business tuning mountain bike suspension down south where the soft lads live. Pete Tomkins was there too. Will Longden and me were good mates. We had travelled together a fair bit and ended up in the same room. That was a plus. We had the same interests and he's a good lad to chat to; we're now more than thirty years into our friendship. But it was the first time I'd spent time with the other riders, certainly with Rob and Jason. I'd only seen them at races but had never spoken to them. It was Rob's first worlds too and he'd qualified by getting a result at the national championships in the Malverns earlier in the year.

Making friends with them was a big thing for me and we all got on really well, even though Warner moaned like fuck about everything, and I do mean *everything*. I got used to that after a while, but it took me a long time to figure Rob out. Jason was a more open book, straightforward. He

FORGED BY SPEED

was also our figurehead, and although we would all be competing against each other, JMC, as we called him, shared all his experience with us. He wanted us to have a good experience at the worlds. JMC willingly helped me with any advice and tips I needed even though he knew I really wanted to beat him. Little things like line choice and how to save energy might seem small, but together they add up to a much faster run down the hill. Jason told me all that stuff. I guess as I was a few years younger than him he saw me as a young pretender, a position that suited me.

JMC and Warner were like chalk and cheese. Rob used to get pissed off when the tracks we were racing weren't to his liking, if there was too much pedalling or not enough tech sections. If the track was no good in Rob's eyes, the whole weekend would be an emotional roller coaster for him and anyone in close proximity. In contrast, I'm the kind of rider that will race anything as well as I can, whether I like it or not. I'll always try to make the best of everything. I guess that's one of the differences between us. If the track was crap, he'd rather have been at home, while I just loved racing anything. Despite our differences and the fact we'd all come into downhill from different disciplines, we all got on immediately and became the greatest of friends very quickly.

When we arrived the first thing I did was check the track. That was already automatic for me. In trials, a rider will walk each section of the course before they ride it. I'd watched my dad doing it. When you're a kid, maybe you don't pay close attention, but by the time you're racing world cups you know every rock and root, every braking and gear shifting spot. The Métabief course started above 1,000 metres, so not high enough to really drain your lungs but still high enough to make a little difference. The resort was amazing. It had looked pretty good on all the media info I'd seen for the race, but when we got there we were greeted with weather similar if not worse to that in the Lake District. It was pissing down and the whole course was almost unrideable for anyone not used to mud. Even if you were used to it, conditions were still *almost* unrideable. It was hilarious watching competitors completely stuck on the course unable to pedal because of all the crud that had accumulated on their bikes. It would have been near impossible to race in those conditions. We settled into our digs.

The energy and vibe around the race was electric and despite the crap weather the fans were out in the tens of thousands. There were 60,000 spectators at the cross-country event alone. There were TV crews all over the place beaming coverage all over the world. From a distance, we all looked like bees, moving about in a swarm all over the hillside. Luckily, by the time the cross-country and downhill finals were scheduled to run, the downhill

86

track had dried out considerably and was good fun to blast down. It was fast and had some technical sections up in the woods that could easily catch me out – and did until I got my lines right. It was mostly grassy on the bottom half, with some really nasty, wide, off-camber turns and challenging corners where if I didn't keep my speed up they would suck seconds out of my time, seconds I couldn't get back. I was pretty good on the off-camber bit as there was similar terrain at home. I knew how to weight the bike so as not to lose too much speed.

There were also some big BMX-style jumps that not everyone could handle. Some riders weren't that good at jumping in those days. One of the obstacles was a huge step-down gap with a double jump that if you got it wrong would suck lots of time out of a run. I'd only seen Cully – Dave Cullinan – do it, so I made sure I could do it too. Rob didn't even attempt it. The obstacles were deep too. I know jumping and getting rhythm on whoop sections is an art form because not everyone has the skills to ride them properly. I liked them even though I found them hard to jump cleanly. Riders who had backgrounds in BMX like Cully, John Tomac and Mike King made this kind of challenge look easy compared to less skilled pros. I knew I'd need to get those jumps right to have a good run on race day, and I needed to clear the step-down and doubles to get a good time. It would take a fair few more practice runs to get them right, so I was using the chairlifts regularly.

There were other challenges too. A wide off-camber left-hander caught a lot of riders unawares. They finished it off the course and off the bike. It was hilarious watching them, left leg out like a pole trying to steady the ship, as they drifted further and further and out through the tape. There were plenty of riders having trouble with the more technical sections of the course too. I was pretty comfortable on most of it and felt that it suited me. I was fit as a fiddle and the pedalling parts of the course weren't any trouble. I was quietly confident that come race day I could go fast even though I was a bit sketchy on that big jump.

Tracks in those days were really fast and quite dangerous. The average speed on this track was high and the technical aspects weren't that tech at all by modern standards. Crashes when they happened were fast and there were some bad ones at this race. The ambulance and medics were busy all weekend. Protective gear was also non-existent for the most part. Although some riders like Philippe Perakis were padded up to the eyeballs, there were others like me, Rob and JMC who were just in shorts and a jersey with cross-country lids and fingerless gloves. Not great coming off on the rough when you're doing fifty miles per hour and can barely see where you're going.

FORGED BY SPEED

As far as looking like an elite athlete was concerned, I was a tall and skinny cross-country kid, similar to how long-distance runners look, although more Liz McColgan than Seb Coe. I didn't have a lot of meat on me yet. Even my British Cycling Lycra top was baggy on my arms. The pro downhillers, like Mike King, François Gachet and Jürgen Beneke, were all well-built, strong athletes, deadly serious and a little intimidating: quite the opposite of me, who was a more chilled-out gazelle. I think Jürgen's calves were as big as my thighs in 1993. The only downhiller I could see that was as skinny as me was Nicolas Vouilloz. He was also really fast, winning junior races. Little did I know that Nico would be the man to beat, but it was clear that he was way more experienced than me on the mountain, and younger and faster. Our paths were destined to cross.

I enjoyed the build-up to the race. There was lots of banter with my teammates and Tim had a wealth of knowledge, having raced both downhill and motocross. He'd been on the scene way longer than me so was good at sussing out lines on the mountain and discussing tyre choice and tech stuff that would be helpful.

Spending time with everyone helped build a good camaraderie. We were pioneers and it was the first world championships for some of us. The newness of it all pulled us close together. Practice is where all the hard work goes into making the day go well. Unlike the UK races I was used to, the overseas races had ski lifts to take the riders to the tops of the mountains. At Métabief this made things much easier and allowed for plenty of runs to help us familiarise ourselves with the track to see how it changed as it dried out and got hammered over the weekend. Given I was riding a simple rigid bike, I had the set-up I wanted and was ready and excited for my turn on the hill.

Before I'd packed my bags for the trip abroad, JP Saville at Kona had called me and asked if I wanted some suspension forks for my bike. They were Marzocchis, he said, and would really help me control the bike on the high-speed bumpy sections. Marzocchi were impressed with my riding and had been in touch to offer me suspension forks for the world champs. Being a stubborn Yorkshire youth, I turned them down. I remember thinking, *I'm doing fine on my rigid bike, I don't need forks to make me faster.* Big mistake. Who heads to Europe's most gnarly and challenging mountains on a fully rigid bike? Me, as it turns out.

So, I rode the downhill on the same bike I would have ridden if I'd done the cross-country. How much of a disadvantage it was I never got to find out. I hit the biggest jump on the course that King and Cully had jumped, nailed all the tech parts, pinned the huge off-camber with my left foot

88

hanging out, but on one of my practice runs got it all wrong on a simple left-hand turn at the bottom of the track. I lost the front end and crashed really hard, putting a big gash into my kneecap, which promptly swelled like a balloon. Knowing I couldn't continue with practice or do my qualifying run was dreadful. I came off the hill thinking I was all done.

I went to the medic's tent and got the wound dressed. I was pretty beat up but I did think it would be possible to ride the next day. Trouble was, I needed to qualify. Then I got to thinking and hatched a cunning plan. It was simple but also reckless. I asked Alistair McLean, another of our teammates, to qualify for me using my race number and by wearing enough headgear that no one would notice it wasn't me. No one on the circuit knew me at this stage – I was unknown to everyone in Europe and further afield. The plan worked a treat. Al qualified for me and almost no one found out. Tim was suitably outraged, but he did wink at Al after telling us off. Plan executed, no one the wiser. Cheers, mate.

I went to bed that night sore as fuck from the crash but also after learning I'd made a name for myself by jumping the big step-down a few times before my crash. I had a beer or two with dinner to take the pain away and fell asleep. You know what it's like waking up and hoping you're better and you're not. That was how I felt on race day. I lay awake, pretty early, with a swollen knee that had got slightly infected from the cut. It hadn't helped that in the night I had needed a wee. Getting up I knew there was something wrong. I felt like I was moving through a hazy treacle dream that throbbed between my ears. The blood rushed to the infected knee and – boom! – I was out like a light. Lucky for me, roommate Will saw the commotion and leapt out of bed to catch me before I smashed myself up even more. What a star. He laid me back down so the blood could get back to the right places and once I'd come round we started laughing.

Inside though I was screaming with frustration. I knew I'd blown my chances of competing at my first world championships. For some reason I also felt really sick and knew it wasn't a hangover. Next morning, as soon as I tried to put weight on my knee, I fell over and passed out again. I went to have it checked out but I already knew it was infected: antibiotics, crutches and bed rest. Oh, and no biking. Race over. Despite Al's gallantry and my skulduggery the day before, my first worlds finished in the blink of an eye.

It's hard to recall much of what happened at the race. I know the course had dried out before the cross-country finals but it was still slippery and muddy in places. That made the race far more interesting as the technical parts of the track caught a lot of riders out. I watched Henrik Djernis win his second consecutive world title, and in the downhill Nico destroyed the juniors for a second title. He looked really good on his bike, in control and efficient; his French-made and designed Sunn bike looked the business. He easily looked as fast as the seniors. That event was a win for Mike King, making it two years on the trot for the Americans since Cully had won in Bromont the previous year. I do believe Mike got a little lucky as he was one of the last to descend and the track was drying out fast. Italy's Paolo Caramellino came second and America's Myles Rockwell third.

As for the British team, Rob finished a creditable twentieth in the seniors, and that was without a chain for quite a bit of the run. He would spend hours – in fact *years* – telling us how he beat Tomac with no chain. He's probably still milking it now. Helen Mortimer managed a superb third for a bronze medal in the women's junior downhill. After the race Tim arranged for all of us to have a big slap-up meal, which was basically pizzas and gallons of beer followed by very drunken bowling where Rich Vickery was completely naked for some reason. We popped him in an industrial wheelie bin and rolled him off down the road. I have no idea how he got back or if he found his clothes, but it was a great way to end what had been a shit weekend for me. I came away disappointed but with a powerful sense that I wanted more of this international racing.

With plenty of time on the way home to think about my week in Méta-bief, I vowed to myself that from then on I would keep a training diary and take things a little more seriously. I'd work on my skills and fitness in the off-season and 1994 would be different. I'd keep making progress and keep pushing on. I had done well in 1993, but had not won a national downhill race yet. I wanted to beat the likes of Rob and JMC. Though I would never have said that out loud, being fairly shy and quiet. It was more my style in those days to be quietly confident and stay under the radar.

So, with a couple of national titles in the bag, some overseas experience, a battered knee and a bunch of new friends to ride and race with, the days and weeks before the new season went fast. I carried on working, went on training rides after work and raced when I could as the season closed out. Fitness-wise, I think I'd probably reached a plateau and needed a bit of a reset. I'd got as far as I could with my gung-ho approach, and despite being very active needed more structure to my programme if I was going to make progress. I'd got to know my body over the past few years – what happened to it if I pushed too far or not far enough, and how to deal with injuries and setbacks to training.

Looking back, this period seems to me now as though I was standing on the bank of a wide river that I needed to cross. I was looking at the far bank, trying to balance work, rest, play and riding bikes. I was turning up at races, winning stuff and people were starting to notice me and give me stuff for free. It only made me hungrier for more success. There were not enough hours in the day to keep it all up and still progress. The candle as always was being burned at both ends. I started to see this. I saw also that there were riders making enough money out of mountain biking that they didn't have to work regular jobs. The bike companies and their sponsors were able to support big teams. Cannondale received a huge cash investment from Volvo and there were similar deals floating about. I looked across the river and wondered to myself: *How do I get across to the promised land of a wage and expense account? What do I have to do so I can sack off my job?* I felt I was on the verge of a new journey. It was going to take a lot of work to get there, but it felt like I'd already come a long way.

First, I had to navigate the off-season. I was still living at home with Mum and Dad and working my arse off to save for a snowboarding holiday. Winter in Chapeltown slows things down if you need to do things outside. The weather can be torrid, freezing cold and wet. It got so bitter that I often came back from training rides unable to feel the extremities of my body and with hands that couldn't undo zips or laces. My riding clothes were filthy seven days a week. The washing machine didn't stop in our house, what with Dad's trials gear and my bike gear on constant rotation.

When I was training there was no Strava or Zwift in the front room with a screen that you could immerse yourself in as you raced with others in the comfort of central heating. Back then and for ninety per cent of the time I would be out on my Jack Jones in all weathers, half-freezing to death. Usually, around once a week, I would team up with Will and sometimes Chris Horsfield and have a belt around with them. Rides with the club, my pals and on my own were sporadic thanks to the snow, ice and hail. But I kept at it while waiting for the New Year so I could start meeting the new goals I'd set myself. One of them was to win a BMBF national, irrespective of who was racing.

I wanted to beat them all.

18 route guides reviewed p104

BRITAIN'S BEST-SELLING BIKE MAGAZINE

Mountain Biking UK

Shred sleds
How to ride hot in the snow!

Scoooop...

1st ProFlex **955** on test!

Pinball WIZARD!

Steve Peat's Vert style

KNOW:

- Why NEW Shimano's GREAT (...and no-mix is a myth)
- Which high-end bike is best under £2,000
- Vote for MBUK best of the year awards

£2.50

January Vol 8 no 1

Your guarantee of value

future

9 770954 869046

01

CHAPTER 10
AMATEUR DRAMATICS

I had been messing around on the bank of the river long enough. In 1994, the year I turned twenty, I would figure out how to get across. I felt I'd done my apprenticeship. Now I needed to see what I could do with the knowledge and skills I'd got. I could feel myself becoming serious. I was more confident in my speed and technical ability. I also knew I needed some stepping stones to appear if I was going to make a career out of bike riding and get on to the world cup circuit. There was lots of work to do after a winter that had been atrocious even by Sheffield standards. Injuring a hand in a silly crash in January didn't help.

Races in winter were few and far between so I raided my savings for a week's snowboarding in Val d'Isère with Titley and some mates. It was a lot of fun with the usual mad nights out. Somehow we lost one of our gang on the way to a club and he turned up hours later back at the hotel drenched to the bone and with icicles hanging off him. The nice French police had half drowned him when they found him on the road and then dumped him in a tunnel. When he reached us he was hypothermic, just stood there shivering, his jeans stiff as a board with ice, so we popped him in a hot bath. Those days in France got me hooked on snowboarding. I knew it offered me a distraction at the end of each year when the bikes got too much.

With my hand healed, normal bike duties resumed. I headed to Titley's when I could for some rides in Shropshire. I love his mum and dad; they are basically my second parents. I spent so much time down there hanging out, riding, drinking and getting up to no good with Titley. I'd stay for weeks at a time; probably outstayed my welcome a few times but I wouldn't have known as they were so kind. I felt right at home there. The weather was also

93

better down his way. Training was going well enough, but I kept being dragged down by a lingering chest infection. I'd suffered bouts of asthma as a kid, so was used to managing that. Riding in damp air in the Yorkshire winter wasn't helping.

I knew my body well enough to know that if I could accelerate after I'd reached the top of a climb I was improving, instead of getting to the top and gagging for air. When it wasn't snowing I got out on the bike, but riding was inconsistent and counterproductive at times. I started running and doing some circuit training because the snow got pretty bad and it was dangerous on the roads. I was even doing push-ups to fill the time, which shows you how bored I was.

I was still hitting the clubs and pubs though. My diary entry for 5 February is fairly typical: 'Drove to Titley's. Went to Shrewsbury club dinner. Went clubbing. Titley and Crispin had a fight with a bouncer. We got chucked out for slam dancing. Excellent night. Stayed up all night, left for Sheffield at 10 a.m. to meet Steve Behr for MBUK photo shoot.' Those sorts of nights would be a regular feature in and out of race season for the next twenty years. Hands up, that wasn't going to change! I was mirroring the behaviour of a 1970s footy player as best I could. I still haven't worked out if that was a good or bad thing, and have never felt the need. There was too much going on outside to worry about inside.

In early February and before the season started, Will, Titley and I did a cycle sprint test. This involved six minutes on a stationary bike when all our vitals were measured and fed into a computer. Mine surprised me because it showed I'd made some progress over the previous year's numbers. Will had been coming to circuits with me too and that was good fun, having him there. It kept us fit. We both suffered through the fartlek programmes they gave us. We got dizzy together at the intensity of it all as we crawled up the wall of fitness improvement step by step. When I could get out on the road bike, I'd be getting in a hundred a week, usually in twenty-five to thirty-five-mile sessions at around eighteen to twenty miles per hour. Not super fast, but pretty good for a mountain biker. My resting heart rate was going down and my recovery from effort was happening quicker. I still wasn't free of my gloopy chest though. Running and riding in bad weather and not getting warm enough after, and the drinking which doesn't help the gut biome as we now know, would have hindered my recovery somewhat. That cough went on all February and into March – bloody annoying!

I kept at it. I rode a few cross-country races in March, which showed me I still wasn't anywhere near where I needed to be fitness-wise. Then I got a second place which told me I wasn't as out of shape as I thought. The race

AMATEUR DRAMATICS

was called Jack's Challenge and I picked up a back injury that would follow me through my whole career and flare up when I really didn't need it. It's a problem I still have to this day. Weekends off the bike in Chap and Sheff continued unabated. I remember being out in town and having a fight with someone and then getting CS-gassed at a club we visited. My diary entry read, 'Great night out with the lads'.

The first NEMBA of the new season was in Nantwich on 9 April and I knew I'd have to get some better form in my legs if I was going to start where I'd left off in 1993. I wanted to win one. The time of being bridesmaid to the likes of Warner and JMC was going to come to an end sooner or later. Sooner the better, I thought. Consistency was important, but you got noticed way more for a win than for a few safe thirds. Despite the weather improving along with my form, I'd now had a bad chest for nearly three months. I had no idea what Warner and JMC were doing since I only went out with my crew. I just kept my focus, thinking that they must be training as hard as I was, and that if I was doing all I could, then I couldn't do more. There was no time to indulge myself thinking they might be having their own troubles. I just had to keep my head down and do my thing. When the NEMBA came around I'd know where we were.

In the off-season everybody worked on deals for the coming year. Warner and JMC had got good contracts with salaries on the new MBUK Nike team. I wasn't there yet. I wanted to be, but I'd have to wait. I didn't warrant enough interest to have money chucked at me. All I had was a phone call from Jay Hardy to see if I wanted to race the Malverns and to let me know that he might be able to help me get a deal. When Jay's contact got in touch to see what was happening with my contract at Kona, JP put his foot down and that was the end of that. I didn't hear again from Jay's contact.

His interest did get me a bit more from Kona though. I had a couple of new bikes to ride, one for cross-country, a titanium Hei Hei, and an alloy full-suspension Verlicchi for downhill. This was a frame several bike brands had put their sticker on. This happens sometimes when brands don't want to develop a bike that may not be a big seller, or don't have the facilities to develop one. I would get the cross-country bike in mid-March, but wouldn't get the downhill bike until late April, so would have to ride the Hei Hei at the first two downhill races of the year.

My entries were being paid for too and I had a bonus scheme based on my performance at certain races. Later on in the year Kona set up a bonus for if I won the NEMBA overall again. Kona would use me for some ads and *Mountain Biking UK* were happy to send down Steve Behr to shoot me for articles. Coverage meant I'd be seen and that might mean a better deal the following year. JP said they'd help out where they could with expenses but there was no cash for a wage, so I still had to work nine to five. I fitted my first bathroom that year but also had to attend college, which I hated. I knew I'd have to find time to go abroad a few times so the season ahead looked pretty hectic.

The bikes I had to race were free, but they weren't that great. I didn't take to the Hei Hei at first, but after changing some stuff on it at Langsetts I started to warm to it a bit. The downhill bike on the other hand was like an elastic band and horrible to ride. The swing arm, the suspended section which holds the back wheel, moved all over the place when the bike was pushed hard. If I was on the limit I'd be too often in danger of crashing. And I did crash because I wasn't willing to back down. There was no rigidity around the bottom bracket and the cranks drifted as well. It felt like pedalling in glue and the bike really limited my speed. Warner and JMC's GT bikes were way better but this didn't stop me pushing mine to its limit and beyond, trying to put the negatives out of my mind. JP did send me better kit to use on both bikes, which helped.

With the off-season over my shoulder and at least some semblance of fitness in my legs and lungs, the first big test of the year was upon me. I remember the week leading up to that first NEMBA of 1994 like it was yesterday. On the Saturday before, 2 April, Langsett called me to say there were some new Marzocchi forks at the shop from Kona and they wanted to fit them. As I'd be racing cross-country and downhill on the same bike, these new forks would be better than the ones currently on my bike, more rigid and adjustable. I also had some heavier-duty downhill wheels made up too that I could use on the following Saturday for the downhill race.

Having picked up the bike, Longden and I headed to Bolehills BMX track. It was windy and I should have left the bikes in the van, but no, of course I didn't. I came off over one of the jumps and landed hard on my shoulder. I was meant to be racing the next day at a local event but next morning I couldn't even hold the bars so called that off and went to Titley's in Shrewsbury, got bladdered and then played frisbee in the town square before squeezing Titley so hard he fainted. By Tuesday I was back home and ready for some snowboarding at Sheffield Ski Village. I didn't need my shoulder for that crack. I didn't ride the bike all week and got to Nantwich early on the Saturday for the NEMBA.

I did six practice runs and my shoulder was agony. The bike felt okay though. The track was excellent, good at the top, rooty and nasty in places, with two pedally sections where I could really get some speed up, then a massive jump into a field to finish. I had a good run in the race but was slower than I might have been, despite the shoulder injury, and felt annoyed about that. But I still won. My prize was some Pace handlebars and other bits I could sell. I raced the cross-country next day, got a great start but then faded back to ninth after blowing up on the third lap. I was so knackered I was hallucinating afterwards. It was a great start to the year. I was on such a high after the weekend that on the Monday I went for a thirty-mile ride to Penistone roundabout and back. Kona and the gang at Langsetts were happy with my results too.

The second round of NEMBA was the following weekend in Beddgelert, North Wales. This was not my favourite course. Titley and I spent all day Friday practising with Warner, Longden, Simon 'Kipper' Kipling and a few others. Will battered himself during Saturday practice and I already had a black eye after a scuffle the night before with some Welsh fella. On Sunday, race day, I suddenly experienced a new emotion: nerves. People kept coming up to tell me I was going to win. I felt real pressure as the favourite. I soon put their minds at rest, crashing out not far from the start line in a riverbed. I hit something really hard, one hand came off and I was catapulted right over the bars head first, bashed my thigh really hard and gave myself a dead leg that took a week before I could walk on it again. It took another week before I had the feeling back. I finished in seventeenth. The high of the previous week was all forgotten. I took some consolation from how fast I had been in practice, which was why folk kept saying I would win. Of course, no one remembers the consolation prizes.

By 1 May I was back in the groove and riding good vibes having won the first Karrimor BMBF downhill of the year at Eston Hills on Teesside. I even got sixth the next day on the cross-country bike. Two weeks later I was down in Plymouth at Newnham Park for the cross-country world cup. That was a 10.3-kilometre loop and I bonked on the third lap because I wasn't used to the distance. Dave Hemming liked to tell people he smoked me on the downhill, but I was lying in a bush begging for a banana off a marshal! The week after was a cross-country in Sandy Balls in the New Forest, where I came in fifth, which earned me some prize money. I think I even beat Rich Thackray. I could feel myself getting fitter and the Verlicchi had been delivered. The plan was to spend a few weeks dialling it in on all the gnarly stuff around Chap and in my beloved Wharncliffe Woods.

Riding the full-sus bike as often as I could, I started to get used to its ways. I was bending a lot of wheels though since the ones that came on the bike weren't up to much. I got a new set from Langsetts with stronger rims, heavier-gauge spokes and better hubs. They gave me a bit more confidence in the bike. Another problem was my pedals. As good as they were, I was coming out of them too easily, especially when I was pedalling hard. The pedals contained a mechanism that used spring tension to keep the shoe's cleat positioned correctly on the pedal. There was a certain amount of float to allow the foot to move on the horizontal plane. If the spring was worn or too weak then as you shifted your foot it could pop out. The technology was still in its early years, and this was a problem for all riders, not just me. It can be pretty scary coming unclipped at high speed with one or both feet out of the pedals. When the only parts of my body touching the bike were my bony arse and hands, there was no control at all on bumpy ground. Overall, the bike was okay. Not the best, not the worst, but it did affect my race results.

Titley, Kipper and I got our heads together and decided we would race a world cup. Having checked out the calendar we entered the round scheduled for June in the Bavarian mountain town of Bad Hindelang. In true Titley and Peaty fashion, we bought lots of schnapps and other booze at the airport, but in remembering the essentials we forgot to book a ride to our digs. An expensive taxi ride was our next best option and en route we drank all the schnapps and started on the rest. Titley and Kipper soon crashed out, which left me to pay for the cab. I was so drunk I couldn't find our accommodation and then we were so plastered we had to book Titley into another hotel, where he slept solidly for two days. Kipper wasn't much better but at least he had a team to snap him out of his self-inflicted stupor.

We did arrive with enough time in the week to get plenty of practice runs in and set up the bikes. The track was very good, so much longer than UK tracks, more technical and faster with really challenging terrain. Things all went swimmingly until it was time to qualify. During my run on the Saturday my chain bounced up and off the rings into my crankset which then jammed. I ended up freewheeling to the finish line in ten minutes dead. My weekend was over. That was the one thing with downhill I was still getting used to. I could look forward to a race for weeks, travel halfway across the world, and then during qualifying have a mechanical or make a little mistake and that was it, weekend over. It was brutal, but I was determined to ensure it happened less often.

I watched the finals on the Sunday which pissed me off even more as I knew I could have been up there. François Gachet won the men's and Missy Giove the women's. By Monday afternoon I was back home having caught a flight from Munich, back to the reality of getting up at 7 a.m. next morning for work with Steve Coleman. The positive takeaway from the weekend was all the Brits out there telling me how fast I was going before the chain had jammed. Another positive was being kicked out of the after-party for kicking apples around, one of which accidentally flew into the leg of a UCI official. After asking us between gritted teeth for our licence numbers, me and Titley made up some numbers. Then we smiled, apologised and made our way out into the night.

―――

I was proud to be chosen to represent Great Britain at the world championships in Vail, Colorado. I hoped I'd do a lot better than I had at the worlds in Métabief the previous year. Yet I didn't take it too seriously. When racing abroad I did the same as I would at races in the UK: check the digs out, go to the track, scope out the terrain, put a plan together with the other UK riders at the race, spend as much time as possible on the mountain, then get pissed with Titley and the others for the rest of the weekend. It was pretty simple. I can't remember a time when I wasn't partying the night before qualification at a world cup. My off-track antics didn't always go down well with the powers that be, whether that was sponsors or the lanyard-and-trackie-top British Cycling crew. They didn't like or even understand anomalies like me. I didn't worry about what they thought. I was doing this on my own terms and didn't think about anything but racing.

The magazines played up this reputation of mine. I was often portrayed as this off-the-bike laidback surfer dude, a party animal with a few beers in him, and then an absolute maniac on a bike. They also had respect for the fact I was a pretty decent cross-country rider and that made me seem more serious. *Mountain Biking UK* had a young male readership so the image of me they presented focused more on the partying and crashing. The good results I was getting and how dedicated I was didn't seem as important to them. I was mostly just glad for the coverage though, as it was getting me noticed and would make getting sponsored easier. The penny hadn't – and actually still hasn't – dropped that it might have been better to lay off the partying a bit to focus on performing well. The difficulty was how to separate the party scene from the downhill race scene. As far as I was concerned, the two always went hand in hand. That was one of the reasons I stopped racing both cycling disciplines. Doing well in cross-country was impossible with my lifestyle.

In late June, just after I got back from Bad Hindelang, I had a snowboarding accident at the ski village and damaged my wrist. That put the kibosh on riding for a week. And on top of that, I seemed to have developed

FORGED BY SPEED

hay fever. Ignoring the pain in my wrist, I went up to Hamsterley Forest in County Durham for a downhill race, but the wrist was so painful and weak it gave way as I hit a rock and I was fired over the bars and got stuck in the trackside fencing. I still came second though, to Dylan Clayton, an ex-BMX racer. I slept in the car that night and didn't race cross-country the next day as my wrist was killing me. Then I found out I had chickenpox, which explained why I'd felt like shit all week.

I'd recently upped my nutrition game by switching lager for Guinness on race weekends thinking it would increase my iron levels. I have no idea if it helped or not, but I thought it did at the time. And with the Kamikaze Downhill at Mammoth Mountain two weeks away I thought I'd better have a week off work and get well again. Jim McRoy had put the Kamikaze trip together in late July for me and Paul Plunkett, with Kona paying for the flight. JMC and Warner would already be out there having raced a world cup the week before in Canada. I was excited to be hitting the USA for the first time, especially California. JMC's success there the previous year was why I wanted to go; he'd really stamped his name in the history books.

Two days after landing and while doing as many runs as I could, I hyperextended my ankle, which swelled up like a grapefruit. I strapped it up and kept at it despite not being able to bear any weight on my ankle. But that was nothing compared to Steve Jones, who smashed his nuts on his saddle and cracked a ball. While still high on the pain meds, he showed them to us in the pub. The size and colour were a sight to behold.

The bike was taking a battering too. The speed on the course was so high that one run could leave a bike unrideable. Mine certainly needed a good tune up, but I foolishly ignored that, focusing instead on getting runs in. So, by the time I'd had my first qualifier on the Thursday, my front wheel was wandering all over the place at fifty miles per hour. I should have fixed it after that because the spokes were loose. Of course I didn't, and 300 metres into my final run on the Sunday the front wheel collapsed, folding like paper. I sat at the side of the track for a few minutes crying, consumed by feelings of utter despair and stupidity. I knew the bike needed fixing. I'd had the time to fix it. There were no excuses.

The words 'if only' ran through my head as I took the walk of shame. By the time I got to the bottom the tears were flowing. Waiting there were JMC and Karen Van Meerbeeck who greeted me with a big consolatory hug. I still felt like a complete dickhead. It was bad enough going to Germany and having a mechanical. This one was worse because it was my fault. I had also skinned my back and nearly ripped my nipple off on the volcanic rock of Mammoth Mountain. Those scars would last a lifetime as a reminder of that

AMATEUR DRAMATICS

day; one of my boobs is still slightly bigger than the other. On the eleven-hour flight home, I couldn't sit back in the seat as my grazes seeped through my clothes and stuck me to the seat. I stuck to the bed sheets for a week.

Things changed quickly though when my schedule had a race a week in it. By the following weekend I was in the Malverns in apple country winning £500 after beating Dave Hemming in the Psychosis dual eliminator. If that event showed me anything, it was that mountain biking was in good health. There were thousands of people there ready to watch and party. I was even asked for my autograph. That was weird but I liked it. The Malverns Classic was a right laugh and one I'd look forward to every year. I spent the weekend in a haze, if you know what I mean. It picked me right up after the lows of the Kamikaze and Germany, and started off a run of races in the UK which led to the national championships at the end of July in Shropshire, where I stayed for the weekend with Titley.

Downhill practice went perfectly on the Friday. Race day was a different story. I wanted to beat JMC really badly and came out of the gate hard. Then everything started to unravel quickly. I hit a tree and just about came to a dead stop. Then I completely mistimed some switchbacks and came unclipped all the way to the finish line, ending up in third just behind JMC. Rob won, annoyingly. I was fucking livid. JMC's time was only a tad over two seconds slower than his time. If I hadn't come unclipped, I'd have won even if I'd still hit the tree. Next day I did the cross-country and punctured with no spare tube. Again. No double break-fast to blame this time, just stupidity and a lack of prep. The cross-country course was really good too.

In July I was approached about the possibility of a big money racing deal that would take me to the world cups in 1995. The approach came from a guy who was trying to put a team together with some non-bike corporate sponsors. I'd see him nosing around at the races in the UK a few times in the coming months, but put it out of my mind and focused on what was real right now. Getting paid to ride though sounded perfect. I got a couple of races under my belt in the coming weeks and then bumped into him again when I was really stoned after having a bong hit after winning a PORC race on the first weekend of August. On the Saturday he offered me a deal of three grand, plus expenses for all the races abroad including the Grundig world cups, plus a car. I said we'd talk some more, and then spent the Sunday unclipping from my pedals. I still won overall after coming second to Longden. The PORC tracks were good fun, though short, but that doesn't matter when they're a crack to ride. At most of the UK races, when I stayed on, I'd post really good times and knew I was getting close to Warner and

JMC. They were gettable. I just had to figure out how to stay on the bike more.

Looking back at my diaries a pattern emerges that I didn't see at the time. I'd regularly come down with flu or have problems recovering from illness. In 1994 that was particularly true. I know now that alcohol and sugar affect the immune system and brain function through the gut's microbiome. They cause inflammation too. I'm sure some of those weeks I was ill and run-down were to do with the effects of excessive drinking and overtraining lowering my immune system. Hindsight is one thing, but would I have changed anything? No, I wouldn't. In fact, I think I was doing a great job having fun and racing. Things couldn't have been any better. Though that naivety must have cost me some race results I reckon. Although I have a sneaky suspicion it may have also helped me calm my nerves and blow off steam, so I may have benefitted from it too. I wouldn't recommend it though.

In early August, Dave Mellor called to say he could help with money to get me to the worlds. The French round of the world cup in Métabief was coming up in the middle of the month and me, JMC and Warner would be out there again trying to put a decent run together to get on the podium. We had all week to practise. The track was good, rougher than the year before, and now I was on the full sus I was determined to go faster. I felt so at home that on the first day I didn't bother putting race gear on and just wore a T-shirt, surf shorts and a cross-country lid. On the Tuesday JMC arrived, so I kitted up and did some runs with him. Wednesday's practice was amazing and it was such a laugh with Warner, Longden and Titley on the mountain with me and JMC.

Thursday was qualification. I fell off on my run but still managed to finish in a good enough time to get me through to the finals on Saturday. We all practised like mad on the Friday afternoon, checking out the track as it got cut up. I didn't party that evening and on race day I was third fastest until the halfway point when I crashed and buggered up the run. I missed out on the final by two seconds. My plans for getting a result at the world cup were once again scuppered by a silly crash. I was so pissed off I didn't stay for the Sunday and caught the earliest ferry I could back to the UK, tail between my legs. My breakthrough ride was going to have to wait.

Racing in GB colours at the world championships in Colorado was a big deal, even if I was a bit blasé about it at the time. I was excited to be going and felt I had a point to prove. Vail is a beautiful and popular ski resort in the Rockies, with the mountain rising a thousand metres above the village. The resort sits at altitude and I knew it would make sense to get there early

AMATEUR DRAMATICS

and spend time acclimatising, so Titley and I headed off a month before the race to get used to riding at 2,500 metres. We rented a small apartment and set to familiarising ourselves with the terrain and nightlife. That four weeks was time well spent. We got used to the way the soil was and how grippy the rocks were, and basically sharked every run we could find. By the end of those four weeks I was pretty confident that I could hold my own on the downhill course. Titley and I also went shopping to buy anything we couldn't get back home: Oakley glasses, shorts, hoodies and T-shirts mainly. We were out partying with the locals too, which helped pass the time. In fact, we were having a right old laugh.

The downhill track was already laid out and took six to seven minutes to get down. There was lots of pedalling, which was fine, but it wasn't as technical as I'd have liked, although it was fast. Like Métabief, the event was huge with TV crews and thousands of spectators from all over the world arriving daily. Bicycle brand rigs were everywhere, team areas were allocated for riders, mechanics and team managers, and media tents were set up with complimentary food and phone lines ready to transmit news all over the globe. Sponsor banners were all over the cross-country and downhill courses, and the UCI had a huge presence. It really was a great spectacle and being there in the weeks beforehand not only got me excited but also let me see what goes on behind the scenes at such big events.

The first race of the weekend was on the Friday night, the dual slalom under the lights. Brian Lopes won the final against Myles Rockwell, while Anne-Caroline Chausson beat Leigh Donovan in the women's event. It was great to watch but I was glad I wasn't riding. You couldn't see a thing in the dark with the spotlights on as you tried to make out where the corners were – the lines down the hill were deep in shadow. Then on the cross-country course there was a crazy bit of technical downhill for the racers to navigate called the Bud Light Bailout. Lots of riders crashed there in the race, as did a marshal on a trials bike who was following the race. He ended up going straight over the bars. We were supporting our GB riders, particularly Tim Gould, who lives locally to me and had a chance of doing well.

When it came to my turn in the downhill, I qualified easily enough. The track had some pedalling sections that I knew I'd be able to motor down, but I always tried to use the terrain to my advantage rather than just attacking everything without any thought to making each run as efficient as possible. It might not have looked like that when people saw me crash, but I was always trying to focus my rage into a beautiful and mistake-free package of radness. It was hard in Vail though. Some parts of the course were so fast and studded with rocks they really did hammer the bike a fair

103

bit. It was really hard for things not to get sketchy, and to stay just on the right side of out of control. It's such a fine line.

I have always been quite good at finding lines down a course that can be ridden differently. Using undulations to gain speed, jumping, 'going light', as I call it. In Vail, I'd look for ways to use the terrain to increase speed, like on rooty sections where I'd ride them neatly instead of hitting them hard, thus eliminating the chance of sliding out. That's what I think I've been good at: running high or tight lines and using body weight to get the bike to grip where others struggle. On parts of the Vail track that precision was impossible though. It was just: pick a line, commit to it 100 per cent and ride it out.

When it came to the final, I was ready to give everything. This was the world championships. It was a one-off race, I had nothing to lose and no series points were at risk if I blew it. It was do-or-die time. I even decided not to wear kneepads. I look back at pictures of that race and think *what the hell was I doing?* Me and Longden were Yorkshire boys and we egged each other on sometimes to do things like that, thinking we were tough. It was with that mentality that I arrived at the top of the mountain and off I went.

I'm not sure it could have gone much better. I rode a good run with only a few minor mistakes, didn't blow up in terms of energy and really attacked the course. When I got to the bottom I was blown away. The feeling was incredible. It wouldn't last long, but I'd set the fastest time on the hill. When I hit the finish line the silence from the crowd was near total. There was just one person in the stands shouting for me. Tim Flooks, downhill team manager at the time, was screaming his head off. No one else knew who I was, and no one had been expecting that to happen, except Tim and me.

In a few minutes the feeling of being the world's fastest would be gone as the cheers resumed for Myles, America's golden boy, who crossed the line right after me and was six seconds faster. When everyone had come down the mountain and the dust finally settled in Vail, I placed twelfth, thirteen seconds down on the winner François Gachet. Tommy Johansson was second and the late Corrado Hérin, who tragically died in 2019 in an ultra-light aircraft crash, was third. Gachet's winning time was six minutes and twenty-two seconds, but I knew where to find those thirteen seconds that separated us. In a strange way I was really stoked. My brain started to compute. *I can do this*, I told myself. *I'm meant to be here.*

I'd also beaten JMC, who came thirty-eighth, ten seconds behind me. He was on a better bike than me too. Myles had come fifth. I was pretty chuffed to say the least, and to celebrate I did what I always do. I knew there was still a load of work to be done to get to the podium. JMC had done it at

AMATEUR DRAMATICS

Mammoth Mountain the year before in the Kamikaze. Between him, Warner and me, one of us was going to make it to the top of the box soon. I badly wanted it to be me. The flight home at the end of September was easy. I was in a great mood. I knew I'd helped my chances of getting sponsorship and had made lots of helpful connections in the USA too.

At Vail it became clear that the bike set-up I was rocking for downhill was not as advanced as that of the top downhillers, the new junior and senior world champions, Nico Vouilloz, Anne-Caroline Chausson and François Gachet. The Sunn and GT bikes were really good. The Sunn Chipie bikes had wider bars and stiffer, more adjustable Bossard forks, as well as rear suspension with a special linkage. Those bikes were way better than my narrow cross-country bars and flexible Marzocchi forks and elastic band frame. They gave their riders an edge over everyone else, including me.

Competing in Vail had also shone a bright light on specific areas of downhill where I needed to improve. That was glaringly obvious given I was getting beat by ten to fifteen seconds. My bike skills weren't there yet, and neither was my confidence, but they were building. I was making too many silly mistakes on a bike that couldn't go as fast as I knew I could. That's why Olivier Bossard was such a huge deal for the Sunn team; he was a suspension genius and the rest of the mountain bike industry was trailing behind his understanding of the available technology. His riders could go faster because his bikes could cope with the terrain better. Clever bugger.

Although I capped off the year with a few wins in the UK and won both the NEMBA and BMBF series, something needed to change. I knew the next year would be different, but I couldn't possibly have known just how difficult 1995 would be.

CHAPTER 11
A HEART OF GOLD

Towards the end of 1994, my boss Steve and I were driving to a job, chatting about this and that. It was Steve who had lent me the money two years before so I could buy a better mountain bike, the Rocky Mountain Hammer, as I was short by more than a few quid. I got my bike and worked overtime to pay Steve back. Everybody needs a boss like Steve. Now I'd been offered a deal to turn pro, riding for the Saracen Coors team. I was three years into my apprenticeship; this would be my last year and then I'd be qualified. I wondered about taking a year off to give the Grundigs a shot. What did he think?

'How much are they going to pay you?'

'Well, they started at three grand, which I wasn't happy about, but as I've done well in the last half of the season it's now at seven, plus a fair few perks which should bag me around ten.'

Steve didn't hesitate.

'A job on the tools will always be here for you,' he said. 'This opportunity won't.'

That was it then. I'd say yes to the deal and start my first year on the circuit as a pro. Then we'd see what happened after that.

The excitement of being able to pack up work and the realisation that my bike-riding talent was being recognised and rewarded by a brand willing to pay me was pretty fucking stratospheric. Three years before I'd been just a skinny lad from Chap on a Muddy Fox with a poorly paid YTS apprenticeship dressed up as a real job. Now I was on the pages of the magazines I'd read as a kid and about to do a full season on the world circuit as a member of the global Saracen Coors mountain bike team. Even better, some of my

107

friends were on the team as well, including Titley and Warner. When I agreed the terms of the contract it felt like I was signing my destiny. All the things running through my head were predictable cheesy sound bites – that I'd hit the big time, that I'd made it and was on my way. If I was American, I would have high-fived the whole of the Cowley estate. I was so bloody happy.

Of course, the Saracen deal was not all it seemed. The team manager and I tired of each other very quickly. In fact, I lost faith even before the season started. Our first team camp was in Madrid and he invited us to stay at his house in London before flying out of Heathrow next day. Me and Titley set off down south but when we got close the guy wasn't answering the phone. He left us for hours not knowing where we were going to sleep. When he finally got in touch we discovered he'd been hanging out with another crowd instead of us. That didn't sit well with me. Nor did the threat of fines for wearing the wrong logo on some casual clothes. I logged all this and more in the memory bank to save for when I eventually phoned to tell him I was off.

The team may have started out with the very best intentions, Saracen being a UK bike brand and all that, but the deal went tits up pretty quickly for all sorts of reasons. Emptying the minibar in three different rooms and arriving at breakfast with a bottle of champagne in my hand and calling him dodgy was a highlight of that doomed Madrid trip for me. Between me, Warner and Titley, we made his life as awkward as we could, and abused the expense account while it lasted. We had no idea what was going on behind the scenes. All we knew was that halfway through the season we weren't getting paid and were having to pay our own travel and expenses, whereas before it was all an open chequebook. Being the age we were, the way our dissatisfaction manifested itself was not especially mature, but it was effective. The team manager loathed me and the situation broke down so badly that we ended up speaking through third parties.

To numb out the frustration I began treating every day like I was living in a non-stop party. Being sponsored by Coors helped, as at least the beer was free. I drank my way through so many minibars I lost count. Having free crates of Coors available and on tap from our title sponsor was not helping matters of lucidity. I was clearly going through my Keith Moon phase of having champagne and beers for breakfast. The frustration of riding for the team didn't bring out the best aspects of my usually good-natured upbeat character, and when I was home I was getting into a few too many fights. I seemed to be dragging a cloud around with me wherever I went. Opportunities were lost at races where I could have done better. That first year as a pro on the circuit I injured myself more than any other year in my career. While it seemed like I was having fun at the time, I'm not sure now that it was the best way to carry on if I wanted to achieve what I needed to on the circuit.

In between posh hotels, hangovers and injuries, mostly sustained on photo shoots for magazines and adverts, I did get some pretty good results at the races. If I hadn't buggered my foot taking press photos at the fourth round of the world cup in the Canadian resort of Mont-Sainte-Anne things might have gone better. Having a more competitive bike than the Verlicchi I was riding would have been the icing on the cake. It might seem strange that I was riding a bike made by a different brand to the one sponsoring me, but at that stage a lot of manufacturers didn't have a competitive bike ready so they would buy in someone else's.

In the sixth and final round at Kaprun in Austria I had a breakthrough ride that restored my confidence. I realised I had become too focused on the team's problems and not enough on riding well. I also had Warner in my ear telling me everything was shit. At Kaprun I decided to ride for myself again and that paid off. The course was bone dry with a lot of pedalling, so my cross-country fitness came into play. Despite coming unclipped a few times, I rode well when it came to the finals. I was down the hill in seven minutes and 3.67 seconds which was enough to get me tenth place. Myles Rockwell won with a time of in six minutes and 51.34 seconds. Nico came second and Tomi Misser third. I was now only five seconds off the top five. The field was stacked with talent and when I crossed the finish line I had a feeling I'd done well. It was a taste of things to come. I was making progress despite all the mess around me. And thanks to Eurosport's coverage, the world was getting to see more of Steve Peat.

———

After Kaprun and back in Sheffield, I had a party at my parents' house in Chap. A lot of my mates came, including JMC, Titley, Longden and Helen Mortimer. In the evening Jason announced he was off home to New Mills on his Harley-Davidson to see his girlfriend, Sophie. It was dark by then and we all pleaded with him to stay and come to the pub instead. It was typical of Jason that he wouldn't change his mind. Not long after, travelling west along the A628 Woodhead Pass, a lorry overtaking him knocked him from his bike and he slid into an oncoming lorry. He didn't stand a chance. My last image of Jason was of him turning left out of Mum and Dad's estate,

FORGED BY SPEED

looking cool as fuck on his Harley. He gave us the horns as we turned right to go to the pubs in Chap. Next morning I got the call from his mum, Rose.

It's very difficult to explain the hole left by Jason's passing. He had shown us the way. He was the first of us to hit the big time, both in terms of getting a pro deal with Specialized and also as a great character who transcended all that earthly bullshit. If he'd ridden a Honda step-through and raced a Raleigh Burner, he'd still have been cool as fuck. The UK downhill scene in 1995 was an incredibly close-knit community and Jason was its figurehead. The best thing about him was that he had a heart of gold, and you can't buy them. Lads like Jason don't come along very often.

Despite how competitive we all were, nothing would get in the way of a good piss-up after race day. We really were one great big family. Jason's dad, Jim, put some of Jason's ashes in a couple of his film canisters that Warner and I taped to our bikes at the 1995 world champs in Germany so Jason could ride the course with us. All of Jason's mates will say the same thing I'm sure: it's like he's still here in some sense. I don't know or even want to know how that is; I just like the feeling of having him around to keep an eye on us from the 'big out there'. I think of Jase very often, he always brings a smile to these old chops of mine. Every time I pass his memorial on the A628 I give him a beep on the horn. British mountain biking changed on 24 August 1995. I lost a great friend, and Jim and Rose lost their amazing son.

My inability to understand or deal with Jason's death was a seeping wound. I became acquainted with melancholy for a while, as the loss worked its way through me. To block out the pain I took every minute of every day by the scruff of its neck and wrung every last drop from it. It didn't matter whether I was having fun or not. I was always running in the red. Instead of grieving I was celebrating Jason. I put the grief away, buried it under good times, but it was there all the time. The hole that was left after he passed would never be filled, I knew that deep down. Yet each day I moved a little further from the edge of that hole until I was able to miss him and not be drawn back down into that hole and the behaviours I used to manage the pain.

Despite the personal loss, my racing career was looking up for 1996. Before the end of the season, I was relieved to know I'd be leaving the Saracen team. I wouldn't have to ride that piece of shit Verlicchi again. But the best part about leaving Saracen was a new deal that meant I wouldn't have to go back on the plumbing tools. Towards the end of 1995 the chiefs at *Mountain Biking UK* put together a deal for me on the MBUK GT Nike team. Being UK based, they knew early on I wasn't happy with Saracen, and we had already been discussing terms when the team collapsed at the end of

110

1 Andy, Jonny, Mum and me outside the family home in Chapeltown.
2 Jonny, me, Andy and Dad on the bikes outside our house on Woodburn Drive.
3 On a family holiday in the late 1970s.
4-5 With Dad and Mum on our Fort Bill holidays.

6 Racing downhill on the fully rigid Kona at Penshurst, Kent, in 1993. © Steve Behr/Stockfile
7 Racing downhill at the world championships in Vail, Colorado, in 1994. Now on the full-sus Verlicchi. © Steve Behr/Stockfile

8   Jim and Jason McRoy at Sea Otter.   © Malcolm Fearon/blissimages.com
9   Me and Warner on a photoshoot for *Dirt* magazine.   © Paul Bliss

10   Me and Warner having breakfast in California in 1997. © Steve Behr/Stockfile
11   Titley with a wheel clap we'd managed to get off my van after I'd been clamped outside the *MBUK* offices.
     I ended up getting a legal letter from the clamping company and had to give it back!
12   Will Longden and me outside Anaheim in the States.
13   Just some hire car damage…

14 The award ceremony at Panticosa, Spain, in 1996 — my first world cup podium and the point at which I entered the big time. © Malcolm Fearon/blissimages.com
15 Driving the Golden Princess to the trails in the States with Adele and Nige Page. © Paul Bliss
16 Winning the Winter X Games in 1998.
17 Shaun Palmer in his gold tuxedo after winning the Big Bear Lake world cup.

18 Adele racing dual at Sea Otter.
19 Me and Adele with Mum and Dad at Fort Bill in 2002. © Steve Behr/Stockfile

20 On the top of the box at the Les Gets world cup in 2002.
21 Racing in Vigo, Spain, for Orange in 2005. I placed third, behind Mick Hannah and Nathan Rennie. © Victor Lucas

22–26 Finally winning the Fort Bill world cup in 2005. It's still one of the biggest sporting moments I've ever experienced. The noise of the crowd blew me away that day. It was great to have my family and baby Jake there to share it with me. All photos © Steve Behr/Stockfile

24

25

26

27

28

27+28 Vallnord, Andorra, 2009. My seventeenth and final world cup win.
29 Canberra worlds in 2009. On the upper technical section of the course. All photos © Sven Martin

30·31 The agonising wait (top) to find out if anyone would beat my time, and the aftermath of winning the biggest race in the world.

32 On the podium with Greg Minnaar and Mick Hannah.
33 I love a one-man party! Seventeen years in the making – I wasn't going to share this champagne with anyone else!
34 No caption needed. All photos © Sven Martin

35+36 My final Fort Bill in 2016. An emotional end to my career at my home world cup. It was great to be able to share it with friends and family, including young George.

37–39 Signing off from world cup racing in Vallnord, Andorra, in 2016.
40 The Syndicate crew and friends at Vallnord. L–R: Andy Kyffin, Jason Marsh, Joe Bowman, me, Rob Roskopp, Kathy Sessler, Greg Minnaar, Josh Bryceland and Doug Hatfield. Luca Shaw, who hadn't yet signed for the Syndicate, is lurking in the background! All photos © Sven Martin

41+42 Me (left) and Dad riding the Pipeline section in the Scottish Six Days Trial over thirty years apart.
43 Riding in Avoriaz with Adele, Jake and George. © Kéno Derleyn

A HEART OF GOLD

the season. The GT LTS bike was really good; Nico won the worlds on one. There was more money from *Mountain Biking UK* too and a lot of familiar faces, and I was still living at home and managing to bank some cash. As a bonus for being on the *Mountain Biking UK* payroll, readers would see me in the mag all the time.

After Saracen, Warner managed to get a good deal with Giant, very much a European brand. Rob and I would eventually become household names in the world of UK mountain biking. I'm eternally grateful to *Mountain Biking UK*, not just for the financial backing but for the exposure as well. Both Rob and I really benefitted from that; it set us up for life. There were some bloody daft things that *Mountain Biking UK* got us to do for articles, but that was a small price to pay for being plastered all over a magazine every month. I said yes to everything they suggested, and I expect Rob did too. The money arrived when they said it would and we could concentrate on making a name for ourselves on the circuit. We both had great bikes now, but truth be known my GT was better than Rob's Giant, which pissed him off.

Thanks to GT and a stable team, the potential I'd been showing began to come to fruition. My top ten finish in Kaprun the year before had been a great stepping stone and the first round of the 1996 world cup season at the Spanish spa town of Panticosa would confirm I'd made it all the way across the river to the other side to become a bona fide contender on the circuit. Everything went well leading up to the race. The bike felt good. I'd broken a few STS models, but GT were on the ball in replacing them. They made some improvements to the frames too as we went along, and Tim Flooks was able to get the bike to handle right. My fitness was good. I'd been focused and getting on with learning how to go faster and make fewer mistakes, in contrast to the year before. I was in great form. I had more confidence than ever.

I made sure to get to Panticosa early in the week before race weekend. The course was rocky as hell, slippery and muddy. Straightaway I felt at home. At this point in my career, I didn't really know too many other pros. Warner had been doing world cups a year longer than me, so he knew a few, me not so much. One day I ended up on the chairlift with Franck Roman, a French rider with a huge personality who was on the massive Cannondale team at the time. We chatted on the way to the top and he suggested I take his wheel and follow him down the track. I snapped up his offer and then tried to hang on for dear life.

The downhill technical sections were super-fast and really difficult to negotiate, with rock outcrops all over the place. There were some

FORGED BY SPEED

switchbacks with 180-degree turns that could sap my speed if I didn't get the lines right. It took all of my nerve to ride them as fast as I could. Franck was bouncing off trees, walls and rocks, carrying great speed everywhere down the course. I hung in there and although it was proper sketchy something clicked. Kaprun was a much longer course than this so keeping a laser focus here was going to mean the difference between a good run and a great run.

It rained in the week, but I managed six or seven runs on the Thursday and Friday. On Saturday it was still pissing down and the track was a mess, cut to pieces from all the runs during the week with lines so deep they would grab a wheel and take me in the wrong direction. On race day I didn't bother with a practice run and went straight to the qualification run, where I promptly fell off going through the tapes at the top but still finished fourteenth. I knew I was going fast. The track was starting to dry out, so I thought I'd get a few sneaky practice runs in before my final run. Then I went up to the gate at the top of the mountain for my start time of 1.37 p.m.

In less than five minutes I would be catapulted into the consciousness of every Eurosport viewer watching that weekend. I pedalled my arse off out of the saddle where I could and felt I was going to do well. I was even styling on the course, chucking in a couple of cross-ups for the fans on the most gnarly downhill bits and some kick-outs on the techie corners. Spectators trackside cheered me on as I ripped down the mountain in four minutes and 36.56 seconds. I then had to wait for the favourites Tomi Misser and Nico Vouilloz to come down after me as they had qualified better.

Waiting at the bottom of the course after a good run was always the worst part. I would be so nervous that the relief when the last rider came down was immeasurable. It wasn't joy. With everybody down at Panticosa, I was two seconds faster than Nico who was in third place and less than two seconds slower than Tomi. It suddenly sank in that I was second. I had beaten Nico. I remember being on the podium thinking, *How the hell did I do that?* It had been a big day but one I knew I had in me. GT and Nike were really happy. The result in Kaprun the year before had lifted me to a place that felt great, but this was different, a whole new level: my first podium against the best the world had to offer. Let me thank Franck for dragging me up to speed that weekend!

Another thing I remember about that weekend was my first encounter with Shaun Palmer. Being a keen snowboarder in the off-season, I bought all the boarding magazines and looked forward to the videos coming out. Palmer was a big character on that scene as well as riding downhill. The Whiskey boarding videos were hugely popular then, featuring the

A HEART OF GOLD

somewhat antisocial character Boozy the Clown and his antics. There had been reports in the media that Palmer, whose nickname was Napalm, was going to have a boxing match with Boozy. While I was prepping my bike for the competition in the hotel's underground car park I looked over and there was Shaun Palmer prepping his bike. I was still a fairly shy young fella, six years younger than Palmer, but couldn't resist trying to start a conversation.

'Hey, Shaun, how are you?'

'Good, man.'

'I hear you're going to fight Boozy the Clown. How's that going?'

There was no answer. I could see he was pissed off and he just carried on fixing his bike. I left feeling a little wounded and thinking he was a bit of a dick. Fast forward to after the weekend and me and Palmer were in the RockShox truck driving to Nevegal in Italy for the second round of the 1996 world cup. We shared a few beers and chatted. After my second place he now knew who I was. I've always said that that second place took me places I would otherwise never have known. Before that weekend in Spain, I had a few mates on the circuit. Afterwards, hundreds of people knew my name and would shout, 'Hi, Steve!' as I walked through the pits, although I had no idea who any of them were. On that long drive to Italy, me and Palmer hit it off and he remains one of my best mates to this day.

Downhill can be a harsh mistress to coin an overused phrase. A week after my success in Spain I was in Italy for round two and the course was mint. Foolishly, I didn't bother to do a practice run on the Saturday and then crashed my brains out in qualification, still somehow managing nineteenth. On Sunday, due to some slapdash prep, the previous night's MTV party and a few bevvies, I once again experienced a recurrence of nerves, duly crashing twice in my final run. I still finished twelfth but it was a bit of a let-down and I only had myself to blame. There were upsides though. The food in Italy was amazing and I did remember to wave to the Eurosport cameras after I crashed. I'd saved a bit of money too, so when I got back to the UK I treated myself to a Tag Chronograph for £540.

A month later and back at the Quebec resort of Mont-Sainte-Anne I got seventh and Warner ninth, the first time there had ever been two UK riders in the top ten. With two uphill sections, the track sucked a little, although the rest of it was fun to ride. My decent result wasn't the high point though. On the Friday before the finals I discovered a naked criterium road race. I was like a kid in a candy shop on a sugar rush. After that, Warner and I sloped off to a party that Palmer was hosting, although in contrast to ninety-nine per cent of all his other parties this one was quite restrained, and we ended up watching BMX videos and drinking beer.

113

FORGED BY SPEED

A year on from losing JMC, being on a team that was properly professional had helped me. I was still misbehaving, but after Panticosa and with the world a little more familiar with the name Steve Peat, my confidence was growing. I had also got to know Warner better and felt that I'd finally started to move out of his shadow. Being younger and less experienced, I'd looked up to him in the past. Like JMC he had been the man to beat. The year at Saracen had jaded us both and I'd seen a side of Rob that was different to the image the public knows. He gets down when things aren't going great, and while I was at Saracen with him I let that affect me too for a while. I sussed this eventually and coped by playing him at his own game, just to manage the mood swings. Now we were both on solid teams with some good people around us he seemed a lot more relaxed and less destructive. We both were. Having a really great bike also made a massive difference. The non-stop partying continued but it was now more for celebration than frustration.

Tim Flooks was a big influence on me at this time. In 1996 he was working with RockShox so having him at the world cups to look after the suspension on my bike was a massive help. I had never realised how much faster I could go when the bike was set up properly and I felt good on it. I was glad that I'd spent the previous three years honing my craft on a rigid bike and that crappy Verlicchi; it had taught me to be nimble on the bike and the importance of momentum. These skills are lost on modern downhill riders who haven't had to endure the technical restraints we experienced in those early days of downhill.

There were also fewer nights in Chap getting pissed up and more days out on the motocross bike I'd recently acquired after having had a go on Will Longden's. I'd never ached so much in places I didn't know existed until I started riding the motocross bike. Sometimes I was so sore I couldn't bend down to go to the toilet or get in the bath because the pain was so bad. It left me sore all over, but it was a massive step up in terms of fitness and skill, which I brought to the mountain. Motocross joined BMX and a bit of enduro as part of my training programme.

The great unspoken question in 1995 for me, Rob and Jason had been who would be the first Brit to win a world cup? We all secretly wanted it to be us. Yet we all knew we'd be happy for whoever it was. The three of us were so close that year. Then there were no longer three, but two. I'd come close in Spain, yet it was Rob who grabbed the prize in 1996 at the last round in Kaprun, despite not having had the best season. Rob is a really good rider; he can make anything with two wheels do whatever he wants.

114

A HEART OF GOLD

On a technical course, like Kaprun, he's right at home, even if he wasn't always so strong on the physical side.

The build-up to the race was less than ideal. It's mountain biking folklore how we almost got arrested in Morzine while celebrating the end of the previous round. We'd gone to a nightclub called the Monroe that had a full-sized statue of Marilyn as its centrepiece. After many beers, Rob jumped up on to Marilyn's plinth and pretended to make out with her. So I jumped up and grabbed her skirt from behind. Not exactly the most mature move, I know. When Rob stepped back down, I lost my balance and brought Marilyn down with me, where she promptly smashed into a thousand pieces. The statue, we later discovered, was worth thousands of francs, but we didn't stick around to pick up the pieces. The cops came looking for me at our hotel, but Jim McRoy helped me out by stuffing my gear in a bike bag and chucking it out the window.

With us in the car was an American lad who thought it was funny to keep grabbing the handbrake and making the car slide. As we set off up the hill to Les Gets, he grabbed the handbrake again, the car slid sideways and then he let it go and we fired off the road and down the hillside where the car got stuck in some woodland. We had to walk back to Les Gets where we hid in Palmer's hotel room and then we went back the next day with a tow truck. Then I realised that the car had come to rest on the edge of a field and I figured I could extricate it myself. The car had a flat so we put a space saver on it, and there was a big dent where it had hit a tree, but it still worked so we drove across Switzerland and over the border into Austria for the next round of the world cup at Kaprun.

Out of all this chaos, Rob managed to snatch the prize as the first British rider to win a world cup downhill. On race day, Rob had a great run, and when he crossed the line the clock read seven minutes and 15.32 seconds. That time wouldn't be beaten. After Rob's run the weather took a turn and it pissed down on the rest of the field. So, in a way the race was decided by the weather. Rob had come down the hill early as he'd had a really bad qualification round. On the other hand, his time was about the same as Jürgen Beneke's, and Jürgen is a great rider and hard-arsed competitor; he's not easily beaten. The famous off-cambers at the bottom of Kaprun were torturous in the wet conditions so everything bode well for Warner's early run. He had to wait a few hours for us all to slip and slide down, but at the end of it all he was still in front.

I'd had a problem with my bike on qualification day. A shock absorber bolt had come out on an earlier run so there was a bit of a panic going on. When I fixed that and went back up for my run, I came fifteenth so I was on the hill after Rob when the rain began to fall. I went as fast as I could, but I was also struggling with a season-long shoe-clip issue. As I came down into one of the most technical parts of the course, I came unclipped and lost all control and came off. I got going quickly and then came unclipped again and crashed in a gully, then came unclipped and crashed again. That was that for me.

Rob had a pretty faultless run and won on flats wearing his white socks. He was speechless at the end, a first for him! I was genuinely happy for him, painful as it was. I wanted it so badly to be me on top of that podium. Yet it came to pass that Rob Warner – gobshite, soft southern bastard, poseur, mardy git – became the first Briton to win a mountain bike world cup and he's been surfing that wave ever since. He was for the longest time the voice of downhill at Red Bull, the Murray Walker of downhill racing, the main man commentating on the world cup circuit. He's still my mate, a good trials rider too, despite having a stiff back when he rides, which we used to tease him about. As for me, it would take another two years before I finally stood on top of the box. In the meantime, I would be sharpening the blade of my will even more precisely, using moments like this as inspiration to train harder and go faster.

With Rob and I becoming the poster boys of the UK downhill scene, the energy and interest around the sport was really gathering pace. Now there were big teams like Animal coming into the sport run by former BMX-er Steve Kitchin. They had a very fast female BMX champion on their team. Adele Croxon was a great rider who like me had grown up under the influence of two wheels, desperate as a kid to ride motocross but channelled instead into BMX. Now after thirteen years she'd decided she needed a change, and when Kitchin offered her a chance to ride downhill she took it. She was smart and knew how to ride properly. Adele and I first bumped into each other at a NEMBA race up at Hamsterley Forest. It wouldn't be until late 1996 that we finally got together, but when we did we knew it was serious. Twenty-eight years and two boys later, it turns out we were right. Meeting Adele was pivotal for me. She was and is the rock that anchors me and gives me a life I never dreamed would be possible.

My first two years on the pro circuit had been like chalk and cheese. Going from turning up to a race and the other pros not knowing me, to turning up a year later and having this huge new group of friends from all over the world was pretty weird. The transition took some getting used to, and like a new set of clothes it took a while for some stuff to bed in and be comfortable. Some of it never did and remained uncomfortable and

A HEART OF GOLD

annoying. I spent my time focusing on the comfortable side; the rest took care of itself.

Spending time away from the UK also fractured the hold that home and the people there had on me. I now had a much wider circle, and the benefit of that was direct interaction with team managers and brand owners. I was now where the movers and shakers of the sport were. During 1996, I built a fortuitous relationship with GT's Doug Hatfield, aka Hattrick, who is still a point man for me at the Santa Cruz Syndicate. We just clicked. Doug would go out of his way to get me new stuff that made my bike better, and I quickly built a good partnership with him. By the end of 1996 I had some big money deals on the table, all direct from the manufacturers. It was a long way from getting a bit of support from Kona through my mates at the local bike shop.

Now the season was done it was time for the snowboarding holidays to start. The plan was to sign my new contract, let MBUK know I was not going to ride for them the following year and have a few months off to recharge, and focus on the snow and ride my motocross bike. Then, in the first week of October, I crashed hard at a local motocross race near Doncaster and broke my collarbone. I was told there'd be no bikes for six weeks. What the fuck would I do for six weeks? It would be torture. Then six weeks became eight weeks. On top of that, I got a throat infection that lasted all the way through December. So that was that for 1996. No snowboarding for me that year.

By the start of 1997 I was on a flight to Los Angeles having signed for GT. It was like winning the lottery and the FA Cup at the same time. Gary Turner and Richard Long put GT on the map in the early 1980s, having had the genius to sign legend Greg Hill as the figurehead pro for their BMX brand in 1981. Fourteen years later and they'd gone from a tiny little workshop smaller than my current garage, to being one of the biggest brands in the world. Shaun Palmer helped me with the negotiations and gave me the confidence to ask for way more money than I had planned. GT stepped up and said yes to everything. Full factory GT, a salary, a win bonus, expenses, mechanic, team manager and a tyre guy. Mountain biking was funny like that. One minute I was racing a crappy slow course on the hills of Yorkshire for a national race with a few dozen spectators standing in the freezing cold shouting 'Go Steve', the next I was on an uplift to race down a premiere snow resort in the Alps with 20,000 spectators yelling and screaming and blowing air horns. Now I was going to be living with Mike King in San Diego riding for Santa Ana's greatest bike company.

CHAPTER 12
THE MECHANIC

Stability for me is Chapeltown. Family get-togethers. Nana's birthday in October. Christmas at home with Mum. The certainty that the old man would say no to storing 208 crates of continental beer at home after a trip to France. My mates. The pubs. The predictable stuff matters the most. The way tea tastes, local fry-ups, nights bladdered down Chap or in the Leadmill. The pubs. Did I mention the pubs? Wharncliffe and Grenoside woods. For a smidge over twenty years at the end of every world cup season this was where I retreated. I slotted back into familiar habits to recharge.

Those routines though were just for home. Life on the circuit chasing world cup points and racing at major events worldwide involved a lot of travelling and time away from all that. I'm lucky in that I can completely let go of home and focus on the job in hand. As soon as the UCI set the diary for the coming year, the next twelve months would become wholly predictable. I knew where I'd be going months in advance. I knew who would be there. As soon as I was on the plane or in the car, the adventure would begin, and I slowly and methodically morphed into the battle-hardened warrior I needed to be to compete on the world stage.

To race well at the world cups and for it still to be fun takes a state of mind that doesn't suit everyone; nor is everyone able to make it fun. After a fair few years, I got to know the circuit as well as it got to know me, and I like to think we complemented each other. It was becoming a home from home. There are some incredible mountain bike riders who won't ever be seen on a world cup circuit. I'm not writing this to explain their reasons for not wanting to race. They can do that for themselves. I just knew early on that this life was for me. I could do it. I liked being in different countries on different courses, making these places home. I wasn't like Warner who would spend hours moaning about how the pillows in the hotel room weren't comfy. I travelled to race, not to moan about anything.

The circuit for me was a bit like an empty house that we riders filled for six months of the year with our experiences and battles, stories that only we could know because we were there. Some told, some untold. Next year there'd be a new house. We'd furnish each one with our dreams and see what happened. When the season was over, we left it for posterity with that year's furniture and decorations up. Condemned to be judged by history but strong enough to stand on its own.

Most of all I wanted to win. I always wanted to win but usually I didn't. Not winning for me was the work, the work I did to make losing happen less often.

As soon as bikes started to get more technically advanced, two significant things happened. They became more expensive, and to race them at world cups required a support team. This was no longer a job for one person. After my shaky beginnings with Saracen, everything since had been pretty straightforward. I'd not really had to worry about having good people around me, or coming up with ideas about how to get where I needed to be. Some years were harder than others, don't get me wrong, but in the grand scheme of things I'd been pretty blessed. One example was how Shaun Palmer helped me negotiate my contract for the 1997 season. His help was invaluable and the reason I was able to buy a house on the same estate I was brought up on. The year before I'd negotiated my contract with the MBUK team myself. All along the way it just happened that I attracted the right people, or they attracted me. Relationships with people and brands have to function smoothly to achieve success. It's no guarantee but it's a big help. A good crew, good mates and hard graft equals great times.

The 1990s were a great time to be involved in mountain bike racing. There was such a fever about it, not a lot different from the rave culture in the UK at the same time. The bike industry loved mountain bikes because there was more money to be made from them than BMX bikes and road bikes. They were more expensive than both and added a fat amount of money to the top brands' profits. The riders who had been the first pros in the sport were still involved and they mainly came from different bike sports. Roadies and cyclo-cross racers struggling to get rides for pro teams in Europe as domestiques fitted right in to the cross-country teams as their pro events were five-lap, one-hour races at a high tempo. That was a sweet spot for the domestiques, a grafter's delight and even better if you could handle a bike off road as well, like Chris Young for example. As for

120

THE MECHANIC

downhill, it was basically the opposite. Racers came primarily from motocross, trials and BMX. Of course, there were newcomers who had never ridden MTB at all that were drawn to it too, but the groups I've mentioned had a distinct advantage. I arrived with a taste of all of those disciplines but was never absorbed by just one.

So, as I was coming up through the ranks, moving from national level to making the podium at world level, the races were already full of serious talent. There were multiple winners of national and world championships at every race. The field was stacked with talent, and they weren't just going to roll over for little old me without putting up a fight. In 1996 and on a decent money deal with MBUK Nike GT for the domestic series and selected world cup races, I was halfway through a rigorous and comprehensive apprenticeship. Competing at that level week in, week out takes some commitment and can wear both mind and body if you're not careful. I'd previously pushed too hard on and off the track and was learning how to temper both, so that I finished races and still had a good time. To be a player on the world circuit after my breakthrough second place in Panticosa would still take a lot of work. None of that would be possible without a good team and a great mechanic.

Putting it all together wasn't luck, although I would need my share of that too. Planning for six months on the road with regular testing in between races required specific contractual obligations on the part of brand and rider, stuff I was still a bit green about. Luckily during that 1996 season I'd got on well with the GT guys Doug Hatfield and team manager Doug Martin and they had started to talk to me as 1996 came to a close. We were trying to work a deal out but there were a couple of other brands sniffing about too. When it came to it, Shaun Palmer's advice changed my income drastically. He sent me into those meetings prepared to ask for a six-figure sum and not be shy about it. I still couldn't get around my shyness and when the big question – 'How much would you like?' – came along, I thought of my mate Palm and the words just came out of my mouth like they were his. He also educated me on the finer details of contract negotiation that I then had very little clue about. He had gleaned that knowledge from his time snowboarding. So, with Palm's guidance and my past experiences, I finally signed the contract Doug Martin at GT faxed me on 10 October 1996. GT was the one I wanted, and although the six-figure sum wasn't quite met, it wasn't far off and I had Palm to thank for that. Doug wanted a big-time team and he backed that up with a salary to match his aspirations. I set up a dollar account in the USA and the money rolled in. I was now on the world's most high-profile mountain bike team, riding with

121

FORGED BY SPEED

Mike King. The GT LTS was good but maybe not the best bike, but it was the best I'd ever ridden and I was ready to make it talk my language.

As I came in to the official GT squad in 1997, Nico Vouilloz was leaving for the French Sunn-Nike team having won the world championships in Cairns on the GT LTS package I'd be inheriting. The Sunn bike was miles ahead tech-wise of where we were at GT; the change from alloy to composite frames was a failure and all mine broke. The suspension linkage on the back end of the bike wasn't brilliant, so we needed to get that sorted. The suspension on the Sunn was far superior to ours; the RockShox gear we were using was good but not great. Sunn's state-of-the-art clutch rear hub made even Chris King's amazing hubs look outdated. In 1996, riding with MBUK on the circuit and running the same bike as Nico, I got a lot of help from Tim Flooks on the RockShox rig at the world cups. I spent that whole year setting the bike with assistance from Tim and North West Mountain Bike Centre. It wasn't as smooth running as the factory deal Nico was on, but I did have a year to familiarise myself with the GT set-up.

My package with MBUK was good but not on a par with Nico's. I knew I'd need to be on a factory team with a full-time mechanic if I was going to make podiums regularly on the world cup circuit. So, my friendship with Palmer had other benefits. On the party side he made my shenanigans seem small-time; on the business side, he didn't just get me a great salary, he made sure I understood contracts. He knew that I'd have to stipulate in my new contract with GT that as well as having two bikes ready at every race in case one got buggered up, I'd also need to ask for a full-time mechanic in writing. Before the ink was dry on the contract, I was already on my way to ask the character I wanted to be my spanner man. Nobody makes it to the top without someone they trust implicitly with their bike, and my guy had already been helping me out on a regular basis. He was from Manchester, but I chose to let that slide.

Just like my parents' union of Yorkshire man and Wigan woman, my relationship with Andy Kyffin was a marriage of sorts too. Our trans-Pennine partnership was bound by a mutual love of motorbikes, mountain bikes and perfectionism. Andy had been around bikes all his life, as his dad had established North West Mountain Bike Centre in 1967. On top of that he had raced cross-country in the pioneering era when John Tomac was the name everyone knew. Andy was also mates with Jason and Jim McRoy. JMC had moved down from the north-east and was living near Stockport, close to Andy's shop, so they often rode together. Andy got Jason into time trialling, one reason JMC was so fit. This was around 1991, the same year Andy drove to Italy on his own to the world championships in Italy where

122

THE MECHANIC

he qualified second behind eventual winner John Tomac. Pro cycling would not be his path though. While racing cross-country he was hospitalised twice due to an undiagnosed health condition that made it difficult for him to convert fats into energy. The issue first appeared when Andy rode a cross-country world cup at Crystal Palace in 1988. A decision had to be made about riding cross-country, and so with a prod from his partner Fliss, who preferred him alive, he packed it in but continued with the downhill and motocross.

Without really thinking about a transition, Andy had made a name for himself by fixing bikes for his mates or riders he sponsored through his dad's shop. He was already a great mechanic when I approached him for the 1997 season. When he was first on the spanners, he mainly worked with JMC. Jason rode some world cups in 1992 with Andy as mechanic, including an eighteenth place finish in Lillehammer. A year later, on a trip to Vail with Jason, Andy had a really bad crash and broke his ribs and sternum. After being given a truckload of drugs by the medics, he spent the week fixing bikes for Jason, Tommy Johansson and Nick Craig, which got him noticed as someone you could trust. He did it all: setting up suspension, rebuilding wheels, groupsets and gears, cable changes and the rest. When Jason was sponsored by Hardisty Cycles riding a GT bike in 1994, Andy was his mechanic. As a racer who understood the issues we were all having with throwing chains, he invented the 'Goat Gobbler' chain guide, which Jason, Will Longden and a few others used to stop the chain from hopping off the front ring. He was and still is a great problem solver.

Despite me knowing Jason well enough early on, I'd yet to meet Andy although we'd raced a few of the same downhill events. Then as I got to know Jason a little better, he started telling me about Andy and what a great mechanic he was and how helpful he'd been, about how a good mechanic could make things on the circuit a lot easier and allow me to focus purely on racing. Jason was going to more world cup rounds than me at the time and Andy was with him; they both gained experience and insights that Jason was happy to share with me.

Andy and I were both at Jason's funeral. After that we started talking more as time went on. Andy helped me a fair bit in 1995, but just as a friend. In 1996, the MBUK deal was well paid, but it required me to arrange travelling and logistics, which was a pain in the arse. So, it was really helpful that season when I was in the UK that I had Andy to work on my bikes. There was still a lot of stuff that took my time away from testing and training, but the deal with GT would sort all that out. Andy had worked on Jason's GT and like me was getting to know the GT guys on the circuit. That was a

123

double bonus for me. I got to know Andy better as a mechanic, and acquired another post-race party animal on the world cup scene, which was as important as his mechanical skills.

By the end of 1996 I knew Andy well enough that I could pop in to see him at the shop if I needed my bike fixing and setting up. He was my go-to guy. With Jason's death hanging over us both, I was cautious about asking him if he'd be interested in being my mechanic. I wasn't sure he'd say yes. He'd been so close to Jason it felt a bit weird but at the same time it also seemed appropriate. When I did ask him, I had my fingers crossed, but he agreed. It was like a torch had been passed to us to carry on what he and Jason had been doing. Without knowing it then, we were on our way to becoming one of the most successful rider–mechanic partnerships in the history of mountain biking.

Andy is a very conscientious hard-working fella. The fact he raced downhill competitively was a massive help because it became clear very quickly that he had more to offer than I had originally realised. He would be happy to scour the mountain when I was practising to see how the lines were developing. He not only understood how the bike worked mechanically, all the suspension, gears and so forth, but he also had an eye for what I needed from the bike that differed from other riders. I didn't approach a track in the same way as some other riders, so I wasn't looking for lines on the mountain that were the same as other riders.

Of course there are lots of riders that are the same, but due to skills I'd picked up at home in the woods of Wharncliffe and across the border in Innerleithen, I would usually pick my way down in a different way to the competition. That put different demands on the bike and the suspension, and Andy knew how to take what he saw me doing and translate it in a way that the head suspension guy at RockShox, Roy Turner, would understand. If Roy didn't get what we were trying to achieve, Andy and I would take him to a track so we could show him. We made a lot of progress in setting up the bike by challenging how GT wanted things to be done. It caused a little friction to start with, but as soon as they saw how much faster I was going, they knew they could trust us to do good things.

There is so much I could write about Andy that I could fill another book, but if I had to explain what our relationship was built on it's this: 100 per cent trust in each other for everything we set out to achieve. My bike was always perfect. I could batter one to death in a big crash, destroy wheels and pedals in practice sessions, and know that every time I went back to the top of the mountain the bike would be immaculate again and I'd not have to touch it. There's not one thing or one occasion during our whole time

THE MECHANIC

working together as a team between 1996 and 2004 that I would want to change.

It's very difficult for me to try to explain the little things that matter, but try to imagine how many hours I spent riding the same bike, week in, week out. It was an awful lot. The muscle memory of it has become part of who I am. I rode so many hours over such horribly technical terrain that I could tell if my tyre pressure had gone down one p.s.i. I knew exactly where I wanted my front and rear brake levers placed – not to the nearest millimetre, but *precisely* where they should be for me to feel comfortable. The point at which my brakes would bite had to be correct; the pressure I applied to the levers to make the brakes work had to be just where I needed it to be. Andy understood how the bike needed to sit when I was standing on the pedals in the gate ready to go. The cleat position on my shoes had to be exact. Grip diameter and glove material had to be perfect. There were so many variables Andy was responsible for, and I needed to be able to explain to him what I wanted and for him to understand what I meant and why they were important. When we got it all right, if we had found a good suspension setting for the track I was racing, for example, then I could really start to relax and attack the hill.

Andy was responsible for so much when we were working together, and it was an even harder job then than it is now. Products were developing and evolving so fast that the notes we'd taken and the settings we'd used that worked in Val di Sole one year would be out of date the next year. At every race and during the time in between we were either testing our current gear to find a good setting or testing new gear to see if it was better. There was no let-up on that front. Any advantage we could get we would go balls out to get it dialled before the next world cup. It was exhausting work, and Andy wouldn't stop working on something until the job was finished.

In contrast, there were plenty of mechanics whose attention to detail and work ethic were nowhere near as committed. I was so very lucky to have him in my corner. There were things he did to the GTs I raced that GT had no idea about, and some which rubbed them up the wrong way until he proved to them his modifications made their bike better. There were some harsh truths that didn't land well on the desks of tech designers who thought they'd just designed the best bike ever, despite me breaking one a week and the suspension linkage being crap. He was brave enough to stand his ground and I was happy to stand by his side as we fought to make my bikes better every year.

With Andy on board, the stage was set.

CHAPTER 13
3:55.23

3:55.23. This number tells the story of a bright summer's day on a mountain in the Pacific Northwest of the USA. It's the time of my world cup run on 28 July 1998 at the ski resort of Snoqualmie Pass. I was there racing for GT, wearing the number 10 plate on my bike, and the course was in perfect condition. When I crossed the finish line, that number told me I'd over-hauled the interim leader David Vazquez by five whole seconds. Still on the mountain was French rider and current world champion Nico Vouilloz. When I posted my time, I had a strong feeling Nico would think he would beat me even if I was at the top of the leader board. And Nico would know my time. He would have been told somewhere on the course. Nico had a group of helpers at every race to give him feedback on lines and times, and this race in Washington State was no different to anywhere else. His whole set-up was on another level to the rest of us.

As he crossed the line in his world champion's jersey on his brilliant Sunn Radical bike I could see the expression on his face. The lack of cheers as he finished would have let him know it was not to be his day. He had expected to beat me with that run but let me give you another number: 3:58.13. That was Nico's time: 2.9 seconds slower than mine. A little over four years earlier I'd raced my first world cup at Bad Hindelang in Germany. I came down the mountain that day in a poor state, my chain jammed and I didn't qualify for the finals after posting the awful time of ten minutes. A little over two years earlier I'd come second at Panticosa in Spain. There was now a lot more experience in these skinny legs and in this head of mine.

I would finally stand on top of the box. I'd won my first world cup.

FORGED BY SPEED

I've always regarded Panticosa as my breakthrough race. Everything changed after that. But it would take me a fair few rounds of the world cup to go one better and win. Let me spin through the races in between. That race in Spain on 12 May had been the first round of the 1996 season. A week later, in Nevegal, Italy, I fell off and hit a tree, finishing twelfth. A month later, on 15 June, we were in Mont-Sainte-Anne in Canada where I had a good run and finished seventh. At round four in Les Gets in August, I suffered a puncture and finished fifty-fourth. Having escaped the attention of the police and made it across the border to Austria for the fifth round in Kaprun, I got nailed by the sudden rain, suffered issues with clipping in and crashed twice, failing to finish. My diary entry reads: 'Warner won. Bastard.' Three weeks later we were in Hawaii for the final round where I came eighteenth. ('Nice place,' I wrote. 'Shit track.') I finished sixth in the overall, one place and just one point behind Shaun Palmer. The prize money only went down as far as fifth.

That year the world championships, the seventh ever, were in Cairns, the first time Australia had hosted the event. I had a great practice run but it rained the day before the final and I mucked up all my turns on the race run. I was five seconds behind the winner, Nico, and totally pissed off. Palmer got second and stepped on to the podium wearing a Stars and Stripes tuxedo. I had a meeting with an executive at Trek and got so nervous that I drank wildly at the after-parties and got in at 7.30 a.m. My diary reads: 'Longden lost his wallet. Warner smashed window in apartment. Destroyed rental car. Bought a boomerang.'

The 1997 season, my first with GT, opened in mid-May at Stellenbosch in South Africa. The track was poor and not at all technical. I saved too much energy for the bottom when I should have pedalled like mad all the way down. I finished twelfth. A week later I was back in Nevegal where the course had been improved from the year before. Despite getting a flat in the final run and coming unclipped I was within a whisker of finishing third. I won $950 and was up to fourth in the overall rankings. Then it was back to Panticosa where I'd come second the year before. I was slow qualifying, suffering a bent chain guard, which meant I couldn't pedal properly. I was nervous on race day, desperate to beat Warner who came down in four minutes and twenty-six seconds. Happily I did, by less than half a second, but I was only four-hundredths of a second behind John Tomac who came in second. Fine margins indeed. Corrado Hérin got top spot. Palmer finished twelfth, which meant I was still fourth in the overall. GT were happy.

They were even happier when I came second in round four at Mont-Sainte-Anne at the end of June. I thought I'd won until Hérin came down

128

3:55.23

and beat me by two seconds. Bastard. Warner was fourth, so a good day for the Brits and we partied hard, with fancy dress and the biggest food fight in history at the end of the weekend, dancing all night into next day. Then it was off to Virginia for the next round. At this stage I was second in the overall and well placed. The world cup at Massanutten though was a disaster. I suffered badly from hay fever and then got a flat during qualification, missing the cut by five seconds. It was a poor result all round for the British contingent, with our top-placed rider being Tim Ponting in forty-first. Drowning my sorrows with Palmer, we were arrested for being drunk in public. Thanks to Palm's previous arrest record, we were put in the cells for the night and I had my mugshot taken. I don't think GT were as pleased with me after that. On the forty-hour drive back to California in Palmer's pimped-out party bus, we blew a tyre at seventy-five miles per hour and went off the road, almost totalling the bus as we narrowly missed oncoming traffic. It took another seven hours to get the tyre sorted and by Thursday we were back at Palmer's place in Lake Tahoe.

Five weeks later I was back in Europe for the final round of the 1997 season at Kaprun. I was not in the best shape. The week before I'd damaged my foot during the UK national championships where Warner beat me by five-hundredths of a second. I hadn't wrecked my foot cycling though. That happened in a drunken play-fight with Matt Farmer, who landed on it from a height. I had massages, painkillers and cream to numb the injury, but by the Thursday it was still agony. Andy had to rebuild the bike because of cracks in the rear of the frame, and with all the pedalling required my foot was burning. The track though was as fast as it could be and despite it all I was flying.

Starting the final round, I nailed the pinball section and was totally on it but then crashed coming into the David Baker turn. I went down hard on my arm and head but sprang up and carried on. I didn't panic but then let it go a little too much into a right-hander, went over the tapes and landed on a rock right on my hip. It hurt so bad I could only just get up to carry on. It was pointless anyway. I'd fucked up big time and finished sixty-sixth. At the bottom I rode straight back to the van. As I was getting undressed, I found a big hole in my elbow. The UCI doctors came over and told me I had to go to hospital. The doctor there treated me like he had lead hands, grabbing my arm roughly. He had to cut my bursa sac out and put a half cast on me, which wasn't good news. Then I found out from Alexa, one of the GT crew, that I had dropped to eighth in the overall. That hurt more than any injury. I was so pissed off I didn't want to drink with Palmer and Warner. Instead, I went back to the hotel and just lay there. Adele found me and gave me a hug and I cried. A week later a Swiss doctor that cross-country racer Chantal Daucourt had recommended said the arm was healing fine and I began to relax a little.

I started 1998 in Huntington Beach, California, planning to get a winter's training under my belt before heading home for the start of the UK season. That plan went tits up after six weeks. After getting some steady ground-work done, I dislocated my hip in mid-February at a place called Tom's Farm where Eric Carter had built a new track that still had soft ground in places. Jumping over a soft mound my wheel got sucked in and I went over the handlebars. That happens a lot in mountain biking, but this time my foot stayed stuck to the pedal and while I went one way, my leg went the other. When I came to rest, the leg was sticking out at a weird angle and I was in agony until the paramedics arrived and started pumping me full of morphine. It was a silly little crash and I hoped they would be able to pop my leg back in, but they couldn't. A helicopter was called but then the head rescue guy said they could carry me instead, but they weren't the fittest and kept needing rests. Each time they put me down I'd be in agony. After five hours, I was starting to feel hypothermic as we finally reached the roadhead to find five fire engines and three ambulances waiting.

Little did I know then that I'd still be lacking the strength to ride four months later and two world cups into the 1998 season. I was off the bike altogether for a few months; the only training I could manage a month after the injury was on an indoor turbo trainer. Hospital and physiotherapy appointments were strictly observed, but it was a bloody painful rehab that couldn't be rushed due to the severity of damage done to the surrounding tissue and tendons.

Back home in March, I then managed to almost kill myself when the brakes on our VW camper failed on the motorway as I was collecting Adele's bike from Andy's shop. I hit the central reservation barrier at about eighty miles per hour – in preference to piling into the car in front – but it took two smashes and a hard right on the wheel to bring me to a stop in the fast lane, and not before I'd overtaken a few cars that were slowing down to the left of me. I then bought myself a BMW 316i that turned out to be a money pit, partly down to me driving it like I stole it (which I hadn't).

By April I was feeling a little more optimistic, but I was still weak in the middle of my body. On the doctor's advice I skipped the first round of the world cup at Stellenbosch in South Africa at the start of April, but was fit enough seven weeks later for round two in Italy at the rad course of Neve-gal. It poured on race day but I really thought I could win. I crashed in the rocks and got my hands wet but was still only a second down. Then I crashed again in the woods and covered my hands in mud. I still finished sixth, though in my diary I wrote: 'Totally gutted, started drinking immediately.'

The next week I was practising at Les Gets. I was flying on the course at that stage but on race day it rained again. My run was going well until I greased off my saddle on the top section and crashed badly. I slid on the ground for over ten metres through the puddles and had to take my glove off to grip the bars properly, which left me riding too cautiously. By the end of the run I couldn't feel my fingers to brake and I finished in eighteenth, once again disappointed at a missed opportunity.

Three weeks later I was back in the US for the fourth round at Big Bear Lake in Southern California. Qualification was a nightmare as I caught some course markers in my cranks and couldn't pedal. The final went much better though. Thanks to my issues in qualifying I had an early run and posted four minutes and twenty-six seconds, which led for a good hour until I was caught and began slipping down the board. I finished seventh. I knew I could have gone quicker and pretty soon I was, racing back to Palmer's place in Lake Tahoe at a hundred miles per hour in his Cadillac.

A month later, on the last weekend in July, we convened in Washington State at Snoqualmie Pass for the fifth round. The track was gnarly. I did two slow runs before qualifying and then went back on the course to take another look. After that I nailed it, topping the leader board in the first qualification run. Back in the pits everyone was suddenly talking about me. That was an uncomfortable feeling; I always preferred to be the underdog.

I was up early for practice but only managed one run because there were huge queues. I rode well and pretty hard but had to stop dead high on the course and so finished fourth. I was still confident for the final. I headed back to the hotel to rest with Adele. Then it was time for my run. I was seven seconds up by the split and went into the lead by five when I crossed the line. Everyone went crazy. I held on to the lead. Then Nico came over the line thinking he'd won. He shook his head when he saw the time; he couldn't believe I'd beaten him. I was stoked and kept choking up and nearly crying. All the Brits there were excited for me. That felt amazing. It was good to hear the national anthem as I stood on the podium. Then I did loads of interviews, went back to the hotel and packed my bags before having dinner downstairs. Everyone bought me drinks and we went to the bar where I got beer poured all over me. Andy and Adele drank so much they were ill all next day. Surprisingly, I only had a few. Instead, I called friends and family in England to tell them I had won.

There was a five-week break before the series resumed at the end of the first week of August in Spain's Sierra Nevada. It was stupidly hot and I immediately got sunburnt. The course was great but I had a flat on the first practice of race day and almost missed qualification. I didn't even have time to do my helmet up. I had a disappointing final run. My feet were all over the place and my legs felt tired. The course changed so much as it got worn. The berms, the banked turns on the course, had dried out and crumbled. I did manage to ride half a second quicker than I had in practice, which put me in eighth. But Nico creamed me by eleven seconds. I was frustrated but I did move up to fifth in the overall. The Spanish crowds were insane and I signed loads of autographs. I ended the weekend running around naked with a gang of others before ending up in a spirits-only bar called Club Astro.

A week later we were in Kaprun where the heat of Spain gave way to heavy rain. I practised hard and finished fourth in qualifying. I had a pretty good run but missed fifth in the final by three-hundredths of a second. The final round was a fortnight later in Japan, a long way to go for a race. The weather was even worse than it had been in Kaprun. Thunder and rain on the mountain closed the lifts on the Thursday but it cleared at the weekend. I loved being in Japan though, especially for the rice bowls. The fans there were so excited. I rode well in the final but had spike tyres on, which proved to be a mistake, as I crashed crossing a road going full pelt. I still finished eighth but that crash cost me; I dropped off the podium for the overall, from third to fourth. Nico, of course, won the world cup. A little more than a day later I was back at Adele's house and glad to be home.

With the 1998 series over it was time to focus on the world championships, to be held that year in mid-September at Mont-Sainte-Anne. I drank a fair bit in the run-up to the race and felt a bit jaded by finals day. It was the same course as the world cup; still tech and gnarly but also now wet thanks to the weather. That left me feeling tired as well. I was still up for the win, but I crashed hard on both my practice runs and during the final I crashed again near the top and lost twelve seconds. I had mud all over my hands and that was it. Finished. Done. Nico won *again*. We drank champagne all night and smoked cigars. World championship after-parties were always mint. It was an amazing weekend with Warner and all our mates and we capped off the month, once we were back in Britain, by watching the Motocross des Nations, held that year at Foxhill in Wiltshire.

Although I had finally won a world cup, the direction of my career was still more a subconscious desire, a great underlying force of which I knew little about and was often unaware. Looking at my career to this point, it was like I was on a river, on a journey; I was just seeing where it took me and having some fun along the way. The one thing I can say confidently with hindsight is that I never really had a goal to be the best, or even to be the champ. I hoped these things might come and wanted to win. Yet that's not the same as being focused on those goals to the exclusion of everything else. My motivation was more naive and innocent than that, which I think probably helped a fair bit.

I don't see myself as others might do. I'm a flawed regular fella who just likes going fast down mountainsides on pushbikes. As long as I can do that, I'm happy. I love my family and friends; they mean everything to me. I've never been one to have people around me that blow smoke up my arse, although there were a lot of people not close to me who did that. They were usually the ones who came up to me at a British championship to say how easy it was going to be for me to win, when in fact winning in the UK was really hard. I was in front of my home crowd and the pressure was actually greater than at a world cup.

I've always been lucky to have a close-knit group of mates that either know me from school or early mountain bike days, mates who will tell me the truth, like Andrew Titley. I've never felt the need to have a full-time coach or any of that bullshit. I had a manager once for a very short time but that just wasn't right for me. I've been fortunate enough to have good people help me out with good advice but mostly all the work I did on training and racing I found out myself and just kept adding bits to my programme when things got a bit boring. It wasn't this great big plan. As you've already seen, I've struggled with injuries but had the patience to rehab them.

Of course, there were some big decisions and I didn't make them without some thought. As my results improved, I definitely got more professional, taking what I was doing more seriously and not letting down sponsors who were investing millions of dollars in running world-class teams on the downhill circuit. And not letting myself down by not doing the work needed to improve. My downtime was my time though and I never felt guilty about that. I clocked on and I clocked off. I guess it's a working-class work ethic. I always wanted to be busy when I was getting paid because I didn't know when it was all going to end. I wanted to keep it going, I knew I was on to a good thing. Panticosa and Snoqualmie were two peaks I'd conquered, I liked the way they felt and naturally I wanted more. So I worked even harder.

A lot can happen in four years, but that first win was the cherry on top of the cake. The deal with GT was the real turning point. Of course, the cash was amazing, but I really felt GT was the best home for me. I think Doug

FORGED BY SPEED

liked what I brought to the team, and I liked them too. Winter training was now in California, not freezing, damp Sheffield. I soon passed my California driving test and stayed out there for a few months with Mike King, indulging in the Southern California lifestyle of beaches, bikes, motocross and the crap nightclubs that pro cyclists go to. Thank God I was mates with Palmer because he made the lack of nightlife bearable. The upside, and there were many, was the predictability of the weather that meant I could ride and train every day, have barbecues, eat at Hooters and drink almost every evening.

Riding motocross was helping my fitness, especially the ability to take more of a battering than I ever thought possible. I'd ache for days after a hard session with the lads. Randy Lawrence was one of the crew I'd hang with, and Randy went on to be Jeremy McGrath's mechanic. The US motocross industry is based in California and I was not only knocking about with legends like McGrath, who started off racing BMX for GT, but was introduced to brand owners like Mitch Payton at Pro Circuit, and Troy Lee who would sponsor me for helmets. Back in the UK it would be impossible to have such a direct line to the biggest movers and shakers in that world. Despite being a fan of European motocross stars like Dave Thorpe and Stefan Everts, there was no getting away from the glamour of the American supercross indoor racing. Los Angeles for a few months every year was predictable and fun, the perfect way to prepare for the coming season.

There was another reason the USA felt like a home from home. The UK's BMX racers had been hitting up the Huntington Beach area each year in a sort of pilgrimage. I rented an apartment there in 1998 and the following year a house with a yard. There was a revolving door of characters moving in and out of our beachside residence. It had at one time or another housed Derby's 1996 BMX world champion Dale Holmes, and X-Games gold medallist Stephen Murray and his older brother UK national champ Martin, who is now the commerical director at Peaty's Products. UK British BMX champ, US rider of the year and rockabilly lover Neal Wood was living there too with some other US and European pros. Neal and I had a connection straightaway as he was the least uptight of the UK pros living there. We both liked a beer or two so there was always some mayhem when he and I were in town at the same time. Paul 'Grotbags' Roberts was a regular too.

It was a typical BMX dosshouse, but it had our own MTB twist on things. That didn't stop it from gaining notoriety on many fronts, none of which I can repeat here without the threat of legal action. I would head to Dale's house for a cuppa and to chat about things that lads from Sheffield and Derby talk about when they are far from home, like getting a decent cup of tea. We would hit Gold's Gym in the morning, Sheep Hills in the afternoon and Laguna Beach for downhill in the evening.

When the supercross season kicks off in Anaheim in the first week of January, that's when you'll find most bike-loving Brits over there. California was where I could avoid the cold and get in the laps at the Orange Y BMX track, where on any Wednesday night you could be rubbing shoulders with upwards of twenty world champions practising for their upcoming national series events. It suited me because I was racing four-cross and dual slalom and my gates were pretty awful, so I was there with my GT teammates, ex-BMX pros Eric Carter and Mike King, who would kick my ass out the gate just about every time. Dave Cullinan and Pete Loncarevich were there as well, and depending on the state of play and who was hungover or not, the BMX racers in the Huntington Beach house would be there too. It was a vibey scene full of energy.

My trips to the USA were handy on many levels. My sponsors were all in California and getting my bike fixed was easy. Hooking up with Andy for the UK races and world cups wasn't interrupted. I could race some of the US national downhill series where the bonuses for winning were good. Palmer was a good foil for me and I'd spend plenty of time up at Lake Tahoe with him whenever I could, blasting around the woods on mini moto bikes and generally causing a different level of mayhem than I was used to back home. Luckily it was never anything worse than destruction of property, speeding and acting like complete twats when we were drunk, which was a lot of the time.

I'm not sure Adele really understood what she was getting involved with now we were going out seriously. Even in 2024, I think she still feels the same sometimes. I'm bloody lucky she loves me. Much as I liked the USA, I love her and Sheffield more.

SATURDAY 25 DECEMBER

TRAILS IN SAN DIEGO.

1999   359th day – 6 days follow   Christmas Day

HAD A DIP IN THE SEA THEN PACKED THE CARS AND DROVE TO SAN DIEGO. TO STAY AT MICHELLE'S MUM'S HOSE. WE WENT AND DO SOME TRAILS IN MISSION, THEY WERE PRETTY GOOD. GOT BACK AND HAD ANOTHER XMAS DINNER THEN PLAYED SOME PLAYSTAITOON. I DIDN'T DRINK TOO MUCH, BUT EVERYONE ELSE DID.

CHAPTER 14
APPETITE FOR DESTRUCTION

As confidence grows, so does appetite. Having won once, I was hungry for more. I wanted to annihilate the opposition. I wanted to be the world's fastest on any terrain. I was growing into a can't-touch-me-motherfucker kind of mountain lion veiled in my usual underdog approach. I would never be unbeatable, but I wanted to get as close to that as I could. I'd spent the last two years putting the walls up, now I was ready to start decorating the house how I liked it. It was time to make the head for the crown I wanted to wear. The first year I actually felt I could win a series was 1999, assuming all the ducks lined up. They did for a while but not for long enough.

Six years of graft and grind were behind me. I felt like a beetle pushing his dung ball up that hill. Reminders of roads I had almost walked down were everywhere when I was back home in Sheffield, but I had too much going on to be mithered by what anyone else was doing now. Winning was the task at hand, being the world's best. The only distractions I allowed were those I needed to release stress or help me relax. Everything else was focused on winning. Looking back now at my diaries from 1999 I can see just how the entries became more focused. Every day I logged how many hours I trained.

The race season taught me what was required to get a leader's jersey and the pressure of keeping it. I learned about consistency and making better decisions, although it took a fair while to filter through my hard-headed no-compromise approach to balancing partying and racing. In truth, they never could be balanced. I just did both and got better at both. It was a matter of fine-tuning, of knowing when to turn off the tap and when to let it flow.

That wasn't easy with so many distractions. The pull of a half-life in the US was strong: the Americans liked me and I liked America. And for some reason, unlike the Stone Roses, Oasis and Blur, I cracked it there. Sorry, lads.

Despite Sheffield being my home, I was spending less time there. The US had become my second home and I was racing more of their nationals than I was in the UK. The American domestic series was organised by the National Off Road Bicycle Association (NORBA). Their tracks were superior to the British ones and far more useful as a foundation for world cups. So it was a conscious decision. There wasn't enough money in the UK bike scene without a brand sponsor. Life would have been much harder for me if I'd tried to do everything from there at that point. Just riding every day with pros I was faster than would only get me so far. I needed to compete with riders that could beat me and push me. I needed better weather, amazing terrain and my teammates. In America that was the UK BMX crew of Dale Holmes, Neal Wood, Stephen and Martin Murray, and American Robbie Miranda, who were all racing BMX national and freestyle circuits. Being a full-time pro allowed me a life where I spent my day with others in the same boat. I still went back for the UK national championships though – to try and kick Warner's arse after he told me I'd never beat him on home soil!

With the bungalow in Huntington Beach as a base, designer Troy Lee's place wasn't far away and I was now sponsored by Troy to run one of his famous custom-painted helmets. It really felt like I belonged. There were teammates on the mountain bike side too: Eric Carter and Mike King. Palmer was there and Brian Lopes too. Life in America and specifically California is made for mountain biking. The terrain is pretty good, but the biggest factor is the weather. It just doesn't rain, or at least hardly at all. The winters are like British summers. It allowed for uninterrupted training and testing. Big Bear and Mammoth Mountain resorts weren't far away and both were amazing to ride. There were some awesome trails dropping off Top of the World down to Laguna Beach and we always ended up on the beach after every ride. It would be great to know how many runs I actually did while training there; it was a *lot*. The West Coast bike industry revolves around this area and some of the big clothing brands were there too. It had its downsides though. I wasn't getting to see Adele as much as I'd have liked, but there was nothing I could do about it. I was lucky she had a sponsor too so she was getting out to California a fair bit.

Clothing designer Nick Bayliss and I started our own little project that year. I fancied doing something clothing-wise so Nick and I hatched a plan. We'd set up our own label and use some of the profits to set up our own team, a kind of academy to bring on young talent, a way to put something

APPETITE FOR DESTRUCTION

back into the sport. Adele chose the name Royal Racing while we were sitting around in California deciding what we should call it. We had a bit of a hassle registering the name, but got there in the end. Royal is still around today and until recently I had shares in it, though not the involvement I once had when it was just us two fools trying to change the world.

Early in 1999 I took part in the winter X-Games at Crested Butte in Colorado, riding in the Biker X category. It was like a huge frozen snowed-up BMX track. I raced in the final against Palmer, John Tomac, Jürgen Beneke and Eric Carter among others. The prize money was about $5,000 so I wanted to at least give it a shot and was hammer down to do well. I got a good gate and with the frozen state of the track felt like I could rail all the insides easily. As the track got steeper I started to gather momentum and carry speed. Palmer had fallen off earlier and I could see Carter and Tomac in front. Tomac went for a huge jump the skiers would do and ended up going too high and lost speed. I decided to keep the bike low.

As I set up for the next huge right turn I could see him overshoot the jump then run wide in the right-hand turn after. He almost came to a stop and Carter got stuck with him somehow. As I was coming down the hill with them in front I could see what was going to happen, so as they went wide I hit the inside of the turn flat out, taking a much tighter line than they did. I knew we would meet on the exit and I ended up taking Tomac out with my pedal. I think I overtook Carter at the same time and went on to win the five grand. Not a bad day's work that, I thought. So now I had an X-Games gold in my possession too. I celebrated by driving with Andy straight through to San Diego to watch round two of the supercross.

Despite not having a full-time trainer I was getting a bit of guidance in 1999 from GT's Dean Golich. Dean now has had a hugely successful career training all manner of cycling, motorsport and Olympic athletes. (Dean once said: 'In the end, even when you are considered really successful, there's a lot more failure than there is success.') That year was the first I felt I needed some structure to what I was doing, and Dean helped with that. If I was going to win a series or the world championships I was going to need the help of people who were as good at what they did as I was at winning. Back home in Sheffield I'd bought a house not far from the family home and had that set up as my base in the UK. The ground floor was essentially a Scalextric Grand Prix track and the garage had all my bikes and toys in, like my YZ250 motocross bike, trials bike, snowboards and jump bike; even a little petrol scooter for flying round the estate on.

A couple of things had also happened back in the UK that would be good for downhill. Alex Rankin and Milan Spasic had started a video

139

FORGED BY SPEED

project called *Sprung* when they were both at university down in Plymouth. They were really good at documenting all aspects of the sport, the riding and the fun, and added a banging soundtrack. The result instantly hit a nerve. *Sprung* became the media for our tribe and it was great to be a big part of it. It also helped that it was nowhere near as slapstick as the media *Mountain Biking UK* was promoting.

To help matters further, alongside the *Sprung* videos came new magazines called *Dirt* and *Grip*. Both were in the same vein as *Sprung* with a real step up in photography and a different look from anything that had gone before. *Mountain Biking UK* and their *Dirt* VHS was the MTB equivalent of *Smash Hits* and covered all aspects of mountain biking. Its editors were a bit older than these new lads who were all my age and more connected to the scene. *Sprung, Dirt* and *Grip* were like the golden years of the *NME*. Journalists like Jerry Dyer, Paul Bliss and Mike Rose knew exactly where the sport was headed and they focused on the bits they were interested in. Their media fitted how I was living my life: partying, going to gigs, ripping on motocross bikes and mini-bikes, riding hardtails, BMX bikes and racing downhill. They followed the downhill circuit all around the world and reported on it.

Journalists would make regular trips abroad and to the USA to film and talk to riders, including me. They'd spend a few weeks with us in the off-season, filming and taking photographs, doing interviews, making the life we were living look so good. You'd open the mag and on one page you would be at a supercross race in Anaheim, next page was a feature at Troy Lee's place, then a shoot of Pete Loncarevich doing gates, then I'd be up on the trails blasting around in my GT gear. I also loved it because I was on photo contingencies. I was always happy when they showed up because my sponsors would send me cheques for appearing in the media. I never turned down a photoshoot. Not only did the contingencies help, being in magazines and films kept my name out there and gave my sponsors more coverage than they could poke a stick at.

No matter how hard they tried, the other magazines weren't as cool and insightful as these UK kids. When Alex Rankin moved on from *Sprung* to film the world cups for 4130, making the *Earthed* films for them, downhill racing acquired a visual culture. If you ever get to any of the resorts that we race on the world cup circuit, at some point you'll end up in a bar with one of Alex's *Earthed* films playing on a big screen. In the US the Transcontinental Headliners videos were of a similar vein, great behind-the-scenes interviews and hip-hop or metal soundtracks; it was just a shame only a couple were made. It was a fertile time for downhill and this flourishing of media signified us breaking away from the cross-country crew and standing on our own two feet. I'd not hesitate to say that downhill had become the blue riband of all the mountain bike sports.

The incredible cross-pollination of sports going on in Southern California meant that when riding or going to the gym I'd usually bump into other bike pros. Turning up at the trails could mean a session at Sheep Hills with Jeremy McGrath, 'Pistol Pete' Loncarevich, Eric Carter, Mike King, Shaun Butler or Cory 'Nasty' Nastazio and the UK contingent of the Murrays, Dale Holmes, Neal Wood, Grotbags and whoever was dossing at my house or Neal and Dale's place. When California was the destination, it was our houses everyone stayed at, either in tents in the garden or on the sofa. It was so easy to get a posse together to hit either Mammoth Mountain, or more often Big Bear for a weekend on the snowboard too. A ride at the Glen Helen motocross track would be the same. No matter where I went there would always be a session going on somewhere. At any point I could pick up the phone and in ten minutes have a crew to ride with, on whatever bike I wanted. I loved that. Much as I missed home, I'd spent too many lonely hours there pounding the woods in the freezing cold and pissing rain. I also met Mike Redding who quickly became one of my best mates. We would hang in the pubs and restaurants of Huntington Beach, and do beach rides and downhill runs together. He also became my main man at Troy Lee Designs.

GT would call me in now and again to talk about bike developments and the new stuff they were making, and I would give plenty of feedback based on the work that Andy and I had been doing on the bike. One example of that for the 1999 season was our decision to ride the I-Drive bike instead of the Lobo. The I-Drive pedalled better, which suited me on the tracks of that era. The world cup series that year turned into a war between me and Nico. He was by then a seven-time world champ. I'd won bugger all except for one world cup, which still felt a big deal for me. He knew how bad I wanted to beat him, and I knew how bad he didn't want to be beaten by me. It was to all intents and purposes, in my mind at least, hedonism versus a much stricter approach to racing and social life. I wasn't about to lose that fight. I loved the way I lived and raced. It suited me. The tension between us was real and not just about racing bikes. For me, a life of no booze would have been the end of fun. Those two factors, our rivalry on the track and our approach to life, summed up the races to come.

The first round in Les Gets was wet, which made it technical and really tiring. Cédric Gracia came down before me and set a really good time despite crashing fifty metres from the finish line on the muddy, rutted-out

FORGED BY SPEED

soft berm that had developed on the last corner. I didn't have the greatest run but slogged it down, nearly crashed more than a few times as the front end wouldn't go where I wanted and was a little all over the place. There was a harder chalk base on parts of the course, which meant it was like riding on ice at times. Andy and I had decided on WetScream mud tyres with the spikes cut down enough to roll well but with enough spike left to still bite into the mud. I also felt a WetScream was a little narrower and would cut through the deep ruts better. Despite going a bit wide to avoid some sticky mud on the corner Cédric crashed on, I just managed to sneak in front of him and win. Nico came third. I'd made the first move. More importantly, I'd proved that the previous year's win in Snoqualmie was no fluke. I felt I could taste a top-three world cup result, possibly a win if the wind blew right. I knew more wins would come, I just didn't know when or where. I did have my favourite tracks though, which was always a bonus.

Being on GT with Eric Carter was great. He was racing both downhill and dual slalom; I was racing dual slalom too but really didn't bother to try that hard to get much better at it. It was always a bit of a slamfest and some of the crashes riders suffered were really bad. I didn't want to jeopardise my downhill results by getting fucked. My attitude was to do it if it seemed fun and back off when it wasn't. Eric on the other hand, coming from a BMX background, was a dab hand at dual slalom. He was also good fun and we got on well. When I was travelling for world cups we'd always be knocking around together. He won the dual series in 1999 and if I had managed to win the downhill world cup series GT would have been happy. Due to an amazing bonus scheme in my contract my bank balance would also have got fatter. When Eric told me how much he'd won it was pretty mind-blowing. Sadly for me it would be a while before those bonuses kicked in.

Pushing through a season when the races arrived quite close together made life pretty easy for the riders. It's not like we were racing in twenty-one different countries like the MotoGP guys. Our races were in mountain resorts and so were dictated by the weather. That made the window in which we could race in Europe pretty narrow. At most, there would be a week or two between races. Sometimes there would be a longer gap to fit in each country's national championships, but that was it. If I managed to get home to Sheff it was only for a few days at most and that was eaten up with Andy and I testing a few parts and getting ready and packed for the next race. Any spare time was spent in the gym. When I won the national championships that year, I flew in two days before the race and was gone for the world cup two days later. I still managed to get locked up for a night in the cells after being wrongly accused of causing havoc with Titley in Eastridge.

APPETITE FOR DESTRUCTION

A police officer claimed he had seen me wrecking some hanging baskets and for that lie I was incarcerated at the local pigpen. I was released without charge eight hours later after witnesses were found to verify it wasn't me. In fact, said hanging basket had actually landed on my head and covered me in dirt. Why would I do that to myself? I was still shaking soil out of my hair when he arrested me.

My approach to downhill racing might have seemed a little primitive or wild to some, but 'unfettered' would better describe it. I would take pride in making my first run of the weekend as close to a qualifying run as possible. It kept it fun for me and also got me up to speed a lot quicker than most of the other guys. I was good at going fast without having to spend hours on the track. That feeling, that focus that comes from the adrenaline, that keeps me from hitting something hard and killing myself, that's my drug of choice.

As far as my bike was concerned, it didn't take long for me and Andy to set things up well enough. I didn't like messing around with something that was already working. I wasn't one of those riders who needed the best bike to win races. As long as I was happy with it, I reckoned I could win on it. The other little habit I built into my routine was having a nap after practice on race day. Those little power naps would be my time to focus on the track, the lines and features I had not nailed in practice. In my relaxed state I would visualise hundreds of runs and the track was all I would think about. I was thinking about where to save time and where I was already on my limit, although the latter rarely happened. After that, I would take whatever result came my way. The most annoying ones followed a mint practice run when, for whatever reason, I'd fuck up the final. That's what lost me the overall title in 1999. Two easy-to-make mistakes and the season could go to shit pretty damn quick. Maybe it was a blessing in disguise as the frustration set me up to win three world cup series gold medals. I guess that old saying of what doesn't kill you makes you stronger is true for me.

The first three world cups in 1999 went well for me: a first at Les Gets, then a second in Maribor, Slovenia. I was leading by nearly ten seconds until a certain bloody Frenchman came down and beat me by three and a half seconds. Even more annoying was that Nico had said that if he hadn't been told my time before he had set off, he didn't think he could have beaten it. When he found out, he knew he would have to ride the whole course at 100 per cent to beat me. Although it was flattering to hear how hard it was for him to win, I still lost and was pretty pissed off. Making a few mistakes on the way down hadn't helped.

Nevegal was next. I set the fastest time in timed training and had more

143

FORGED BY SPEED

in the tank but fucked up in the rocks and lost my rhythm so finished third. And because Nico won he took the leader's jersey off me, which left me bummed out. I'd enjoyed a month of wearing the leader's jersey and I liked that feeling a lot. Nor could I believe Mickaël Pascal had beaten me for second. After a big crash at the NORBA in Pittsburgh, I'd dropped back to second on points there too. With the next round of the world cup at Big Bear in three weeks, I'm not sure if the vigorous partying I indulged in helped my preparation or not. One of those weekends was my birthday, and when Palmer was around the rulebook on health and safety was puréed with cold American beer and Stoli vodka and then chased down with a dash of Crown Royal.

Big Bear was now my home world cup after a fashion, or my home-from-home world cup. I was really looking forward to it. It's a good track, albeit brutal on bike and body. All the GT heads were there and I'm sure Richard Long was in spirit too. Rich had been a founder of GT but had been killed on his motorbike three years before while on his way to Big Bear. As for the race, I couldn't have done much better. Winning would have been nice, but Palmer beat me by less than a second. Better still, Nico came sixth and I was back in the leader's jersey. Taking that off him felt amazing. Palmer wore the most amazing outfit to the podium: gold lamé, a big crown on his head and teddy-boy creepers on his feet. He looked fantastic. The party boys claimed that weekend two-nil. GT were also happy; doing so well on their home turf was nice for them as well as me. The next three weeks were spent up at Lake Tahoe since the next round at Squaw Valley wasn't far from Palmer's. The area around Mammoth and Lake Tahoe is breathtaking, and cruising around in Palmer's pimped-out vintage Cadillac partying non-stop was an opportunity too good to pass up. Although we did get some riding in, when not busy destroying our livers.

At Squaw I felt amazing and got up early. I'd only had one practice run and qualified second. All week everyone was getting punctures. The track was littered with rocks, but I really liked that. It was technical and fast. To ride it well you had to thread the eye of the needle through the dust: not easy, but it really focused me. I was belting down on the first quarter of the course but then I punctured. Luckily for me I had the Michelin system, or 'Le System' as they liked to call it, in my wheels, a sealed tyre and wheel set-up that was unique to Michelin. On this occasion it got me to the finish rather than suffering a DNF. I was able to continue rolling down the mountain, albeit somewhat slower. The back end was spitting out on every corner, but I still managed to finish sixth. I could have won at Squaw but instead ended up back in second overall to Nico, which was a total bummer.

APPETITE FOR DESTRUCTION

Two memorable parties occurred that weekend, both of which are on Alex and Milan's *Sprung 3* video with footage I shot myself. The word carnage does not cover the behaviour of a house full of pissed mountain bikers with access to unlimited alcohol and flour with pirate Palmer at the helm. A week later, and after spending a lot of elbow grease cleaning up Palmer's place, we were in Mammoth for a NORBA. A mistake there on a practice run on the Friday left me concussed. I felt okay by Sunday but only managed fifth, which put me back into third overall for the series. Annoyingly, Palmer was able to win the dual at Mammoth and he was in way worse condition than I was when we were getting loose. Four hours later I was back in Huntington Beach getting rat-arsed with Titley and Mike Redding and the weekend was already put behind me. I didn't dwell on a poor result. Best to crack on, or crack a beer and try to forget.

The following week I won the UK national title during a quick jaunt home, shutting Warner up, since he only finished fifth. That set me up well for the next stop on the world cup circuit in Mont-Sainte-Anne. Gone was the dust of the California courses. Now we were on lush, grass-covered slopes. I only did ten practice runs the whole week but I still beat Nico by almost two and a half seconds. I was back on the gas and I wanted him to know it. The after-party was fancy dress and for a reason unknown to me now, Warner and I wore bed sheets and I drank so much tequila that next morning it was coming out of my pores. We also sank a gondola. Childish, I know, but funny at the time. I slept for the next two days because I felt so ill from the tequila. Warner wasn't so bad, but all the plants around him were drunk ...

The next round was the following weekend in Bromont, also in Quebec. I managed a game of crazy golf on the Wednesday evening and stayed out till 4 a.m., partying with Lopes and Gracia, both of whom ended up in a strip club after leaving me asleep in a hot tub. Come race day I led qualification by ten seconds. I don't think I've ever felt so confident about winning a race. I had the course wired. I felt invincible, absolutely sure I was going to win easily. Then it rained before my run and after setting off and having a good run at the top I lost the front down a hole. My hands went down first and got covered in mud, so I spent the rest of the run all over the place, unable to hold the grips properly or pull on the bars without my hands slopping around. I know what you're thinking. Of course, Nico won, while I could only manage sixteenth. Back down the snakes and ladders leaderboard to second overall. The only consolation was that I went on the piss with the Aussies that evening and had a blinder of a night. As usual I drank the result right out of my mind.

145

FORGED BY SPEED

Three days later I was in Kaprun having been back to the UK for a day to do my washing, repack all my gear and see Mum and Nana. I also treated myself to my favourite at the time, prawn puri from the curry house. The course in Kaprun was shit, which it usually was. Too much pedalling. I had a hungover practice day on the Friday and only managed five runs. That was enough though since I knew I was quick. Sunday was a repeat of the previous weekend. I'd been first in qualification by three seconds, then it pissed down before my run. Even with the rain I was still three seconds up at the split. Then I crashed on the switchbacks and finished down in fourteenth. That was it. Nico had won the series, and I got second. Second. If that wasn't bad enough, one week later during practice at a NORBA in Vermont I hit a tree so hard I broke my forearm and lower leg. All due to a yellow warning flag being waved in the wrong place, long before it was needed. That was the world championships in Sweden over before I'd even had chance to think about them. The track there would have suited me; it seemed like the sort of place where I could take a title from Nico.

The hospital I was taken to was excellent. The doctor was better still and he even checked up on me after I'd gone home. They sorted me out with a temporary cast and arm support and forty-eight hours later I was back in the UK and off to see a fantastic physio. Not before the hospital in the UK had plastered me up to the bicep though and put a pot on my lower leg up to my knee. I got a major strop on about that, having a hissy fit like a child. Not only could I not drive, they'd plastered my drinking arm. I was wheelchair bound and useless. My old pal Scott was a godsend at this moment. He'd drive and push me anywhere and it didn't stop the left-handed drinking.

I still went to Sweden though, to support the team and go to the parties. It would have been bad manners not to. One bit of good advice the Sheffield doctor offered was to cut the plaster off my foot and arm and let them heal without. I got right on board with that. It meant I could keep everything mobile so I didn't lose any muscle mass while I was sitting around doing nothing. They said my body would send healing vibes if it hurt or if I overdid it, and I heeded their advice. Fifteen days later I was driving the van, still nowhere near good enough to ride but at least I could now get around on my own. I was done and dusted as far as the 1999 season was concerned. It was the only year in my whole career that I missed the worlds.

Each year I raced took on its own character or significance, and 1999 was a growing-up year of sorts. It was also a watershed. I'd left Sheffield for a new home in the USA. I had an incredible salary, a great mechanic and great friends. Palmer was on board the party train. Our scene was a critical mass

146

APPETITE FOR DESTRUCTION

of energy and we had the right people and brands telling the world about it. We raced down some of the world's most beautiful mountains at death-defying speeds risking our lives on every run. We were doing things no one would have ever thought possible on a pushbike. It was a glorious time to be racing downhill mountain bikes. What I sorely needed though was a winner's medal. Close was no longer good enough.

I wanted to win.

CHAPTER 15
NO CIGAR

There's an old interview in *Mountain Biking UK* from 2000 where Justin Loretz asks me about the difference between Warner and me. I talk about how talented Rob is and how he likes to win. Then I say that the difference between us is subtle but nonetheless clear. I am addicted to winning and will do whatever is required to achieve it. It literally keeps me awake at night. I thrive on discomfort and am happy to admit it. I've moved to another country. I train hard. Rob won't do that. He will happily admit that he just isn't made like that. I used Rob as a contrast because we often got lumped together for many different reasons. The point is that liking the feeling of winning and being addicted to that feeling are very different things. Beating an addict at something they are good at is hard; they have done it so many times and can't live without it. It's an endless cycle of repetition, perfection and destruction. Repetition of drills and training programmes, of pushing myself day in, day out; the endless hours mastering every kind of terrain brought a perfection of skill. The destruction came after failure. *Who am I? How good am I? Can I beat Nico?*

While I was in California in 1999 I had a deep conversation over dinner with Mitch Payton, owner of the Factory Kawasaki Pro-Circuit team. Mitch and I were talking about Nico. He told me the reason I was struggling to beat Nico was that I didn't have it in my head that I *could* beat him. The reason for that, he explained, was because I wasn't physically where I needed to be. There was a mismatch between what I wanted and what was possible. I needed to change what I was doing. The conversation we had went into great depth, much of which I'm unable to recall now, but the message that stuck with me was that I had to do the work on me: the grind,

FORGED BY SPEED

the graft, the repetition. That work would mean I could beat Nico consistently. This became a huge driving force for me to knuckle down and get the job done. I had done it a few times already, but I was not yet the master.

Why did I listen to Mitch? If you haven't heard of him and his hugely successful motocross team, let me explain why I was all ears. Mitch was paralysed as a seventeen-year-old while racing motocross in California. He then bought a motorcycle dealership and started to tune Husqvarna bikes. Belgian ex-rider and Honda team manager Roger De Coster heard that Mitch was a master tuner and signed him up to tune the engines of his riders' bikes. Thirty years later and Mitch owns and runs one of the most successful aftermarket tuning brands in the world as well as running his own 250cc race team for the Kawasaki Factory. Mitch had Ricky Carmichael, one of the greatest motocross riders of all time, on his team, along with the UK's Jamie Dobb. That's why I listened, and also because he was mates with Troy Lee and we all liked to drink beers together.

It's important to mention how riders end up respecting each other. We all know the weather can change drastically on the mountain on any given day, so there are a lot of races when a fast time will be set by someone in the dry that cannot be beaten after it pisses down. For some riders – Sam Hill and Danny Hart, for example – the weather makes less of a difference than for others, but generally speaking, it's a fact. So, if I won a race and knew that the course was pretty much the same for everyone then I would come away knowing who did what and how good they were on the day. I wouldn't be leaping with joy after a win if I knew that the times of my rivals were slower because of the weather. The self-respect and joy of winning only came when I knew I'd battled them on equal terms.

As two riders who were willing to go nose to nose, Nico hated being beaten by me. I hated being beaten by Nico. Yet both of us had a huge amount of respect for each other because we knew that the only way we could beat each other was to go faster down the mountain. When the gate dropped and the bullshit stopped there was usually only me and Nico wanting to push that hard every weekend. We forced each other to push far harder and right to the limit. That kind of intensity is exhausting, and considering a lot of the time we were riding with jet lag or hungover, the season took its toll on mind and body. Nico was a phenomenal rider, probably the best of his era. That's why I wanted to beat him, so I could say I had beaten the best there was. It must have been hard for him; I don't think anyone pushed him as hard as I did, and vice versa. I loved that I could beat him sometimes, and when I didn't, I still made him work.

To keep on winning after reaching the pinnacle of any sport is hard.

150

NO CIGAR

It takes incredible motivation and willpower. I won the world cup series three times, Nico five. I never got a run of consecutive wins like he did in 1995 and 1996, and then the trifecta between 1998 and 2000 when I was knocking on the door. Two years in a row I'd be the bridesmaid; two years on the trot I was second to the skinny bugger. My wins came a little later, in 2002, 2004 and 2006. During those years only me, Nico, Sam Hill and Greg Minnaar were sufficiently consistent and fast enough to challenge for the title. To make matters worse, South African import Minnaar was barely out of shorts when he won his first series in 2001 aged only nineteen, beating Nico before I got the chance. I'd met Greg a few years before when he first came to the UK and we got on really well.

My battle with Nico in 1999 had been an epic dogfight and I wanted to kick off 2000 like a bullet from a gun. Things didn't work out like that. Off-season training was a bit of a no-show in terms of solid preparation and miles in the legs. After the broken arm and leg ruled me out of the world championships in Sweden, I did basically nothing for the rest of the year. I didn't even bother filling in my diary for almost three months. In the previous twelve months my training programme had become more focused on skills and terrain. I had not been getting out doing the long old loops I used to do. No more thirty-five-mile rides in Sheffield's winter weather, no more Grenoside or Wharncliffe sessions. To be honest, I really missed them.

I started getting some time into my legs in mid-December, but was mostly drinking with the lads. A week after Christmas I managed a few weeks of road rides but then came off and cut my knee open. Two weeks later it was okay to ride so I started again. I'd also arranged to travel to the winter X-Games again as defending champion. Needless to say, I went to town on the whole thing. The X-Games did a video about me and commissioned a punk band from Los Angeles called Möbius to write a song about me too, which was pretty mind-blowing. I took my GT I-Drive to the paint shop and got it customised in a lovely gold colour with bronze ghost flames running up the forks and rear end. I had special race kits made so the bike and me looked the dog's bollocks. When I turned up, I thought I was the boy, strutting around looking so good.

Warming up for the qualifying round I did some big old turns in the icy sludge and snow but, unbeknown to me, in all this cocky joy I was blasting my gears with snow with each turn. I lined up in the gate with Wade Bootes next to me. Wade was an Aussie BMX guy and could get the snap out of the gate, something I just wasn't as skilled at. Neither did I have legs like tree trunks like Wade. Once the gate dropped though I was surprised to get a fairly decent start. At this stage I wasn't worried about qualifying as I knew

FORGED BY SPEED

I was faster than most of the boys there. Then, as I pedalled down the first part of the steep start ramp, I went to change gear and nothing happened. I was spinning my ass off in the snow going nowhere fast. I carried on pedalling like a lunatic but when I clicked the shifter nothing happened. I was stuck in a stupidly easy gear. Everyone else just pedalled away from me. I felt like a right twat.

Never mind, I thought, *I'll catch them up in the corners*, which I did. Unfortunately, though, when I pulled on to the last straight I started spinning again. Wade Bootes was in the last qualifying position and I got past him in the tech section, but after that he just pedalled away from me as I was spinning my chainring like a hamster on a wheel. I was humiliated and embarrassed. Once the race was over and I was down the mountain, we worked out that while I had been showing off doing those turns up top, my gears had frozen with snow and left me stuck in second. The story went into the history books that the defending champ failed to qualify.

I wanted to put that nightmare behind me and luckily I was due back in the UK for some testing with RockShox. After that in mid-February I was at Will Longden's wedding where I had to give a speech. I was so happy for Will and the speech went down well, despite my panic. Then, towards the end of the month, I was due to travel to Malaysia with Hans 'No Way' Rey on one of his exotic mountain bike adventures. Unfortunately, my passport was out of date and while having a few drinks waiting for a new one in Liverpool, I nearly got the shit kicked out of me by eight really angry Scouse lads looking for trouble. Luckily, I could still run fast. I was in Malaysia three days later. It was such a great experience in such a very different country. We started off in Mulu climbing up and riding down Mount Santubong. The whole adventure was plastered all over the press in the coastal city of Miri, and when I got back it was in the mountain bike press too. Everything we did was filmed. I got my wallet pickpocketed, then got it back minus all the money that had been in it. Then I picked up some godforsaken ear infection.

One very strange thing happened there that freaked out Hans. Malaysia seemed a spiritual place and our guides Malcolm and Eunice Jitam, who were well versed in that sort of thing, warned me that we should be sensitive to the spirits that inhabited the jungle. If I needed to go for a piss, they told me, I'd have to apologise, which felt pretty strange the first time I did it. One place we visited was the Headhunter's Trail, which featured some absolutely massive sacred caves that were full of bats. People would sleep in them for a kind of spiritual detox. A local headman told us that there were still some skulls up there, hidden in a smaller burial cave. Hans got very

152

NO CIGAR

excited and shot off to film all this with the crew. I was all set to follow when Eunice warned me that whatever I did, I shouldn't touch any bones. By the time I got inside Hans already had a skull in his hands. He was mortified when I told him what Eunice had said and later he apologised to the spirits. He was really affected by it.

At the end of the trip we were having dinner together, with a few other tourists, discussing what a great time we'd had, when Malcolm suddenly announced: 'You see, I told you, don't touch those bones or you'll die.' The mood at the table suddenly changed. The colour drained from Hans's face. Eunice signalled something to Malcolm, who got up, walked around the table and touched Hans on the shoulder. Then Hans got up and they both went to the bathroom. I asked Hans what was said, and he said, 'Oh, nothing, but the guy across the table, the Swiss guy, I looked at him and I suddenly saw the devil in his eyes. I had to get up and leave.'

Later, I asked Malcolm what had happened and why he'd said what he said. Malcolm was very matter of fact about it. Eunice, he told me, was very good at seeing spirits and she knew Hans was now carrying some. Malcolm had said what he did to make Hans seem weak, which flushed the spirits out. Eunice then told Malcolm they were exposed and Malcolm, who was more hands-on with the spirit world, then scooped them off Hans's shoulder and took them away, stomped them into the ground and continued on to the bathroom. When Hans got home, he was sure he'd been affected by this and later he went back to Malaysia to try and sort it all out. The whole episode really opened my eyes.

I was back in the USA at the start of March for a big meeting with the new boss of GT, Len Chapman. I think he was the second or third boss I'd had there. Unbeknown to me, GT was not in good shape financially. After Richard Long's untimely death in 1996, the brand hadn't really managed to maintain its place in the market. Len was stoked on the downhill team but he wasn't there that long and a year later someone else was in charge. Then, in June 2001, the venture capital fund Questor Partners who owned GT would file for bankruptcy and I'd be looking for a new sponsor. The contract I'd signed two years before was ridiculously good; my bonus money would be added to the previous year's salary every year, which totalled an awful lot of cash for me. I ended up having a meeting with the same accountant as U2.

Back out training in the California sunshine, I managed a few long rides

FORGED BY SPEED

before the ear infection I'd picked up in Malaysia laid me low. After a week on antibiotics and Vicodin, I was back riding but in mid-March I raced the Sea Otter downhill in Monterey and only finished seventh. I knew I wasn't in good enough shape for the start of the 2000 world cup series at Les Gets in late May. I only had eight weeks to get in shape. Luckily, there were a few UK races to do to get some time in my legs. I won the first two British RAV4 races – but I also should have: I was world-class now and even though the lads in the UK were gunning for me, I could win without having to kill myself. Jetting back to the UK to race at Innerleithen and Pateley Bridge was a good chance to meet old friends. It also coincided with me leaving the house at Huntington Beach. I'd decided to move to Temecula and live closer to Eric Carter, or EC as we called him. The UK races were also a good place for Andy and me to do some testing, and that all went well. It's always a relief to win at home when expectations are high. I even got in some good laps round Wharncliffe again and a few runs out to the Penistone roundabout. I'd missed that.

A few weeks later I was off to France for round one of the world cup. My start to the 2000 season didn't have the same intensity as the previous year. Or rather, I didn't have the same intensity. I was a bit off the pace and it would take a while for me to get going. My results in the first four races were okay but not enough. I followed fourth in Les Gets with sixth in Cortina a week later. I didn't gel with the track there at all. I also had a scuffle with a French rider in the dual category after he rode into me and grabbed my leg, trying to push me over. What a prick! One of the main reasons I was lukewarm on dual racing was its tendency to turn into a slam-fest. Downhill is the gentleman's sport by comparison. No one is trying to force you off your bike.

A week after that I came third at Maribor. The result does seem better, but I rode way too cautiously and was even talking to myself on the way down, worrying about crashing, something I had never done before. Back in the States at the NORBA on Mount Snow in Vermont I came second to Myles Rockwell. Myles is one fast dude but I was annoyed he beat me. After the race, and for the second time ever, I spent hours trying to piss for a drugs test. I had taken a big crash in practice, the first time I'd landed on my arm since I'd broken it. It must have affected me psychologically. Then it was a short-haul flight to Canada for a third place in the Mont-Sainte-Anne world cup. I wasn't riding badly. These results were worthy and consistent but weren't where I needed to be if I was going to win the series. The bike wasn't the problem. I was.

That changed at round five in Vail where I finally got a win. There

154

weren't any more that year. In the final three races of the series I got seconds in Japan and Kaprun and a lowly sixth at the final round in Leysin, Switzerland, where I rode way too cautiously. Once again I ended up bridesmaid to Nico. My consolation came at the European championships in Vars, France, where I beat Nico on his home turf by three and a half seconds. He was well pissed off, but it gave me some much-needed confidence and provided a welcome boost to an otherwise disappointing season.

Getting broken up had done something to my confidence. I just wasn't balls to the wall as I usually was. There also seemed to be a lot more to do away from the track that year and less time for training. Getting our clothing brand Royal going was taking time. I was enjoying seeing Nick and excited that we would be helping up-and-coming riders, but it was another thing to think about and a serious one at that. Nick and I organised a Royal motocross day, bringing together our riders for a bit of cross-training at a track near Doncaster. Those days ran for ten years and expanded into something special that we dubbed the Battle Royal, with huge bonfires and fireworks. And we supported some great riders early in their careers, like Josh 'Ratboy' Bryceland, Brendan Fairclough and Marc Beaumont.

There were loads of other commitments too: bike shows, magazine features and media interviews. I ended up on the *Big Breakfast*, riding around outside the studio. When I got a bit of time off, I did my invoices for bonuses, which totalled about £50,000. That number didn't include my salary, so I bought Adele a new car and invested the rest. There were other distractions back home in Chapeltown. Adele and I had to have mediation with our neighbours who claimed our TV was on in the middle of the night and that we were using exercise machines. The woman next door made her husband come round to demonstrate to me and Adele how to close a door. We were fuming. Most nights we were in bed at 10 p.m., though maybe not at weekends. Eventually they moved away and the woman then did exactly the same thing to her new neighbours.

During all this drama my nana became poorly after a fall, which was rubbish news. I spent a day with her and just chatted to see if I could cheer her up. I also managed the Hillsborough M.C.C. club trial with the old man at the end of the year which was a treat, although I 'fived' too much, meaning I made too many serious errors. Mum was watching too, so it was just like when I was growing up, following Dad to a trial and riding around while Mum looked on. I loved it.

At the start of 2001 I began my last season with GT and my last year in the USA with a move to a condo in Temecula, over an hour's drive southeast of Huntington Beach. It was easier to train with EC out there with our new Slovenian trainer Val and a masseur called Cory. The new place was much nicer than the old digs. I had a pool to swim in and it was easier to get to places I wanted to ride. It was also less BMX focused than Huntington, and as much as I loved living near the beach, I was focused on trying to win a championship or three. Fewer distractions bar-wise were another plus. I'd been in the UK since the start of August and had been doing a lot of motorcycle trials and motocross as well as getting in some downhill practice with the lads. I'd missed being at home. The rhythm and ease with which things slotted into place were welcome.

In complete contrast to the previous four or five months, when I got back to the States I went to see Palmer at New Year and popped a Valium for a laugh. Off we went snowboarding for the weekend, but after that blowout it was down to business. I didn't want the same thing happening to me this year. I was sick of second. Training was coming easy now and every day was filled with something. EC and I were pushing each other. The two-hour cross-country rides were back and I was happy to be huffing my lungs up again and feeling the improvements in my fitness coming thick and fast. I was lifting weights at the gym too, so I knew I was getting stronger. The only difference to the bike this year was a switch from the Michelin tyres to Maxxis. Meanwhile, Royal had hooked up with Orange Bikes on a deal, which was good for the team back home. Nick was sorting all that out. The new training schedule included stuff I'd never heard of, underwater plyometrics being one. The surfer Laird Hamilton is all over it nowadays, but then it was new, at least to me. Swimming, Swiss ball and racquetball were also added to the schedule, along with the usual weights and riding programme, plus motocross.

It was a completely different preparation to the previous year. I was getting drunk way less and the level of commitment to the programme Cory had me on was absolute. I wasn't going to skive a day, not my style. The only hiccup on the run-in to the first world cup was a bad case of poison oak rash at the end of March. I needed a jab, but that was it. I was also refused entry back into the US by immigration after a training trip to Canada so had to go back to the UK direct from Canada to sort that out. I carried on training my ass off though.

I won at Sea Otter, did a race in France where I came second to Nico, then went to Fort William in the new van that GT had bought us; it was the first race of the national series, which had been renamed the National Points Series (NPS). I won that too. The Royal lads did wicked, so we all had a dip in Loch Linnhe before setting off home. Domestically, things were looking up too. I bought a new house for me and Adele above Wharncliffe. It cost

NO CIGAR

£280,000, which seemed terrifying in those days. My old mate Scott, now working as a joiner, fitted the kitchen for me. We drank pints of Baileys to keep us entertained while fitting it.

Somehow, though, I'd hurt my back and now the world cup season was upon us. It started, bad back and all, at Maribor. Adele went to hospital on the first day and Kate Burcham broke both wrists and her collarbone. Not the best start for the women. I felt like shit on race day and nearly came off several times in my practice run, but a cold shower and a two-hour nap changed everything for my race run and I came down the mountain without making a mistake bar tagging a pad on a tree, although not hard. I must have looked bloody stupid though as I'd worn a skinsuit and taken the visor off my helmet. The difference between Nico and me was less than half a second but I was in the leader's jersey now because of my qualification points, which were for the first time being taken into account for the UCI rankings. It was a great start to the season but I felt so ropey I didn't drink at all that night to celebrate. At least that meant I was stone-cold sober next day when Mum called to say Nana had died. I was pretty cut up. I took some sleeping pills and went to bed for a while, hoping I'd feel better when I woke up. I didn't.

On the Tuesday I was heading back to Vars where the previous year I'd beaten Nico at the Euros. Finals day coincided with my birthday. I would turn twenty-seven. It would be bad manners not to win I thought, so I did, ahead of the Aussie rider Chris Kovarik. Even better, Nico came fifth. I'd lost a few points because I only got fourth in qualification, but it made no difference. I was still top. I again didn't drink to celebrate because I still wasn't feeling 100 per cent. Nana's funeral was scheduled for the Wednesday so I flew home from France. Everyone was at Mum's house and it was good to see them all, despite the occasion. We had a good send-off for Nana Dixon. On the Thursday I was on a plane to Pittsburgh and then on to West Virginia for the next NORBA, which I won by eight seconds despite hitting a few trees on the way down. I remember Jeff Steber kicking me and a bunch of other drunk fools out of his rented condo after the race. I didn't blame him. We were all well lit. Next day I was back at the apartment in Temecula. It felt strange, as I was there to say goodbye to the place. The following weekend was the NORBA at Park City, Utah. The course was as dusty as hell but I beat Nico again by three and a half seconds. Then I handed the keys for the Temecula condo back to the agent and on Independence Day flew to Grouse Mountain, Canada, for the third world cup.

Next day, a Thursday, I headed up the hill for practice. The course was pretty short and after a few runs I was getting more familiar with the

157

FORGED BY SPEED

terrain. Then on a really fast section I got the line wrong and hit a tree flat-out with my shoulder. It spun me right off the bike and on to the deck. I have never known so much pain. I was carried off the mountain and put in a wheelchair, which was a stupid decision as every bump reverberated through my destroyed shoulder. I was then put in a gondola. It took an age to get me in the ambulance and after forty-five minutes I still couldn't breathe properly. I was fading in and out of consciousness as they loaded me up and when they eventually got me on gas and air it induced a laughing fit that lasted a while. Only then did the pain go away.

After the X-rays, the bad news was delivered in the only way doctors know: deadpan. 'You've suffered a third-degree separation and it will take six weeks to recover. Here's an injection of morphine, here's more for later and here are some pills.'

There goes my season, I thought. At the best estimate, I was going to miss the world cups at Durango in Colorado and Arai in Japan. Maybe I'd be back for Leysin and Kaprun, but it was highly unlikely. I got a taxi back to my rented place where I spent the next few hours passing out because of the drugs they'd given me. I'd won the first two world cups of the year and had been feeling on top of the world. Now I'd been taken out of the reckoning by a soft patch of track. To say I was gutted was an understatement.

Next day all the Peats from the Canadian side of our family came expecting to see me race. Instead, they saw me passed out or delirious. There was nothing I could do about it, but it was still pretty upsetting. I got a flight that night back to the UK. Two days later I was with my physiotherapist Alison who had helped me recover from the broken arm and leg the previous year. Eight weeks' recovery, she said. It was like hearing a death sentence. All I could manage exercise-wise when I got home were some road rides. And that was only after two weeks of doing fuck all except physiotherapy once a week, along with some shoulder-strengthening exercises with a band that Alison recommended. Nico had finished thirty-eighth in Durango but was back to winning ways in Arai.

I knew my chances of winning the world cup series were done, but the world championships were coming up in Vail in September and I wanted to see if I could race at Kaprun, which was only five weeks after my crash. Of course, I'd have had no downhill practice at all in that time. Four weeks after the crash, on Wednesday 8 August, I flew to Kaprun. It was the first time I'd seen Adele in a month so I was much happier. On the Thursday Andy set the bike up well and I was excited to see if I could manage a run. I ended up doing five and couldn't stop smiling. It felt great to be on the bike again. It pissed down in qualification on the Friday but I managed to get

158

NO CIGAR

fourth. Saturday's run was in the rain again but I still qualified third. Race day went well. I did just two runs in the morning and then finished fourth. Nico was third. South African legend Greg Minnaar won and went on to win the world cup series, the jammy bugger.

I flew home on the Sunday and on Monday picked up the keys for the new house and moved in. Dad helped move a load of my gear, which was a big help. Next morning was beautifully sunny and it took me four hours on a sit-down mower to do the garden. After that I did a bit of sunbathing. I loved my new house but was only there for two days before I flew out to Mount Snow for another NORBA. That Friday in practice I suffered a huge crash and buggered up my shoulder again. This time it wasn't as bad and I could ride again after a week, but no racing and only non-technical cross-country and road rides. Two weeks later it was weak as a wing in a gale, but I hadn't stopped getting the miles in on the roadie. Four weeks later it was okay: not great, but okay.

In mid-September I was in Vail for the world championships. I had a good week leading up to the finals with plenty of decent practice runs, and to top it off Troy had painted me a new world's helmet, which was mint. I won the seeding round on Thursday by four and a half seconds ahead of Minnaar and Kovarik. That was something to celebrate. But the confidence was gone by race day and my first three runs were shit. I crashed on the first one, rode badly on the second and only marginally better on the third. I just didn't feel right at all. When it came to my race run, I felt like I was fighting the bike all the way down. All I can remember was thinking I shouldn't have got shit-faced on the Thursday night after I won seeding. What an idiot. Nico won by two seconds and, yes – you guessed it – I got second, again.

By the end of the season the demise of GT had become clear, and with the company looking for a buyer I was going to have a busy few months ahead of me sorting out a deal for the coming season and beyond. It was the last year I'd live in the US, and I was back home in Sheffield on 30 October. A day later, Lester Noble and Michael Bonney from Orange came to see me. I'd been talking to them on and off for a few months and had an idea that something might be possible. It would mean taking a massive pay cut, but a Yorkshireman riding for a Yorkshire brand was appealing. I was about to spend the off-season rustling up some money to see if I could pull it off while keeping my foot on the gas when it came to training.

The GT years might have been over, but I was no less desperate to win.

CHAPTER 16
THE ORANGE YEARS

Don't ever let anyone tell you I'm not a romantic at heart. Yorkshire born, I was now on a Yorkshire bike brand with a mission to lay a few ghosts to rest. With no contract at the end of 2001 and without a team, I put most of my energy into making something happen with Orange and the sponsors I'd had while riding for GT. The enormous cost of getting me to the races, developing a bike I could win on, maintaining a training programme, running the Royal mountain bike team to bring on those up-and-comers, plus all the other stuff that goes with being competitive, it was going to be a hard feat to pull it all off. One of my best mates, Brian Lopes, had run his own deal the previous year. It gave me confidence that my team could work from the success he'd made of his own self-funded outfit. And so, Team Orange England was born.

Michael Bonney ran a tight ship financially at Orange, and Lester, Orange's owner, was also a shrewd guy. I knew I'd not get anywhere near the salary I'd had with GT – they both made that clear early on – so I came away from the first meeting knowing I was going to have to raise some cash from my other sponsors. After topping up the coffers with them, Orange jumped on board with the project. I'd invested well during the GT years. If it all went tits up, I knew I'd be okay digging holes or plumbing houses and working nine to five. I had very little to lose. I felt that now was a good time to take a punt on what a lot of people thought was not the best deal on the table. Looked at financially it wasn't, but I had other ideas. I agree it wasn't the best on paper; it was the stuff that couldn't be put on paper that was driving me to make it happen. It felt like a quest, not a business deal.

The fact it could be pulled off and be seen as a sort of miracle drove me

161

FORGED BY SPEED

harder to make it work. I'd spent three years developing a relationship with Troy Lee that would go on to become a lifelong friendship. Troy was in for some money for the 2002 season. Orange were into it for a good five-figure salary, though nowhere near what I was used to at GT. Their frugality on salary turned out to my benefit on the bonus front. Since they weren't going to pay me what I was worth monthly, then I made sure I topped it up with my results: if I pulled off a big win they would pay. There was no mechanic's salary though. RockShox jumped in again. I had a long relationship with glasses and goggles company Smith, a photo contingency deal with DC Shoes, money from Mr Crud, and EBC, who make brake pads, came on board. Maxxis lobbed in a few suitcases of cash too. Also on board were Hadley, who makes hubs, Hyundai, handlebar company X-Lite, cable manufacturer Clarks and specialist paint sellers PPG, thanks to my connections with Troy Lee. Last but not least, local brand Hope Tech were 100 per cent all for it. It was complicated but enough for us to go racing in 2002 on a one-year deal with the prospect of things improving financially in year two.

It was curious how getting so close to the world cup gold and the world championships had changed me. It was like getting closer to the light; it put into relief the shadows holding me back. In 1999 I was all about hunger, desire and raw energy. The following year was disappointment and nihilism; I'd been a bit lost. Then at the end of 2000 a regular programme that reconnected me with old patterns built a solid foundation that took me to the next level at the start of 2001 until my injury intervened. I may have wandered off the beaten track a few times, but there was always some kind of self-righting mechanism despite all the frustration and hedonism. Like a lifeboat on the high seas, I always seemed to be able to right myself and come to my own rescue. I now had enough experience to see where I should focus for the coming season. I had got to know my body and how to get fitter, and I was also more emotionally robust. I had the wherewithal to mount an attack on the 2002 world cup series and bring it home. Me, Andy, Orange and the rest of my crewmates were ready for war. I had endured enough high-octane disappointments to pour down the funnel and burn as fuel.

I was back in Sheffield. California was in the rear-view mirror. I'd loved my time with Palmer, obliterated myself in the name of Bacchus and learned a lot. I soaked up all the USA had to offer. I was so fortunate to have Eric Carter and Brian Lopes to call on as best friends. But I'm a Sheffield lad and I missed the sound of water over rocks and trials bikes riding up gullies, like Dad had done. I missed the freezing winters and numb extremities from rides in snow and ice. I missed Mum and I really missed my mates. My

162

THE ORANGE YEARS

heart and home were – and are – in Sheffield. I had found the girl of my dreams. The money from those GT days was banked. Adele and I now had our forever home. It felt like the right time for a crusade to bring back the gold to the hills of my youth.

Our new house was where the assault on the world cup series would be planned: Castle Peaty. Adele and I settled in easily, sharing with a couple of spirits that were meant to haunt the place. I'd heard someone had been murdered over unpaid taxes and buried in the back garden some time in the eighteenth century. I've not found them yet, but I'll keep digging. Maybe they hid their fortune in the garden. Andy was still over the way in Cheadle and together we hatched our plan for world domination. He and his partner Fliss were an integral part of the team, psychologically and spiritually. They were great friends and good fun to hang with.

We felt our time had come. Rock and roll had AC/DC and Angus and Stevie Young, the lead and rhythm guitars of a defining era. Mountain biking had Orange England with Steve Peat and Andy Kyffin. Andy would turn thirty-four in 2002 and I was going to be twenty-eight. We were two fellas with experience of highs and lows and dreams unfulfilled. We were both desperate for a winning year and depended on each other to get it. Despite our mutual love for alcohol we both had a laser focus on winning that was a smidge more intense than our love of mischief and mayhem. Sometimes the planets align, and for Andy and me they were about to deliver the Holy Grail. I don't know if it was fated, but I'm good at following a gut feeling and won't back down when adversity kicks in my door. I get fired up, not blown down. The river was taking us on a ride, but we didn't yet know that all we had to do was go with the flow. Second wasn't happening this time.

I knew I'd got to Nico over the past few years. Greg had won the previous year's world cup series on his new team. If it hadn't been for hitting that tree in Canada, I'd probably have been sitting on a few gold medals and sipping a Stella, but the mountain gods had a different plan. Nico was two years younger than me but was mostly unchallenged early on. He had been so successful. Now there were challengers: Greg, Kovarik, Peaty and a few others. Maybe he felt his time was running out. I had a feeling that he was getting hot under the collar and didn't like the continual pressure I put him under during the world cup series. I was prepared to go to places Nico found uncomfortable. I knew that he grew from me pushing him, but I grew from having him in my crosshairs. I wasn't going to stop until the job was done and he knew that. Was he losing interest? I don't know. I don't know what he was feeling or thinking but I know I lived in his

163

head for a while as he did in mine. I think that's why, despite all that's been said in banter and media interviews that have not aged well, we can both now at this stage in our lives stand side by side and know we did our best and left nothing on the table when we raced each other. We put the chance of death to one side and turned that tarot card over. He was a one-off and you only have to look at what he achieved on and off mountain bikes to see he's an incredibly talented individual. Companies happily pay for his know-how, as they do mine. We're two old buggers who know some stuff about bikes, what makes a good one and what doesn't. Now we're the crafty foxes.

The first world cup of 2002 was at Fort William on 2 June. The six months leading up to it had given me a solid base. I'd done lots of trials and motocross and a couple of months' really intensive training in April and May. I'd got a few UK races in, winning the first two NPS races, and had been to the Red Bull Downtown race in the city of Lisbon in April. I won that too and came away with a couple of grand. Not bad for a course that's not even two minutes long. It reminded me of my early days blasting round the streets of Chap on my Muddy Fox. Four runs is all you get before the final, and that kind of pinpoint focus suited me fine. I broke a few frames along the way, but Orange were working on getting me a new bike for the season proper. There was nothing insurmountable, just the run-of-the-mill stuff that happens when a bike is being developed.

Lots of my time was taken up sorting sponsors, but thankfully by the end of March everything had been settled. I spent hours on the phone and answering emails as the deals came in. There was also plenty to do on the new house. The first three months of the year were spent pulling ivy off walls, and gutting the barn and kitchen, sunrise-to-sunset graft and a little more. It was all hands on deck. After things settled down it was easier to focus on the season. We now had a team van and held a weekend testing on the hill at Innerleithen. The weather was poor and it didn't go as well as it might, but a press event afterwards in Edinburgh got us in the papers and was a boost for Orange and for me.

There was also the Bike Show early in March; these events are a regular for any sponsored rider and I'd worked out my strategy for surviving them long ago. I'd sign autographs and sink a few beers. Royal and Orange had a stand, but I really went to do a bit of four-cross racing. It was supposed to be a bit of fun, but it ended badly. Kelvin Batey fell going over a jump and I landed on him as I cleared it, breaking his femur. Kelvin was left screaming on the floor. I felt terrible for him, even though there was nothing I could have done to avoid him.

I was hyped about the first race of the year being at Fort William. It was

THE ORANGE YEARS

a place I'd been to almost every year since birth. If ever there was a place I felt at home, it was Fort William, and to win the race on my first outing with Orange would be massive. I felt like I was being written into a fairy tale. I'd already been up earlier in the year to do some testing and check out the track, so knew what to expect. Brian Lopes was over, staying with us from the Tuesday with his mechanic Stikman. We had a couple of days' training then drove north on the Thursday. The cops pulled me over on the way up for dangerous driving and speeding. Luckily the cop was a mountain biker and he let me off with a warning.

Fort William was heaving with thousands of people and the weekend was fantastic except for one detail. After comfortably setting the fastest time in seeding, on my finals run I bailed on one of the least technical parts of the course at high speed. I just hit a spot badly that pushed the front wheel one way then the other and that was it: arse over tit I went. I broke my seat off, bent my brake lever down and had mud all over my gloves. My roll-offs, the film in front of my goggles that I could change while racing to keep my vision clear, were streaming off the side of my head like bunting. To top it off, I fell again further down. Seventeenth place and that was my fairy-tale start to the 2002 world cup. Then the wheels fell off the new team van on the way home, the second time this had happened. Poor Andy had to deal with that nightmare. Greg was in a worse position than me though. He'd crashed near the end of his run, landing funny on the big downhill ski jump with his body to the right side of his bike. He flew off the track through the tapes and crashed into twenty-second place. I drowned my sorrows, as usual, getting pissed with winner Chris Kovarik. And, as usual, I had a great night.

Two days later and we were off to Maribor where I posted fastest qualifier and got second place, a hundredth of a second behind Chris. That catapulted me to third place overall in the UCI standings. Mont-Sainte-Anne was next at the end of June. I love that track. Chris had crashed in practice and was a bit battered. It was him I was after. My qualification run was fairly sedate; I didn't pedal too much and finished third. I had planned to wear a skinsuit for the final but broke the zip putting it on. I still won by almost four seconds. My run was near perfect and I still felt I could have gone faster. Cédric Gracia was second, then Greg, with Chris down in ninth. That was more points clawed back on Chris, and I badly needed them after the disaster at Fort William.

Lucky for me I got a five-year US visa sorted because next stop on the tour was Telluride, Colorado. I'd raced the previous weekend at Whistler in British Columbia and got third, although not being a world cup round it didn't count. I had such a good time I was thinking about buying a house

165

FORGED BY SPEED

there. Whistler is amazing and I've been told their weed is the best ever. I had two weeks' riding nearly every day and a week filming. It was a good chance to dial the bike in even more and get our base settings right. I arrived in Colorado on the Thursday with the final scheduled for Sunday 14 July. I didn't get the best start, crashing in practice and hitting my knee. By Sunday things were a bit better. I qualified eighth having slid out going into the woods and losing a little time: no big deal.

As usual, I had a nap before my final and then I took a line I hadn't used in practice. Sometimes I would do that, having visualised the track in my race preparations. Seeing it in my head it might occur to me that I could shave time at a certain point. It had the added bonus that other riders wouldn't have seen me do it. These days it wouldn't work, because riders and coaches are way more on it. At Telluride, I thought I'd blown it so was surprised to end up in first place by 0.15 seconds. That put me in first place in the UCI standings, ahead of Cédric, who finished sixth, and Chris who came in twenty-first. While Chris had won in Maribor, and despite my awful first race, I had been consistent enough elsewhere to lead the overall.

A week later I was back in the UK to race the national championships, winning for the fourth time, not bad considering I'd gone over the handlebars and got back up again just to see where I'd finish after the bail. I certainly wasn't expecting it to be first. Then came the world championships in Kaprun at the start of September. I lost a pedal in the woods and it took about ten turns before I got it clipped back in. Then I rode another bit with both feet off. Even so, I took the lead and kept the hot seat until a certain Frenchman – master tactician, stealer of my gold medals – came down. Nico had done bugger all for the whole year, then beat me by 0.64 seconds. The only consolation was that I got more cheers than Nico on the podium, but I'd have swapped that noise for total silence to win one worlds.

The following weekend was the world cup decider in Les Gets. After Telluride I was in the lead, so I put the disappointment of silver at the worlds behind me to focus on keeping what I had. I flew in to Les Gets on the Wednesday and spent a fun evening drinking tequila with *Dirt* magazine's Steve Jones. I felt fine next morning and got six runs in on the course despite it pissing down. On Friday the Chapeltown posse turned up – Farmer Jack, Ken, Cobber, Stav, Dell, the whole crew – after nineteen hours' driving nonstop. I got another six good runs in and was second to Fabien Barel in timed training. It was a solid start and I was so happy the Chap crew were there. We had a meal together on the Friday night and a few beers. Apparently a TV went missing and their apartment window was open, but I know nowt about that.

166

THE ORANGE YEARS

Race day was Saturday 7 September. I did two practice runs and put spike tyres on because it was raining again. Then I did my qualification run and won by one and a half seconds. That was a relief since it gave me a good cushion of points for the overall. To take the pressure off further I went into town for a meal with Mum, Adele and Brian Lopes and his partner, Paula. That killed a few hours and was a good distraction. There were so many UK fans and Union Jacks everywhere that I was getting a bit nervous, although not bad nervous: this was good. Then I had my nap. It would soon be time.

The Orange and me just seemed to gel. They'd made it longer in the front and the rear so it handled well and was predictable, which suited me. Andy had set the bike up perfectly. That he was there at all was some kind of miracle. Earlier that year I had been struggling to find the money to pay him what he deserved and what he had been getting when GT paid him. Then we had some unbelievable good fortune. While riding one day in North Nibley with a friend from GT and his mate and their kids, we chatted about my plans and I mentioned I was struggling to raise some cash for a full-time mechanic. My friend's mate told me he'd just sold his business for millions and was a fan. This fella, whose name is Gary Salter, who I'd literally only known for those few hours, said he'd pay Andy's wages. I couldn't believe my luck or Gary's generosity and I want to thank him here publicly. Winning this world cup would be a big payback from me to him, and even more so to Andy.

Back at the race, Fabien Barel, a Frenchman at a French world cup, had been in the hot seat for a while. He was enjoying watching a series of failures to oust him as he sat on what he thought was a winning time of three minutes and 38.61 seconds. Nico was 0.07 seconds behind. Another Frenchman, Mickaël Pascal, was 3.55 seconds further back. And just behind him was a fourth Frenchman, Cédric Gracia. I was last man down. The rain had cleared up earlier and the track was running really well. I rode the first half pretty well, kept my lines tight, didn't slip out anywhere and pedalled my arse off when I could to keep momentum up. I knew I was motoring. I knew the high cadence I was known for would help here, as I'd seen other riders not bother. Halfway down I was on two minutes and 44.61 seconds, up on Fabien by 0.09 seconds. That would make the bugger sweat.

I took a tight line three-quarters of the way down on a drop-off that had a right after the landing. I knew that by missing the berm on the outside left I'd carry more momentum and cut off valuable metres from the course that would keep my speed up for the next left-hander. All I needed to do now was keep things pinned and avoid a mistake. It was coming to me so fast it

FORGED BY SPEED

felt like I was being pulled to the finish line by fate. I dropped into the last turn, a fast sweeping right with the finish line on the turn. Crossing it I looked over my right shoulder: *3:38.03*. I'd done it. Ranking points for the year were Peat on 1,002, Gracia on 729, Kovarik on 709, Pascal on 660, Barel on 659 and Vouilloz on 495. I'd won the world cup.

Safe to say we had a party. The UK crew were out in force. Mum cried her eyes out when I was on the podium as the national anthem played. Everyone seemed really happy for me and that was an amazing feeling. I had a problem pissing for the drug test as usual but a few hours later we were all in the Boomerang bar getting pissed out of our heads. Someone tried to headbutt me, everyone bought me drinks, Titley had a fight, then we went to the Irish bar and did it all again. I went to bed at 5.30 a.m. and was up again at 9 a.m. and drank all day to celebrate.

Finally, I'd done it. All I'd been working towards. There was a big bonus from Lester and Michael for the win, thank you very much. It all felt so good. That win set me up for three more years with Orange. I'd also won the UK downhill series, so that bode well for Orange too. Racing on home soil and in the USA was helping them and I was glad to be able to keep the whole thing on the road. *Same again next year*, I thought.

How wrong can you be?

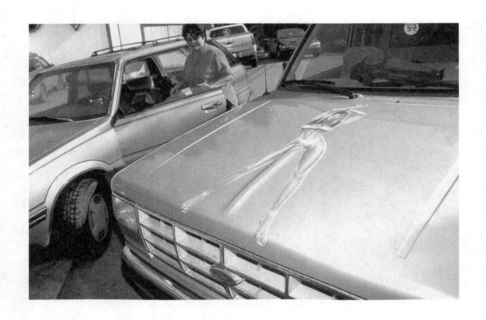

CHAPTER 17
WITH OR WITHOUT YOU

Early in February 2003 I was in the USA testing new RockShox stuff, staying with EC and hooking up with the old crew for a few days. Then I stayed with Lopes and Paula, needing to collect the pink slip for the Golden Princess, the name for the pick-up I drove in the States. I hopped on a flight back to Heathrow from Los Angeles on 6 February and settled into the thirteen-hour flight home. I landed at 4 p.m. and Adele's dad picked me up. On the drive home I had a weird and eerie feeling about my pal Scott, who had only recently fitted the kitchen in our new house. It was a cold, wet sensation crawling from my toes all the way to the top of my head. I didn't say anything to Adele's dad, but I was freaked out.

When we got home, I unpacked my gear, watched some TV and went to bed at 10.30 p.m. As I was nodding off, the phone downstairs rang. I was so tired and jet lagged I didn't bother to get up and answer it. It rang again. Then my mobile pinged. There was a message from a pal saying I should call one of Scott's mates urgently. I got on the phone straightaway and he told me Scott had been found dead. I had a good cry and then just lay there, unable to sleep. I knew he'd had his battles, but he'd been off the hard stuff for ages. He had been to rehab in the Midlands and was doing so well. Hanging out with him had been just like the old times. He'd pushed me round in the wheelchair for days when I'd broken my leg. We'd had such a laugh over the last year. I was devastated. He'd been up at my place nearly every day sorting the kitchen and drinking Baileys. I'd lost my pal.

Next morning we gathered his mates together and went to see his mum and his sister. Then we all went round to see his dad and ended up telling stories and crying. We had our own gathering at his mate's house where we drank and played all the old tunes that reminded us of him and all the good times we'd had. It was a good send-off. I was a pallbearer and sobbed like a baby when they played U2's 'With or Without You'. I'd known that little bugger since I was young. We were muck-about mates, said yes to every adventure, apart from one on my account. There were some brilliant and very funny speeches made that helped us forget the pain just a bit. We ended up in the Royal Oak drinking his favourite tipple, Royal Emblem sherry. I woke up between two mates, then someone's dad turned up with fish and chips and we cried into our chip bags. I went home and watched a movie, just sat there all night in shock. I still raise a glass to him on the anniversary of him leaving us and on his birthday. Silly bugger.

I'd knackered my knee earlier in the year and on a trip to Ireland to train up the Irish lads I banged it again. A few weeks later I hit my knuckle on a tree while riding the mini-bike. I was still training hard despite these setbacks, doing everything I needed to do. Then my mate Nige lost his dad and I felt that being there to support Nige was the least I could do. I nipped over to Portugal and won the Red Bull race in Lisbon again. That was like picking cherries. Last year the money had been two grand. This year it was two and a half, thank you very much. I loved that race. Then I went to Big Bear in mid-May and broke a bone in my wrist. What was really infuriating was that I'd given up drinking for three months to get fitter; after Big Bear I resolved never to stop drinking again.

There was a silver lining though to those grim and grey months, one that's endured. After the emotional and physical battering we'd suffered, Adele and I had a mini-break at the end of June in North Wales. I took her into the garden and picked a red rose, gave her the ring I'd bought and asked her if she'd marry me. Her saying yes was the best thing I'd ever heard. It also made up for what soon became a season to forget. A third at Fort William and a first at Mont-Sainte-Anne were the only decent results I managed all year. As my mate, the recently departed Queen Elizabeth II, was famous for saying, it was our *annus horribilis*, but with a cherry on top. I finished ninth overall for the year and fourth at the worlds in Lugano where I crashed and Fabien Barel beat me, the only consolation being that Greg won. I finished the season with twenty-third at Kaprun where I hurt my leg, which required a pot on it for three weeks. The bonus money from Smith, DC and Maxxis was good though, despite it not being a year to remember.

Everything changed in 2004. We got married on Valentine's Day at a castle in Dumfries. (This followed three stag dos at various races, which I'll leave to your imagination.) It was the perfect day and we went on honeymoon to Mauritius. We spent the week walking and sightseeing, snorkelling, sleeping and drinking cocktails, and I read Howard Marks's memoirs, which I couldn't put down. When we got home at the end of February it was snowing, of course. A month later I won Lisbon again, banking three grand this time. Fabien was second, Mickaël Pascal third and the Swede Felix Beckeman fourth. Gee Atherton, one of the famous downhill family from Salisbury, and Marc Beaumont rounded out the top six.

Consistency wins world cup series. Getting on the podium at every race is vital. Winning two of them is consequently that bit more difficult, which is why 2004 was a pivotal year for me. It was also a year of parting with good friends. This would be my last year with Andy as my full-time mechanic. By 2005, Andy's protégé Giacomo Angeli was my new guy. There were other new additions. Adele was pregnant with our boy, Jake. He was due at the start of 2005, so I prepared myself for acquiring cots, prams and all manner of baby stuff that I never knew we needed.

In the meantime, I had races to win. I started with the first two NPS races. The first was at the Forest of Ae in Dumfries and the second at Moelfre. The Moelfre race was on 30 May, the week before the world cup began at Fort William, and I beat Greg so knew I was in okay shape for the first round in Scotland on 6 June. Greg stayed with us the week before and we practised together. Then on the Tuesday we drove up to Scotland and had a good piss-up with rider and journalist Steve Jones, filmmaker Alex Rankin and Mike Rose on the Wednesday. It rained for several days, was windy too, but by Sunday I'd qualified fastest and all seemed set fair. I really thought I could get the win. The atmosphere was incredible; I signed so many autographs. Yet when it came to it, I rode a bit too cautiously in my final run and ended up fourth behind Greg, Cédric and Aussie legend Sam Hill. In some ways I was glad to get out of there with a fourth. I'd done better than in previous years and it wasn't the worst start to the season. I'd love to have won there, but it just seemed to be as elusive as the world championships.

By Tuesday, Andy and I were driving to Les Deux Alpes for round two. It was a new track, quite old school, not too technical and pretty fast. That Sunday, I punctured on my first qualification run and crashed on rocks on my second, bending my chain guide, but that was still a good run. I had my usual nap before the final run and came down without making a mistake to win by a meaty 5.77 seconds, with Cédric in second and Pascal third.

Thanks to the celebrations, we slept in until 10 a.m. the next day before starting the long drive across the Alps and deep into Austria for the next round in Schladming. The Iron Horse Team were following us, so we stopped that evening in a lovely village to eat gorgeous traditional Italian food before continuing to Austria next day. By Wednesday we were all on the mountain looking at the track. It was long and technical and great fun to ride. That Thursday was my thirtieth birthday. I did seven runs, then crashed and banged my ankle badly before settling down in a bar in town to watch England beat Switzerland in the Euros. Weirdly, everyone knew it was my birthday. Even more weirdly, I didn't drink. By Friday I was exhausted and hallucinating with some virus. Practice was a waste of time. I was in bed by 10 p.m. on the Friday night and only did two more practice runs. The first was to check the track out and the second was to hammer it at full tilt.

Considering how utterly crap I was feeling, I was happy with fourth in the final qualification. I went and had a bite to eat with Cédric in his truck. I knew it would be relaxed; Cédric and I get on really well. I then went back to see Andy at our truck and went to sleep for a few hours. When I woke up I packed up a bit so Andy wouldn't have to do as much, then got my head around going up the hill for my run. I only managed to come down one second faster than my qualification run which put me in fourth, but it was a pretty good effort considering I felt so bad. For the first time I also felt the bike held me back a bit. I didn't know what it was, but I just didn't feel comfortable on it. What was more impressive than my meagre fourth was Gee winning his first senior world cup race and kicking all our arses.

Despite the setback, I was still in the leader's jersey and was beginning to like the feel of it. Unlike in the past, when I felt it was like having a target on my back, I now felt like I'd grown into it. There was no imposter syndrome any more. I struggled with the urine test as usual and at 6 p.m. off we drove to Calais. We were at the ferry at 4.30 a.m. for duty-free, where I bought thirty crates of Stella and Andy bought thirty bathfuls of wine. I got home at 10.30 a.m. having bought Adele some flowers on the way and we spent the evening round a big fire at a friend's house. At 8 a.m. next day we were looking at a scan of our baby. Twenty-four hours after that I was on my way to Canada with Andy and all our gear.

The weather in Mont-Sainte-Anne is inclement at best and 2004 was no different. Practice was delayed on the Friday. I rode with Greg and managed to get five runs in. On race day practice was at 8.30 a.m. There was a rock drop-in I needed to get dialled so off I went to see if I could get it sorted. Then everything went wrong and I crashed, landing hard on the rock on the side of my thigh at just the same place where you give someone a dead leg. My whole thigh went numb and I had to do qualification like that. How I

WITH OR WITHOUT YOU

won by five seconds I do not know. When I got back to the pits the leg had started to balloon. I tried to ride on the rollers but that was agony so went off for a ride with Greg and David Vazquez to see if that helped. It didn't. I came back to get some ice and stick my leg above my heart for the few hours left before my final run. That made it feel better. When it came to my run, it took a while for the feeling to come into my leg and I was down a couple of seconds on Sam Hill at the split, but on the second half I managed to make up the time and some, winning by 0.86 seconds over Sam, Nathan Rennie, Mickaël Pascal and Gee. That was three in a row for me at Mont-Sainte-Anne. By the time I was on the podium, my leg had swollen and I felt sick. I didn't go out that night; just iced the thigh and went back to our condo.

By Sunday I couldn't walk and had the medics apply pressure bandages. Then I flew to Calgary for the next round and went straight to the hospital. My thigh was now black; flying hadn't helped. The doctors diagnosed a huge haematoma that would take a few weeks to go. The Calgary world cup was only five days away and by Wednesday my leg was even worse. I couldn't really walk on it. On Thursday I was so pissed off and bored I put a T-shirt and shorts on and went to check out the course. I managed two very slow runs down the hill but after that my leg stopped working again. I went back to the condo and climbed into an ice bath that Wally the masseur had sorted out for me.

My first run on the Friday couldn't have gone worse if my biggest enemy had willed it. I then managed three good runs but on the fourth caught my arse on the back tyre going over a drop-off and went straight over the bars, landing on my bad leg and hip. I yelped like a puppy in agony. That was it for riding and I waited a good few minutes on the hill until the pain had subsided. When I got back, I had another ice bath, and didn't drink or go out. I woke up on Saturday morning feeling like shit, did one run, felt terrible and went to the medics' tent at the bottom of the course as it felt warm and sweaty. I was told to go to hospital so they could check if I had a blood clot or an infection from the haematoma. The results came back: no blood clot or infection. I would race then.

On Sunday I could only manage four runs and dithered about what front tyre to run. I still qualified fifth. The weather was so changeable that I was still indecisive about which tyre to use and only had forty-five seconds to go before my gate time when Andy passed me my bike with a new tyre on. With fifteen seconds to go I was up there and ready, just in the nick of time. I didn't have the best of runs but it was okay and came easy. When I found out I'd got third I couldn't believe it.

175

Half an hour later as I was getting ready for the podium and doing interviews, Andy came rushing over to me and said he'd just tallied up the points and told me I'd won the overall and that I was now world cup champion for 2004 with one race still to go. They announced it at the podium, gave me the leader's jersey and as usual I struggled to piss for the doping test. We couldn't find a single party or bar to celebrate at that night, so we went back to our condo and drank on our own. Next day I flew to my place in Whistler. I also got the physiotherapist to come round. It was open house at my place, so everyone came and partied for a week before I flew home on the Tuesday.

It was the national championships at Fort William the coming weekend. I don't know what I was thinking but I wasn't focused. I arrived thinking I had it all worked out and was going to win. I won qualification by three seconds then had a final run that was simply complacent. I thought I'd win no matter what. So, it was a shock when Gee beat me by two seconds. I hadn't felt that pissed off in years. A fortnight later, at the end of July, I won the European championships ahead of Fabien and Julien Camellini. In fourth place was Royal rider Marc Beaumont, and another up-and-coming young 'un Brendan Fairclough came fourth in the juniors. I knew Brendan was going to come good; he, along with Gee, Marc and Ratboy were all riders with loads of talent.

As for my season, a week after the Europeans I busted my collarbone into three pieces at a race in Pajares in northern Spain. I flew home and called British Cycling to see if they knew any good surgeons. They were all on holiday so that was a dead end. I went to A & E in Sheffield where I had another X-ray at the Northern General, the same hospital where I'd arrived into the world in the car park. They decided my shoulder blade had a crack in it too. A week later my collarbone was plated. I remember the opening ceremony for the Olympics was on the television. I spent the night on a ward drugged up to the eyeballs with morphine next to a mad man who shouted all night and a woman who wouldn't stop talking. Luckily for me the morphine sent me to sleep but not for long enough.

A week later, with a recommendation from BMX champion Stephen Murray and motocross star Jamie Dobb, I had laser treatment at Brian Simpson's clinic in Ipswich. He had helped numerous athletes to recover through his revolutionary techniques and I had my first session on my broken shoulder on 19 August. A couple of sessions were all I could manage. It was a long drive and he was limited to two treatments each day. But I was hoping it had worked as the doc said it would. The worlds were scheduled for 11 September in Les Gets and the last round of the world cup was a

WITH OR WITHOUT YOU

week later in Livigno, Italy, near the Swiss border. At that stage the worlds weren't on my radar, being just twenty-three days away. Even so, just five days after the treatment I was back on the cross-country bike. The shoulder was sore as fuck and I was riding too cautiously, but I could ride.

On 25 August I watched on TV as my old BMX pal Jamie Staff got disqualified from his Olympic keirin semi-final. The following day I had another cross-country ride then went to the hospital for a check-up on the shoulder. All was good. Adele was in hospital the day after for another prenatal scan which was also good. I didn't do anything for the next four days but on 31 August got some proper downhill runs done at Wharncliffe to see how the body would hold up. I did six on the short track I used and ten on the rocky one. After two more consecutive days doing some cross-country, I was off to France.

It wasn't until 8 September that things got serious on the track when I managed eight runs. That was the day of the opening ceremony. In proper qualification I got first place by two and a half seconds ahead of Gee. A few of the others had stopped on the hill to waste a few seconds thinking the weather would turn in their favour on the Saturday, but it didn't. On the Friday I did a couple of runs and crashed hard straight into the netting, bashing my bicep on a post. That closed the track down for a while. I crashed again on my first run on race day and had a crap second run too. I got stopped on the hill three times for various reasons and that was that in terms of preparation. I went back to the truck and fell asleep.

Fabien was in the hot seat as I prepared to leave the gate as last man down. He was the only thing standing – well, sitting – between me and a gold at the worlds. Greg and Sam were in second and third. I spun on the gate, no biggie, rode okay on the first half, quick, precise and focused, nothing too mad and by the split I was up by 1.06 seconds. Thirty seconds later I'd got through all the most technical parts of the track and was heading down the last but one straight that had a gap in it that you had to jump. It was just before a root-strewn left-hander that led to the straight-ish part of the course down to the finish line. The rest of the story you already know from the start of this book.

I'm not sure what hurt most, falling off and losing, or Fabien winning in his bloody skinsuit. Nine years in and still I hadn't won a world championships. What an idiot. I had it in the bag and threw it away. What really hurt though was that Fabien and his entourage were celebrating before I even crossed the line. I thought that was really poor. I disappeared from the finish corral sharpish and climbed into the back of the van where I cried my eyes out for about ten minutes, thinking about all those years of trying and

FORGED BY SPEED

failing, of training and race injuries, all of it pouring out of me. Then I pulled myself together, stuck my sunglasses on and went out to face the fans to sign posters.

The world cup series was already mine, but I still wanted to put in a good showing. Orange had made me a new bike for the last round; it was super-custom, black and gold. I hadn't tested it so Livigno would be the first time I rode it. On the Thursday I used my regular bike as Greg and I did half a dozen runs. Next day I went up with Greg again with the new bike. It was awful; the head angle was too steep. I did a timed run on it at four minutes and twenty-six seconds and it felt like I was fighting the bike the whole way down. I then did one on my regular bike and clocked four minutes and twenty-one seconds. Everyone else was on four minutes and twenty-six seconds. I had beer cans on my custom Troy Lee helmet but kept knocking them off when I hit some tree pads on the way down. Troy put them on top of the lid so they ended up looking like rockets. I wish they had been. On the Sunday I rode the black bike and just didn't gel with it. I felt like I was going really fast after qualifying fifth, but my sense of speed was a delusion. I was actually going slower and ended up in eighth place and off the podium.

I was really gutted that I did that badly having thought I'd done better. I fooled myself there on that pile of crap. So why did I ride the black bike when I didn't like it? Honestly, I just loved the way it looked and I'd already won the world cup so it didn't really matter. That evening featured the usual celebrations with an added bonus. After getting in at 3 a.m. pissed as farts, Andy and I had an amazing heart-to-heart about our time together, his thoughts about his plans for the future and what we had achieved together. It was the end of the road for us as a team. Of course, we were mates for life, but I was going to miss my main man. A day later I was back in Sheffield buying a pram with Adele.

CHAPTER 18
SAY HELLO, WAVE GOODBYE

I would leave Orange at the end of 2005. I'm a tight Yorkshireman myself, so dealing with two other Yorkshiremen over money wasn't easy. Whether you need forty pence but get twenty, or need a hundred grand but get fifty, there's never enough cash in the pot to do things properly. That was the kind of vibe I had experienced. There was something about the way things were going that I didn't feel comfortable with. I need a certain level of commitment to a project and in 2005 it felt like things were a little more fragmented at Orange than they had been previously.

In 2005 I was a new dad, stretched for time, juggling a new life. A heavy crash at Fort William doing four-cross of all things at the first UK NPS ended my chances of a full season's racing. I separated my shoulder and needed surgery. Running the team, as fun as it was, was also hard. Or rather, running two teams, both the Royal lot and myself on Orange. Life with GT, where travelling and booking flights was all taken care of, had been a very different proposition. My new life was more tiring and frustrating. As great as it was, running my own programme seemed impossible to maintain over the longer term without more support.

I hadn't fallen out with anyone. Nothing much had changed in the time I was there, other than the company growing and finding it hard to keep up with demand. Perhaps nothing changing was part of the problem. It was quite something to do as well as I did on a bike that didn't develop that much compared to those of my competitors. I was proud of what we'd done and how we'd shown the world that the UK was a real force on the world cup circuit. If I'm honest, it felt like that was more down to my riding and

181

pushing Orange, especially in the final season. The three frames a year I was given and the endless effort of planning the season on my own was no fun.

I got on really well with Michael Bonney. Sadly he's no longer with us after a cycling accident in 2015 left him a tetraplegic; he chose to end his own life in 2019 after a very difficult time. Back in the early 2000s he was running the show singlehandedly from what I could see. In 2005, Lester, the owner of Orange, seemed to me to have little interest in the downhill thing. There was little focus or appetite for bike development and technical progress. I think Lester just wanted to go sailing. Steve Wade, who was the brains behind the bikes, had some health issues and wanted to live in warmer climes. This made him less available for forward planning of the bikes for the coming season and the technical development that I desperately needed.

So, my time at Orange was coming to an end. The idea was always that it was down to me to drive the team. It was four years of graft and great times, but I don't feel those years were built on as much as they could have been. Did those four years result in more bike sales? I would have thought so, but I felt that Orange weren't that focused on downhill despite my success. It just seemed an add-on, an expensive, time-consuming sideshow. That fourth year was the hardest. I was thirty-one, not getting any younger, and I felt like after all we'd achieved there would be a bit more oomph to get me signed up for the 2006 season. Instead, it just felt predictably unfocused. That's not a good feeling if you're a rider who needs to feel like you're wanted, that your sponsors are going to be there for you no matter what. Orange felt like that for a while, but in 2005 something felt different that I couldn't put my finger on.

There was no bad feeling, just an underlying disappointment and a little resentment on my part that I felt they hadn't capitalised on my success, for both them and for me. I'm fairly sure they thought I was being overpaid and that had possibly contributed to some tension. I felt regret I wouldn't be finishing my career with a UK bike company. It's difficult to put into words, but these feelings created a sense of unease. I loved my years at Orange, don't get me wrong, but the trajectory of my career changed for the better after the 2005 world championships in Livigno.

The worlds had come at an emotionally intense time for me. A week earlier we'd commemorated the tenth anniversary of JMC's passing on the Woodhead Pass. A big get-together was arranged. The weather on the day was awful but that didn't stop any of the hundreds of friends and family that turned up for the ride out. After we all got drenched, I invited everyone back to mine where we all sat around telling our favourite stories about Jase.

SAY HELLO, WAVE GOODBYE

The sun came out and we had a big fire and lobbed loads of aerosols on it, which exploded like small bombs, people ducking everywhere lest a stray one clobber them. It was great to see Jim and Rose. It was a great way to remember our friend.

The worlds that year proved another bust. I came fourth behind Fabien, Sam and Greg, and was feeling sore about it. I liked the track at Livigno and thought I'd do better. As I was packing up the van to drive back to Sheffield, Santa Cruz Bicycles owner Rob Roskopp came over to ask where I was at with life. And yes, I do mean *that* Rob Roskopp. Although I wasn't a massive skater in the 1980s, his name still resonated with me. I was stoked he'd even talk to me. I told him I was getting ready to drive home to Sheffield. He asked if he could hop in for a ride and have a chat. He had an agenda, of course, and I was all ears. Brendan Fairclough climbed up on the bed in the back and slept the whole way home while Rob and I made plans for a future I hadn't foreseen. I opened up to him about what I needed for a proper campaign, and he shared with me how he needed and wanted me at Santa Cruz. That was how the seeds of my leaving Orange were sown.

Rob told me about his vision for Santa Cruz as a brand, why he called the team The Syndicate and how he wanted a group of like-minded individuals who were free to create space for themselves within the group. He wanted the riders to be the ones to spread the word about his vision. His pitch was compelling and he could back it up financially. His business partner Rich Novak was partner in the incredibly successful Screaming Hand skateboard group. Between the two of them they had a lot of experience about how things needed to be done to take on the big guns in mountain biking. No one at Orange had shown that much interest in either me, or what I thought. I knew that if he could deliver his vision for the brand and its riders it would easily be the best move I'd ever made in my career. By the end of the trip, it was a done deal. I'd leave Orange. Once back in Sheffield, Rob and I rode the dusty trails of Wharncliffe Woods, drank beers, ate fish and chips and sorted out the finer details. Fort William was the following weekend; it would prove to be the last time I'd ride for Orange at a world cup in the UK.

Contract negotiations are rarely easy. Brands say they are interested and then calls don't get answered; things can change quickly. I'd had plenty of interest in my services from most of the big brands, but only a handful ever stepped up to the plate. I never got to know why the others hadn't, but that's the nature of this business. As a pro racer my window of opportunity wasn't big. I never thought I'd have a competitive career lasting close to twenty years. That was unusual; it seems only Greg and I managed to have

183

decent results into our late thirties. When I won the worlds in Canberra, I was thirty-five years old, a milestone. Greg won the worlds in 2021 in Val di Sole, Italy, as a thirty-eight-year-old. That's quite something. These feats are anything but the norm though. Making as much money as I could in the remaining time that I'd be competitive became increasingly difficult.

Negotiating with Rob was unusually easy. He gave me everything I asked for and a ton more. So my fate took me back to California, only this time much further north than Los Angeles. The beachside city of Santa Cruz is seventy-five miles south of San Francisco. My transatlantic journeys would resume. I had a smile on my face and kicked my heels and raced heart-first into this new adventure.

Like any rider, I was always open to other brands but until that chat with Santa Cruz nothing else had materialised. When it came to contract negotiations at the end of the year, I didn't feel bad; I already knew I was going to leave. What was sad was how Orange left it too late to offer the right deal to keep me. And they did try. But it was way too late. I'd moved on months earlier. I really felt it was their loss, but it was too late for me to go back on my handshake and promise to Rob, irrespective of how much they now offered. I'd committed to Rob and wasn't going back on my word. All year Orange could have talked to me. I was in the last twelve months of my contract but there wasn't a peep out of them. They left the door wide open for me to walk into Santa Cruz – and Santa Cruz really wanted me.

Despite this professional uncertainty and all the other pressures that year, I still managed to nail down one of the best wins of my career that year at the Fort William world cup. It would prove the perfect send-off, a goodbye to all the folks at Orange, although they didn't know that then. Back from Livigno on home turf and after a good night's sleep I had my second long chat with Rob on a long cross-country ride in Wharncliffe Woods. Brendan had come too but Rob and I dropped him on a brutal three-hour lap, which gave us time to sort the details on the deal we were making. I wanted to show Rob the lovely views up at ours and when we got back we chatted about the coming year. Then we headed to Leeds for a curry and next morning I drove Rob to Fort William where I introduced him to my usual ritual of several pints of Guinness in the Cruachan Hotel bar.

Next morning, after setting up the van, I walked the track. It was rough and not fun at all to ride. Fort William is different to any of the other world cups. Over half the track is built on peat bogs. To get over these gloopy sections, crushed limestone is laid on top but that soon gets rutted. So some sections are soft and some are hard. They were always bringing in aggregate to fill in the potholes at the top where the track was sinking into the bog.

SAY HELLO, WAVE GOODBYE

Riding it is no mean feat and sometimes not the best fun. The top section is not that wide, only around two metres, so you can't get creative with lines. Some berms are wood slats and there are bridged sections where it's unrideable. After the bog you go into woods and the bottom is a flat-out pedal and not too hard. There's some flow at the bottom. The middle bit is where it's technical. The track is many different things, and they don't all fit together that well for me to have fun on. I suffer a fair bit with arm pump at Fort Bill as it's one of the most pedally of all the tracks. It's not a favourite of mine, not by a long shot. Other riders love the place, so what do I know? I certainly love the event and love the crowds; the place feels like home. Yet as much as I wanted to win, it's not easy if the track isn't one I like that much. That evening I caught up with old friends and met Lopes for a curry. We talked the night away. Next day Adele turned up with Jake. It was the first time a lot of people had seen him so I did the proud dad thing and showed him off to everyone. Having Jake there with Adele was a real treat. It felt good with us together as a family, something I'd not experienced before. I just glowed with joy.

Wanting to win my home world cup is one thing, actually winning the damn thing is quite another. I'd come fourth in 2004, nineteenth in 2003 and seventeenth in 2002. Those results don't make for pretty reading. The odds of a win over the border had never gone my way. I'd won on plenty of tracks that were awkward by the way, and I wasn't short of motivation. I was desperate to win in front of my home fans. I knew a lot of people there wouldn't be able to attend other rounds of the world cup, so this was their one chance to see their favourite racers in the flesh. It was vital to put on a great show. The event, despite the track, was and is absolutely fantastic. If only I could win it just once.

That year as every year I felt I had a chance to win. I qualified first on the Friday after four runs, two of which were timed. The track was already pretty beat up and would be even more so on Sunday. After that I did the cross-country lap with Marc Beaumont, which is a bit of a ritual of mine, and just hung about the pits. I bought Adele a fish and chip supper, and then with the Orange crew I took my chances at getting a decent meal in the hotel. The evening ended predictably with some beers in the bar.

I got a couple more runs in on the Saturday and then spent the rest of the day in the pits with Adele and Jake. We bought Jake a huge chainsaw-carved bear and the fella who made it chucked in a hare for good measure. Mum loves hares so he must have been telepathic. I did an autograph signing for Visit Scotland and then we watched the four-cross. Lopes got bumped on the first turn and that was his weekend done. It reminded me

185

FORGED BY SPEED

that I didn't miss four-cross at all. I ended up in the Ben Nevis Hotel that evening for a better meal and was back afterwards in the Cruachan bar for a few beers. It was a typical steady pre-race Saturday.

Troy Lee painted me a really decent lid with the St George's Cross on top of it; it's one of my favourites that he did for me. I've still got it. The atmosphere in the morning at the track was otherworldly. There was a hum to the day that I can't describe. It seeped into me and seemed to change the way I felt. It was like being lifted and the hum just got louder as the day went on. There's always a risk going off last if the weather changes halfway through the day, but by winning qualification I wanted to nail my intentions for the event. After two practice runs on Sunday morning I was still first, and Beaumont was second. I was feeling the pressure, could sense myself getting a bit edgy but was comfortable enough with the discomfort of it. I'd be last down and was going to have to have the burden of that on my shoulders. It comes with the territory and there was no going back once I'd nailed the fastest time. *Too late now*, I remember thinking.

I had a good lunch with Adele and Jake. Then to calm myself down and not get swept up in too much overthinking I did what I normally do and took a nap in the van. When I woke up I did my regular warm-up routine that was pretty straightforward but spot on for four minutes of hammering down a mountain in Scotland. Everyone I met on the way to the lift wished me well. Usually when I woke after a pre-race nap I felt relaxed. This time it was different. The hum was louder. Riders had been coming down the mountain all day. British rider Tracy Moseley won the women's downhill, which got the day started on the right foot for me. It felt as though I was in another world, carried along by the incredible energy the crowd was creating. I expect spectators in Rome's Colosseum had their favourite gladiators. That's what it felt like, going into battle.

Getting the gondola to the top of the mountain takes twelve minutes, give or take a little for the crowds; this is where I spend some time going over things in my head – how the track runs, bits I want to avoid, places to rest, where I can hammer it, where I need to be cautious, braking points, gear shifts. Years of racing here are now embedded in me. The new black and yellow Orange I've got to match my horrible yellow wheels is hanging on the outside of the gondola, never out of my mechanic's sight, helmet, goggles and gloves at my side. The ritual once I get off at the top is always the same – have a little walk around, crack a few jokes, check out the start gate.

With thirty minutes to go I jump on the turbo trainer, put some Olbas-soaked tissues up my snout, do a good twenty minutes of warm-up with a

186

SAY HELLO, WAVE GOODBYE

few bigger efforts thrown in. This is my time to visualise the track, going from the start gate to the finish line in my head. It helps me deal with nerves. Five minutes to go I jump off and have a pedal around on my downhill rig, pull a few wheelies and get to know the bike again. Two to go and I'm making my way to the start line, pulling tissues out of my nostrils. I can feel my airways opening up.

In the gate I know a few things but there are a few I don't. Greg on his Honda is in the hot seat with a time of four minutes and 13.57 seconds. That's about all I need to know. Marc Beaumont has gone off before me so I'll not know what time he does unless someone tells me halfway down. They don't and I don't care one way or the other. It's my time. No one will come down after me. After I'm done, the tents at the top will be dismantled and the marshals will make their way down. The officials will clear tables and timing equipment and once again the mountain will be left alone. Helmet and goggles on. The bike's tuned to perfection. I roll my gloved hands on my grips to make everything come tight as I bring that sense of anticipation and muscle tension to the bars and pedals. I roll into the start hut, sit down on the saddle, waiting to go. Time ticks on. The numbers are called: five, four, three, two, one.

The whole hillside is waiting for me, thousands of spectators at the bottom, TV cameras sending visual feeds to huge screens. When I leave the start gate there's a small pocket of people, maybe three or four, shouting, 'Go on, Steve!' A little further down maybe six or eight shouting the same, then fifteen, then twenty, then more and more the whole way down. The shouts get louder and louder and I know they are all thinking the same as me. *Can he do it?* I nail the boggy top sections, get across the chicken-wire wood-slat bits and for the first time in a while I'm skipping across the white rocks like a flat stone skimming across a mill pond. I have a rhythm, haven't hit a speed-sapping boggy black hole and have made no silly mistakes. The cutbacks are all done and the danger spots avoided. That's just about two and a half minutes of the job done.

Marc has had a rough one and won't beat Greg. That's another thing I don't know. I'm hammering into the section that runs alongside the ski lifts. It's littered with roots, loose sandy soil and some nasty exposed rocks. These bits are tricky and the speed needs to be kept up. This part of the track is good fun to ride and I really like the way it keeps me focused. Most of this section reminds me a bit of Wharncliffe. I'm so used to riding stuff like this I know how to keep my momentum up and not use too much energy. Although it's hard on the hands and shoulders I can't really feel it. I know I'm having a good run.

FORGED BY SPEED

I'm out of the woods safely and fast. Now comes the pedally bit where there are lots of man-made jumps. There's forty seconds to go and it's all flat-out pedalling, jumping and hauling ass. Then I become aware of the noise and it's not the usual noise of a world cup. This is different. I can actually feel it pulling me down the course. I'm getting faster and faster as it gets louder and louder. All of a sudden I race into sight under the Red Bull arch and down the steps and I can see the finish. The sound is deafening. I can't hear my breathing. The bike's rattling but it's drowned out by the sound of 20,000 fans screaming at the tops of their lungs. What they know that I don't know is that I've pulled out two seconds on Greg. I'm pedalling my arse off flat out to the finish line. I beat Greg by 2.13 seconds.

The place erupts.

If there's another feeling like it, I don't know what it is. I do a few circles at the finish taking in the experience. The crowd is still going mental. This is better than any feeling I've ever had. The crowd is still going bonkers, banging the hoardings, banging the drums, banging any damn thing they can. There's the sound of bagpipes. The yelling of the fans is overwhelming. Greg and Marc come over and give me a hug, then I lift the bike above my head.

Fort Bill is finally mine.

Not for the first time, the urine test took an age. Greg and I were drinking Stellas instead of water, and so we waited to dribble some of Belgium's finest out for WADA. I stayed up partying that night until 3 a.m. then went bush-diving with Ollie Hill before I finally got to bed. I was so happy to finally get that Fort Bill monkey off my back. And that was it for 2005. I had some filming projects to do but as far as racing big events went, I was done. There were new experiences ahead. My boy was now growing fast and things would change again. Nothing stays the same for that long, even the excitement of winning a home world cup.

Let me tell you though, that feeling the next day when you're driving home, knowing that yesterday you were the fastest guy in the world, is hard to beat.

CHAPTER 19
LAST ORDERS

I saved two big gifts from my career to give to Santa Cruz: a world cup series win in 2006, and in 2009 a world championship after a long and barren seventeen years as bridesmaid and nearly man. They might say I've given them a lot more than that, and they would be right, but these two triumphs meant the world to me and I'm glad I could deliver them to Rob, team manager Kathy Sessler and the rest of the Santa Cruz crew. Runner-up was a label I didn't want anyone to read on my headstone when I kicked the bucket. Yet these wins came at times I didn't expect them.

My first year on Santa Cruz coincided with my first full year as a dad and life was very different in the Peaty household. At this point I was thirty-two and a game old dog. Despite my success at Orange, I soon became aware that things were going to be different riding for Rob. By then I'd been racing the world cup circuit for fourteen years. That's a pretty full tank of retained fitness for any season, and having signed for Santa Cruz I was the happiest I'd ever been. Taking that energy into 2006 was kind of weird; I hadn't felt that way for a long time. I was excited and motivated to do well. There was still a lot of work to be done and at the start of 2006 I didn't allow myself to think about winning championships. I was just as focused on being a dad, which was a journey in itself. So with that and the new team I thought I'd just ride the wave and see where it took me.

Having the backup from Kathy and the Santa Cruz crew freed up a lot of time. I hadn't quite realised at the time just how draining running my own programme had been. In the last few years at Orange I had been doing it all, from booking flights and sorting bikes to arranging just about everything else. Kathy just stepped in and did all this and more. I was grateful to be free of it; it allowed me to manage my time better and not rush around like a blue-arsed fly. It would take a while to let things go. I had tons of experience running my own show just how I liked it. But it was great to work with Sessie. We would bounce ideas back and forth, but she would do all the hard and time-consuming stuff. That freedom gave me new energy and a lot more time to train, ride and prepare for each season. During race season I now had a measurable amount of extra time to prepare for each race. She really did make a monumental difference.

It was a freezing cold winter up our way and the weather at the start of 2006 interfered with my schedule. I much prefer to be out riding in nature than be in the gym. I felt like a caged animal and would have liked more time on the bike. As spring arrived, I got to ride a little more. I flew out to the USA to get acquainted with the Santa Cruz family and rode the now famous Sea Otter race, which was nothing too serious but a good crack. I also raced the Megavalanche in Peru at the end of March and won after a great battle with Rémy Absalon, brother of cross-country legend Julien.

The high altitude there almost got the better of me. Coca leaves in my water bottle helped a little, but I spent the race crashing my brains out in front of him. Rémy would then overtake me and I would catch him up again. On my last bail, I was on my arse and he got me again. We then had a mad dash to the finish, where I found a great line that ended with me jumping over Rémy's head to beat him by the skin of my teeth on the line. Winning like that was brilliant and I had a fun time in Peru. Although I visited Machu Picchu two days before the race and must have picked up a stomach bug, because on the podium I felt dizzy and desperately needed a shit. The bug lasted four days and travelling to the USA for a Santa Cruz press day was not a lot of fun. Even worse, I couldn't drink beer.

I loved the buzz of being on a new team, the feeling of having a racing family. The Syndicate's support was second to none. I hoped it would lead to a long and stable relationship with Rob and his crew, and almost two decades later I'm still a contracted Santa Cruz lad. That says an awful lot about how happy I was, and I guess how happy they were. That first year I didn't really think I'd win the world cup series on a new bike against the hardest competition I'd ever faced. I trained like I always did, but I'd been racing long enough not to take anything for granted until I had a few races under my belt and I understood my form.

I think I did more riding on my jump bike and motos than any other bike in the first four months of the year, and kept myself busy with trips to

LAST ORDERS

Mothercare, cleaning sick off my clothes and learning to survive on very little sleep when little Jake cried in the night. No one can prepare you for being a parent, but I was completely committed to doing the best I could. For a while I took the helmet off and got on with more homely priorities while making sure I kept the body in decent shape for the first round of the world cup at Vigo on 7 May. I was riding a fair bit of downhill before the race, at Moelfre near Oswestry in Wales and then at Bringewood near Ludlow, getting in as many runs as I could before leaving for Spain via Portsmouth on 1 May.

The track at Vigo was the same as the previous year when I'd won riding for Orange. I got about half a dozen good runs in before first qualifying but felt a bit tight on the bike and ended up second to Mick Hannah. I then went for a cross-country ride in the evening to watch the four-cross where Eric Carter broke his collarbone. Early the following morning I was back at the track to get some runs in again before second qualification. I then waited fifteen minutes for a timed run and for some reason the UCI let some slower riders on the course during my run. I came up quick behind one of the lads and yelled for him to move. He didn't and I was forced on to a blind line that ended with me flying head first into some roots and rocks. I put my hands out to protect myself and caught the middle finger of my right hand, dislocating it. As I got up, I was still shouting at the other rider. Then I looked at my glove and saw my finger at ninety degrees. I grabbed it and pulled as hard as I could, heard it pop and crack, but then saw blood coming through the glove. When I reached the bottom I took the glove off and realised I'd split the skin and would need stitches. There wasn't much time until my final run so a UCI rep, Kathy Sessler and I went to the medics to get my finger stitched up.

By the time I got back it was time to go up the hill. My finger was still numbed up and I couldn't feel the bars, but I carried on with my warming-up process as normal. Then the finger started to get some sensation back, which hurt like hell but was also a good thing as at least I'd be able to feel my bars on the way down. I didn't have a great run, made a few mistakes and ended up third behind Aussies Mick Hannah and Nathan Rennie. It was Mick's first world cup win. Marc was behind me in fourth and Gee was fifth so it was a fun podium. We were all out partying that night and the Brits got rounded up by the cops and taken back to our hotels because not everyone had identification on them. It was a bit of a relief to be honest. I thought they were going to take us to jail like they did the year before.

After the race I had some good testing with RockShox in the week before

193

FORGED BY SPEED

the Lisbon Downtown race on 13 May. I had another great experience there, winning for the fifth time on the trot. The prize, always good there, was a bonus. On the way back from Lisbon on the ferry we got drinking with some lads from a boxing club in Liverpool. I was getting on really well with one dude and we shared a bottle of vodka. Then he got up to stretch his legs and out of the blue, and for no reason, while I was sat down minding my own business, he lamped me in the head, giving me a black eye. Before I could react his mates had surrounded us. My chance of landing one on him had gone so I pretended to calm down. Santa Cruz teammate Nathan Rennie was my wingman so I knew I had decent backup and I wasn't going to let the lad get away with lamping me for no reason. This lad was shielded behind two mates but as the other lads began to move away I saw a gap between them and took a chance with a big right hand. I hit him so hard his feet left the ground and I knocked him out. It felt good teaching that fucker a lesson. He'd picked on the wrong person.

What I didn't know immediately was that I'd also broken the knuckles on my right hand, the same hand with the dislocated finger. It was so painful I was forced to miss the Innerleithen national champs a week later. Next day I went to hospital where they said it would be a month before I could ride again. I ignored that because Fort Bill was in a week, but at least I now knew how long it would be until it was fully healed.

Before Fort Bill I was invited to British Cycling to meet a British Cycling strength coach and sports psychologist Steve Peters, who wrote *The Chimp Paradox* and advises snooker star Ronnie O'Sullivan. I was working with Sheffield Hallam University at the time and brought along Dave Hembrough, my own strength coach. Women's downhill star Tracy Moseley and her coach were also there to see what the pair had to offer in terms of psychological support and training ideas. I arrived with high hopes of coming away with new ideas and training protocols. This was the period when the track guys were killing everything with Dave Brailsford at the helm. Their programmes were working well. So it was a disappointment to discover I wasn't doing anything different to them. In fact, the strength coach was such a bell end that it left a bad taste in my mouth. Steve Peters then sat me down and asked me to go through what I did on a weekend. I went through everything with him. I told him my routine, my warm-ups, my visualisation techniques and the rest. He then just reassured me I was doing the right thing and told me he couldn't do anything to help. So as nice as it was to visit Steve at the facility and have a good chinwag with him, I'd wasted a day and missed putting Jake to bed. Thanks, British Cycling.

Leading up to the weekend I could only manage a couple of runs each

194

day. The weather was mixed and my hand was killing me. I'd not had broken knuckles before and my no-grip situation wasn't doing a lot for my confidence. On the Saturday Steve Peters and another British Cycling coach turned up to watch the race, so we chatted and I showed them the lay of the land at a downhill event. It was the first time I'd ever seen anyone from British Cycling show any interest in downhill. Usually the sight of them was more rare than hen's teeth. I did two practice runs on the Sunday, ended up fourth in qualification and fourth on the day. Sam Hill took the win. It wasn't a bad result for me considering the state of my hand and the fact I wore the wrong goggles and couldn't see properly on the way down. Fourth put me in second in the overall standings behind Greg and I came away feeling confident things would get better as the year went on.

The next round at Willingen was a week away. I arrived on the Tuesday, which happened to be Rennie's birthday. We had travelled together for the past two world cup races and now had a great night getting up to mischief. The next few days it rained. On the Friday all I'd had were three good runs on the course. There was a big hip jump – where you turn in air – that I hadn't got sussed like Chris Kovarik, but I knew I'd be okay for the finals. I spent all day on the mountain that Saturday, getting two good full-speed runs. I got another two in on the Sunday despite blowing a shock. I got the fastest time too, with Greg in second. So that put me in a good mood.

I had a really good warm-up before hitting the lift for my final run. There was a bloody cold wind blowing on the way up. I was nervous too, not bad nervous though: good nervous. The consequence was I had a great run, didn't make any silly mistakes and kept my rhythm all the way to the bottom. I couldn't believe it when I won by 1.17 seconds over Greg, Gee, Rennie and Chris. It was my fifteenth world cup win and my first win for Santa Cruz. If you had asked me two weeks earlier how I thought I'd do, I couldn't have imagined this. I'd have bitten anyone's hand off for two podiums. I was now leading the overall standings too. Some things didn't change though. The urine test took an age – again.

Mont-Sainte-Anne was next up on 24 June, a good few weeks away. I was able to relax and get in some well-earned time at home with Adele and Jake, and celebrate my birthday. Then, four days before the race, I caught a flight to Quebec. It always rains there and this year was no different. I didn't get a good run on the mountain until Thursday where I got five decent runs in the tank. On the Friday I got another five. My first qualification run was mint until the bottom at the very last section of woods, where I uncharacteristically caught a pedal on a rock that stopped me dead. I was thrown off the bike on to my hip, landing really hard on a rock that cut it pretty deeply.

FORGED BY SPEED

I got up quickly but only finished thirteenth. Greg got the fastest qualification so made up some points on me there.

The finals didn't treat me any better. I fluffed up two left-handers, which normally I'd sail around. I lost all momentum and ended up on the podium but only in fifth. Chris won, Greg was second and I'd dropped 100 points on him. He was now only forty points behind me. It was also the first time Marc beat me and I was as gutted about that as losing points to Greg. That evening unfolded in a way that can only happen when Rennie is involved. Apparently, I ate Chris's sick, which was just following in my big brother's footsteps, since that's his party trick. Cédric ended up losing control of his bladder in his own apartment, which is unusual as he normally pisses in everyone else's. I put that down in my diary as 'a good fun night', which it sounds like to me. More worrying though than ingesting sick was that upon waking next morning the bruise on my hip had spread to my balls and cock, which were now also black and blue.

A few days later I was in Balneário Camboriú for the Brazilian round of the world cup. It was chaos from the start. The airline lost my bike and those of many others. I still didn't have it by the Friday. On Saturday I got another bike built up, borrowed from a shorter Brazilian guy. So, you can appreciate it was only a medium, not my usual XL. It was dressed in Brazilian colours though and consequently looked the coolest. I headed to the course first thing on Saturday and got ten runs in as soon as I could. I knew some of my competition had been on the mountain all week, so I was over the moon to have some time on it myself. That evening I got a call to say my race bike had arrived and I felt immensely relieved.

By Sunday morning the stress of the week was draining away. On my own bike I knew I could improve on the previous day's times in qualifying. I got three good runs in and thought they would be enough, but Sam did better than me at the bottom so I ended up second to him, but Greg finished third so I pulled a few points back on him. I had a lovely lunch on the beach that took my mind off the pressure that was starting to build as this battle with Greg intensified. Then I had a quick nap before my finals run, which was broken by the great news that Rachel Atherton had won her first world cup. As for me, I raced like I did in the qualifier, in that I still couldn't get the bottom of the track dialled but miraculously ended second behind Matti Lehikoinen, the first Finn to win a world cup event. I was only 0.09 seconds off winning so was gutted about that. Greg flatted and then crashed so that gave me some breathing space in the race for points. I now had a lead of 178. Mick was third, Gee fourth and Beaumont fifth, so another big UK

196

LAST ORDERS

podium. Sam got twelfth which would undermine his run of good fortune to come.

The party that night was great fun. I don't know how many *caipirinhas* I drank, but it was *a lot*. Brazil's national cocktail is a simple but really nice drink when it's so bloody hot. It's made of cachaça, which is fermented sugarcane juice, lime and sugar. Gorgeous stuff. Greg and I had so many we ended up having a right good bundle on the sand until we exhausted ourselves, then we drank some more while Rennie tried to commandeer a vessel to sail back home to Australia. I left Brazil on the Monday afternoon and by 10 a.m. on the Wednesday I was in Manchester. It was a relief to be in Chap again with Adele and Jake, who called me 'Da' for the first time.

Back home and still in the lead in the world cup I was on a bit of a high, despite the airline losing my bike. Again. Yet with one more round to go the pressure was building. Being in front put me in an uncomfortable position. Other racers might relish being in the points lead, but I was never able to enjoy it. I preferred it when there was some uncertainty and the pressure was off. Now I knew I'd be worrying about whether I was riding too cautiously, which is a horrible way to approach a race. I liked to be the underdog, not the guy with a target on his back. All I could do was put it to the back of my mind and forget about it. The last thing I wanted to do when I got to the next round was race sensibly. I liked the opposite, just hanging it out and ripping down the mountain. What is riding sensibly? I'll explain.

I usually know my limit on the hill – where I can push, where I need to take it easy, where I can make up a second here and there. I don't ride down 100 per cent flat out everywhere, that's just not physically possible. The art – and it is an art – is how to set a pace that allows me to exhaust myself fully by the bottom of the course. It would be too dangerous to ride half the hill in an exhausted state. That could easily end in a trip to hospital, or worse. Downhill is dangerous. If I don't have enough respect, I'll be spat out and left for dead.

Being able to maintain pace or not could come from not being fit enough, which would mean not having enough air in my lungs, which could translate as less feeling in my legs and arms, or my core collapsing. If my feet aren't strong enough it's impossible to ride well because tendon strength and calf strength are required to maintain perfect foot positioning as I steer the bike down the tech sections, and then ride on the balls of my feet with heels up on the flatter sections. Thighs, hamstrings and glutes need to work in harmony. Even the shin muscles of the lower leg, like the tibialis anterior, have to be trained to maintain total stability.

The upper body is no different. We wear heavy helmets so my neck and

FORGED BY SPEED

shoulders have to be able to support its weight, which, when I'm doing fifty miles per hour down a mountain over rough terrain, weighs a lot more than it says on the box it came in. My eyes bounce around in their sockets so vision is affected. As soon as the neck goes, vision goes. The eyes can't focus. Shoulders, back, triceps, biceps, lats, abs, even erector spinae muscles are all crucial. Arm pump is a killer. No feeling in fingers, hands and forearms means a loss of control. Unless every single muscle and tendon is ready for the hill, they will at some point give way and then more pressure will be put on another muscle, which will then get overloaded and soon I'll be in a big heap on the floor, hopefully missing rocks or tree trunks with my soft fleshy bits. Riding sensibly means riding within limits that can sometimes be hard to gauge thanks to the chaotic nature of a course. But they need to be considered.

In the driving seat I was trying to conserve the lead but not ride so cautiously that the competition gained points on me. So, the approach was simple. What speed could I maintain from top to bottom without the intensity of the ride causing me to make serious mistakes that could result in a DNF? It's riding a fine line, knowing when to push, when not to and when to take a chance. There are so many things to consider and none of them you can plan for perfectly; most of the time I'm winging it to some degree. If I had my way we'd do more runs on the mountain before the race. Once I'm up there I want to get as many runs in as I can. I just love the feeling of getting better and better as the day goes on. Unfortunately, when riding to win a series, specific strategies are required and not all of them suit my approach. They do however help me win championships and riding sensibly is one of them.

On 16 July I was riding the national championships at Moelfre, ignoring the fact I was protecting the points lead in the world cup. I was having a mint run until I made a little mistake and crashed jumping into a stream section where I bottomed out my suspension so hard my rear wheel exploded. The bike slowly ground to a halt but because the gear cluster was dragging on the ground my back foot was also scraping it too and in the process the nail of my big toe was ripped and the toe broken. Oblivious to the pain I ran to the finish line and still got sixth. It was Marc Beaumont's first big win and I was pleased for him.

A day later I ran over Adele's foot with the family Volvo as I was dropping her off for work. She got out to head into the building, then decided to turn back to tell me something. I was reversing and looking the other way. Once the wheel was on her foot I turned the wheel, making it worse. She was in agony and had to jump back in the car so I could take her to A & E.

198

LAST ORDERS

I had to limp into her work to tell her boss I had just run over her foot and we were both off to hospital. Mr and Mrs Peat, two X-rays, please. The docs made a mess of my toe by leaving the nail hanging on by a small part of the nail bed, so it was agony to walk on. Adele's was little better. What an idiot. Now we both had ruined feet. To add insult to stupid injury the last round of the world cup at Schladming was coming up in early September, two weeks after the worlds in Rotorua, New Zealand. Hopefully my foot would be better by then, but it wasn't going to be a lot of fun in New Zealand. I finished fourth there; Sam won gold.

To not win the world cup now would require a major fuck-up. I was nervous as hell, in both good and bad ways. I couldn't afford to make a mistake, not now I'd come this far. Sam and Greg were contenders for gold too at this point, but only if I monumentally screwed things up. Despite my points lead it was still a very stressful day, not helped by Sam being six seconds faster than me in qualifying, which really pissed me off because it showed I was riding too conservatively. Greg was only a second or so off Sam, who was on a roll after Rotorua. If he carried that into the final runs, he would be hard to beat. At the end of the day, I crossed the line with a very safe thirteenth. I know that's not the sexiest way to win a world cup series, but it's a sensible one, and it didn't take anything away from the fact I won the overall. Sam won on the day, which put him ahead of Greg on points in the final count.

It was a good weekend. Loads of my Sheffield mates had turned up to celebrate with me but we had had a few big nights in the build-up and forgetting to pay a bill one night led to the cops temporarily holding all their passports until things got sorted. Winning this third title felt amazing but more so because I had delivered for Rob and Santa Cruz. On a personal level I was a little annoyed I had ridden cautiously in the final race. I had wanted to win in better style than that.

Adele and Jake were also in Austria to watch me, and there is an awesome picture of me, Jake on a tiny little bike and Uncle Greg riding our bikes to our accommodation after the race. Santa Cruz had never won a world title before, and I was so happy at being the first guy to deliver it. I wanted to repay Rob, Kathy and the rest of the team for seeing in me something no one else ever had. We'd done it. The icing on the cake was that Tracy won the women's series too, so we had two British champions.

I never won another series after 2006. I was competitive on the world cup circuit for a good handful of years, but I'd never better those three world cup series wins in 2002, 2004 and 2006. There were seven medals over the years for me: three gold, two silver and two bronze in the overall. I think

199

FORGED BY SPEED

that puts me fourth on the all-time medal list where I'm tied on gold with Greg and Loïc Bruni. Only Aaron Gwin and Nico are ahead on five apiece. Will those records get broken? Maybe. I guess that's the exciting thing about any sport; there's always a chance for someone to make a mark just as I made mine.

That wasn't going to be the end of my winning just yet though. I had one more score to settle.

CHAPTER 20
EVERY KING

Given how shy I was when I started mountain biking, how uncomfortable I felt standing on that first world cup podium at Panticosa all those years ago, it's curious how I became so well known among the fans. Perhaps it was because from day one I was mountain biking's biggest fan as well as a racer. I guess that's why I connected with the fans so well over the years; you'll find me equally at home in the pub before the race or at an after-party, as you will on the mountain. You'll have gathered by now that there aren't any walls around me, and people appreciate that. Yet I didn't want fame nor did I go looking for it. I was always just one of the lads and I always will be. Like any good footballer worth their salt, I welcome a pitch invasion at the end of a hard day's racing. I really love it when fans jump the barriers to mix it up with the racer, get rowdy with their air horns, chainless chainsaws and insane screaming and shouting. The best part of racing is either celebrating a win or drowning my sorrows after a loss. The party is what I live for.

With three world cup wins, three silvers and two bronze, I was well established as a contender for the world championships when they came around each year. By the time I retired I'd been chosen twenty-three times to represent my country, which makes me incredibly proud. I even put up with the horrible race gear British Cycling made me wear and the fact that their interest in what I was up to came but once a year. Yet in all those years I must have pissed off the gods and goddesses of downhill because in the first sixteen years of trying I didn't win any of them. It was from 1996, after that second place in Panticosa, that I really started to get on the gas. From then

FORGED BY SPEED

on, I thought I was capable of a win. Yet my results make for frustrating reading.

In 1993, in Métabief, I didn't finish. At Vail in 1994, I came twelfth. It got worse in Kirchzarten, Germany, the following year, where I finished thirteenth. Worse again in 1996, in Cairns, with fifteenth. I got sixth in Château-d'Oex, Switzerland, in 1997, but was back down to twelfth the next year at Mont-Sainte-Anne, a course I often did well at. In 1999 I didn't come anywhere because I'd broken my ankle. Then came the nearly man peak: second place three years running in the Sierra Nevada, Vail and Kaprun. Back down to fourth at Lugano in 2003, eleventh in Les Gets in 2004, back up to fourth at Livigno and the same in Rotorua in 2006. In 2007, at my home track in Fort William, I came sixty-seventh. In 2008, I was bridesmaid once again with my fourth silver medal, this time at Val di Sole.

At times, I consoled myself with the thought that it's the better champion that wins the series. Given the different nature of the tracks on the world circuit, the diversity of the terrain that we all race on, that's still true. But fuck me, did I want to win one worlds. The frustrating thing about winning the world cup series is that you can't call yourself the world champion. The UCI, our governing body, saves that accolade for this one-off race, and if you win you get to ride in the world champion's rainbow jersey for the whole of the next year. I've been close to winning too many times to remember, but the closest I got prior to 2009 was in Les Gets in 2004, where I was in the lead by a country mile and fell off in a cloud of dust going full tilt with 200 metres left to the finish line. All I could think was, *You idiot!* Of all the world championships I didn't win, that one hurts the most. Even now I still hate thinking about it. After I crossed the finish line, I saw Adele and Mike Redding. Their eyes said it all. I got back to the Orange van, put my bike down, crawled into the back, closed the door and hid under my bedding. I sobbed long and hard. Adele turned up a little later and we both had a good cry. There were hundreds of people waiting outside in the pits for autographs, I got myself together and went out and faced the music. It was the first time I knew I could win the worlds easily and I blew it.

The 2007 worlds at Fort William was another nightmare. I'd knackered my ankle earlier so I got a rugby physiotherapist to tape it so I could ride. I tried so hard there and didn't feel too bad on the day, but on one of the raised wooden sections the chicken wire had gone completely and as I tried to turn and brake on it, the bike just slid out. I was gripping so hard it blew both my feet off the pedals, I slammed down on my seat and broke it off the post. Then I went straight over the berm in front. I was so pissed off I didn't think about the consequences of riding down the rest of the course without

EVERY KING

a seat, so I carried on, firing over the big last jumps with this seat post sticking up between my legs and aimed right at my arse. That was the end of that; I was never going to win the world championships in Fort Bill.

A few years before, at Kaprun in 2002, I was in the hot seat having posted the fastest time. The organisers had us waiting in a Volvo as part of the hot seat deal. It was a nightmare. I just couldn't get comfortable in there with all my race gear on waiting for Nico to follow me down the mountain. I whacked the seats back and finally managed to relax a little bit, sticking my feet out of the window instead of being so bloody cramped up. Nico won and then made a point of saying that because I was looking so smug, cocky and self-assured in the Volvo he was more motivated to beat me. Truth was, I was just uncomfortable but that shows how much we were in each other's heads in those years. We'd use anything as fuel for the fire if we thought it would motivate us. I did think I had done enough there though and was devastated when he came and knocked me down a peg. Cool fact from that race was that it played on the BBC back home, getting an airing alongside football, cricket and tennis. I had all kinds of messages about that from people who wouldn't usually get to see me race.

I've had some great seasons, some shit ones too, like 2012 where nothing went right. I've learned you just have to go with the flow if you want a long career. Things come to an end though sooner or later. My first podium in the world cup was on 12 May 1996 at Panticosa. My last world cup win was at Vallnord on 17 May 2009. My last podium finish at a world cup race was second at Windham, New York, in 2011. After coming second in 2008 at Val di Sole to Gee, the first British man to be world champion, where Sam Hill's run before he crashed was faster than both of ours by a mile, I gave up on ever winning worlds. That disappointment though was a wound that freed me from the bag of self-inflicted torture I had been carrying around all those years. On top of that was the vibe I got every year from fans that wanted me to win one. Finally. It was heavy, *too* heavy. It's just didn't look like it would ever happen, so I let it go, which for me was a hard thing to do. Yet this would turn out to be a blessing in disguise.

In 2009 I was in a monumental fight for another world cup series win. It was also a significant year for another reason that was far more important than mountain biking. Our George was born on 29 April in circumstances that gave me a few grey hairs and must have aged Adele considerably. He arrived safe and sound in the back of the Volvo at the end of our lane at five o'clock in the morning. His birth certificate reads: 'Born at the end of a dirt track leading to our house.'

As for the racing, I'd had a great start to the year with a third in South

205

FORGED BY SPEED

Africa at Pietermaritzburg. That was a bit of a surprise to be honest as I'd spent the previous few months run-down, feeling like shit and struggling with a bad back that had gone way beyond a niggle. Trying to put all that behind me I followed up the result in South Africa with two wins on the trot. The first was in La Bresse, France, ten days after George was born. The second came a week later in Vallnord, Andorra. That was special for a couple of reasons. The first was that I wasn't riding well and didn't feel like I had much form at all due to feeling tired all the time. The second was that it was my seventeenth world cup win, taking me past the record of sixteen that Nico had set. That felt amazing. The win also put me in the overall points lead despite me carrying a heavy cold, about the third or fourth that year.

The season would unfold into a huge battle between me, Greg and Sam. Greg won in South Africa, got sixth in La Bresse and third in Vallnord. Sam's fortunes at the start of the year weren't as good. He had a fourth, a second and a thirty-first. Going into Fort Bill I was carrying a small lead. The previous week I'd also won Downtown Lisbon for the eighth time. (You may have gathered I love that place.) I also picked up a hand injury, so that wasn't so great. Greg was second at Lisbon and was now second in points in the world cup series. I got a poor sixth at Fort William. The week in Scotland didn't start well as the mechanics didn't set the bike up how I needed it. That caused a bit of commotion I could have done without. We got it sorted in the end, but it was a fair bit of stress. On Saturday in qualification I blew up my shock but still got fifth. I hoped that by Sunday the race would come to me, but it didn't. I just couldn't get on the pace and could feel how weak my hand was on such a physical track. Greg won and Sam got second. The BBC were doing a piece on me and having them around was a bit of a distraction. It would have been fine if I was feeling a hundred per cent, but I wasn't and it got to me a bit.

Going into round five at Maribor in Slovenia, Greg and I were just about neck and neck in the points. I flatted on my final run and came down in thirty-eighth. Fabien won, Sam came second and Greg was third. Bang went my lead and I was now on the back foot going into Mont-Sainte-Anne. The only good thing about that was that it's one of my favourite tracks. I was hoping to make up some points with a good result there. It was also great hooking up with Palmer in Canada. I hadn't seen him in ages. I had a good run and finished second to Sam. Greg came twenty-second after an off, and what had originally been a two-way fight was now between the three of us.

We then headed to Bromont, also in Quebec. I had been struggling to get motivated for races that year, and in Bromont, despite the pressure from

206

EVERY KING

Greg and Sam, I was functioning well below par. I rode well considering my mental state but walloped a rock in a turn and nearly pretzled my rear wheel. That lost me a couple of seconds and was enough to put me in seventh. Greg won and Sam got third. I was now third in the points after my poor results in Maribor and Bromont; the chance of a fourth world cup title was, after a blistering start, slipping away.

Shoehorned between Bromont and the last world cup at Schladming was the world championships, to be held that year in Canberra, Australia. World champs is a race where everyone always ups their game. I've had custom-made everything over the years, but when 2009 rolled along I was so far past caring I thought I'd go to Canberra with the Santa Cruz V10 as I'd run it all year and have some fun for a change. I had absolutely nothing to lose and to be honest it was the first time ever that I thought I was just heading to a race to make up the numbers. I knew the series was probably lost and I was unmotivated to get on a plane again.

Throughout the season I'd been speaking with my sport psychologist, Dr Robert Copeland, to help me keep focused. I had really wanted to win another world cup series, but you already know how that was going. I had zero motivation going into the race in Canberra and didn't fancy my prospects, but also didn't want to let myself down. I needed a bit of help to refocus. Rob and I played a round of golf at Hillsborough and I vented on him, saying how I'd got a bad back and had not been able to train properly, so what's the point even going to try and race the worlds? Rob calmly said we should just go play golf and he'd have a think. So, off I went to the other side of the world with not much of a plan and even less hope. To acclimatise I got there a week earlier than normal and when I landed in Oz, Rob had dropped me an email with a very simple piece of advice. Just pick one thing a day to do well, he told me, and build on that as the week goes on. Just tick that one thing off each day. So that's what I did.

Ever since I started riding, at some point during the season I would have to deal with lower back problems, and it had been niggling throughout 2009. I had been to see the chiropractor a few times before getting on the twenty-four-hour flight to Australia and I hoped my back would hold out. We spent the first week in the Blue Mountains, just hanging out and having a bit of fun with our Syndicate crew, with me ticking off my daily goals. When I got to the track, I walked it with Greg, scoping out the terrain. I had an idea I could do okay on it. So, on the Tuesday I got four laps in and set the bike up properly with mechanic Ricky Bobby, another student of Andy's who had taken over from Giacomo. We put some smoother-rolling tyres on the front and rear that felt good. Day two I did three more runs but I focused

207

on nailing the rocky sections, which made me happy and was another of my daily goals. I knew I wasn't as fit as I'd been in previous seasons, which was a first for me, so getting the tech sections of the track sorted would be the key to a good result.

That night we all went to the pump track worlds, which was fun to watch and I had a few beers. On Thursday I walked the track again, did a helmet-cam run following Greg, and then we walked the track again. A steady cross-country ride with Brian Lopes rounded off the evening. By now I was really figuring the track out and was building confidence that I might do okay. It was a long flattish run to the finish and you needed to keep your speed up. Due to my lack of fitness I knew Greg would be stronger than me there. Up top, in the rocks and the switchbacks, I knew I was quick. Another thing I did to keep my motivation up was to write both my kids' names on my gloves as a way to focus my attention on my family and the things that made me happy.

On the Friday, Rob Roskopp turned up, another big building block in my race preparation. I did my seeding run but had a big slide out near a bridge and lost my speed going into the most crucial part of the track where I needed to go really fast. This mistake didn't matter too much though as my top split was great. I also had the other guys' splits on the bottom part of the track. I could physically and mentally feel my confidence building hour by hour. I was keeping that to myself though. I had a relaxing evening, ate a nice meal Kathy had made and answered some emails.

On the Saturday we had a team breakfast with me, Greg, Ratboy, Rob, Kathy and Joe Graney, chief engineer at Santa Cruz and later CEO. When we got to the track the fans were turning up and it was getting busy – there was a hum of excitement that only the worlds can create. Thirty thousand mountain bike fans do make quite a noise. There were loads of old friends too, which was lovely, as they'd spent their own money to get to the race. After a warm-up in the early morning I went up on the hill with British team manager Will Longden. I wanted to get some times on the sections where I'd not done well in my seeding run. We ticked them off one by one and made sure I was on pace or better than all the other guys' splits. I then did three full runs and called it a day. I couldn't believe it. A week earlier, I had been sitting at home thinking there was no point going, that I'd blown my fourth world cup title and there was no point travelling just to get beat. Now here I was thinking I could win the bloody thing. The mind of an athlete can be like a jungle sometimes, an impenetrable forest of conflicting thoughts that can change in an instant. Mine was no different.

The section where I was fastest was quite near the top on the most

EVERY KING

technical part of the course. The big benefit of getting that right would be that hopefully I'd do enough at the top to counter any time I might lose at the bottom. All the experience of carrying speed through horrible rock sections back home was going to pay off there. I felt right at home. I knew I'd lose time at the bottom to Greg. He was my main threat; how much I didn't know. I knew that I'd have to pedal like a bastard all the way to the finish line and leave nothing on the track. Now we'd all have to wait.

After our practice runs, Greg and I changed into our civvies and headed up the hill for a track walk, the last one of the weekend. When we hit the bottom we wandered over to the party that was kicking off in the RockShox truck. Every year at the worlds they do a competition for mechanics called the Boxxer world champs, basically a drinking game played while trying to strip and rebuild a suspension fork as quickly as possible. When we got there, Warner was already off his tits on absinthe and greeted me and Greg in the only way he knows, with two bottles of beer in his hands. 'Here you go, lads,' he said. 'Get one down you.'

'No thanks, Rob,' I replied. 'Not today, mate.'

He fired right back with a look in his eyes I'd not seen before.

'Peaty, don't be daft, have a beer. You always have a beer.'

'No thanks, mate.' Greg had already taken his bottle and had a sip. He looked at me more than a little surprised and put his beer back on the table and didn't drink another drop. That made me laugh. Neither Greg nor Rob knew that I'd told my sports psychologist I wouldn't be drinking at all before race day, another first for me. I kept to my word. That evening we went back to our digs, relaxed and I had a little ride on my cross-country bike. I sent some emails to friends and got some back all wishing me the best. I spent some time going through the track in my head, working out every little bump and jump I could use to maintain speed. That night I went to bed, and if you'd done a scan of my brain all that you'd have seen would be those lines and all the spots I knew I'd have to ride perfectly if I wanted to win this thing.

I got to the race site early on Sunday morning. I wanted to have some time to myself to think and see how the track was running. The British Cycling bods were around, turning up once a year as usual to run things their way. I found it quite funny, given all the success I'd had at downhill was nowt to do with them. British Cycling ignored downhill for decades. But I was glad Will Longden was there to be in my corner. The course at Canberra was on Mount Stromlo, although it's hardly a mountain. Its summit is only 770 metres above sea level and we didn't go down anywhere near that, perhaps 150 metres at the most. Top to bottom it took a little over

209

FORGED BY SPEED

two and a half minutes to race down. It was more like racing on a hillock. It was fun to ride though, quite rocky, and dusty in places.

I checked to see if my bike was set up right. One thing I'm completely obsessed about is tyre pressure. I've been riding long enough to know how much pressure is in my tyres. I can guess within a pound per square inch and am never wrong. I also know that different pumps give different readings, so when we use different pumps I know which ones are accurate. Being one of the taller riders on the circuit I move the bike around differently to shorter riders. In turns I push the bike down hard and ride the edge of the tyre a lot. To do this and not lose the back or tuck the front the pressures have to be spot on or the bike feels like a dog.

I think because I grew up riding rigid bikes and cross-country I learned early on how important pressures are in maintaining a line and being able to rely on grip where others may not know there is any, especially on off-cambers. After practice I was 100 per cent happy, but I needed to be. I was going to ask everything of those tyres to hang on to my lines where I knew I could make up time. Just like a surgeon with a scalpel, I was going to have to be absolutely precise to get down this big anthill. Every cut needed to be perfect. It wasn't one of those tracks where you could make a big mistake and because it was so technical make that time back up with some brave moves. This was a one-mistake-and-you've-blown-it kind of track. Perhaps that's why my focus during the week had just got sharper and sharper.

I hadn't seeded fastest but I knew I was fast. Fabien and Mick went off before me. Sam, Greg and Gee would all come down after me. When it was time for my run, Fabien had just knocked Aussie homeboy and my good pal Nathan Rennie off the hot seat with a mighty fine run. He came down with no kneepads on, wearing his school shorts, compression socks and a super-tight shirt on a Mondraker bike with a single crown fork and suspension lockout system. He'd even cut his number plate down to make it more aerodynamic.

If there was one rider who could make me raise my game to another level it was Fabien. After losing to him in Les Gets in 2004, I'd wanted revenge. In stark comparison with the French federation, British Cycling had shown apathy and near disdain for downhill and were useless as a national governing body in supporting us. The French organisation and their applied tactics were second to none. I took it personally when they came for me at the worlds. I can remember too many times when Nico and Fabien benefitted from the support of their federation. My motivation was always to beat them, and I used the lack of support from our federation as more fuel for the fire here as Fabien hoofed Nathan out of the hot seat with a time of two minutes and 31.17 seconds, over three seconds faster on his special bike. This was war. Mick was down next on his GT. It was his home worlds and Mick is one hell of a competitor. He was absolutely fired up and had a great run top to bottom, beating Fabien by 0.15 seconds. Fabien was booted out of the hot seat in the back of a pick-up after getting the seat warm: great news. Me next.

On my run I didn't put a foot wrong and hit every single line I wanted. I was counting on my tyre choices for the long pedal home at the bottom, and hoped they would work out at the top at race speed, and they did. I pinned the rock section like I was riding in the woods at home. Everything went perfectly on the rhythm sections that switched quickly from left to right in the middle part of the course. By split one, halfway down, I was up 1.45 seconds on Mick. By the next split I was still up by 1.46 seconds. Now all I had to do was not lose too much time on the bottom where I knew my fitness wasn't as good. It was a near-perfect run and although I gassed a bit at the bottom and felt my lungs screaming, I pedalled as hard as I could to the finish and gave it absolutely everything. I was fit to collapse at the end. I'd given every single thing I had and channelled all my disappointment about losing the world cup series into that run. I couldn't have done more. My time was two minutes and 30.33 seconds, 0.69 seconds faster than Mick.

I had no idea if it was going to win me the gold, so I had to sit in the back of the truck in the hot seat and wait for the others to come down. Having one more Aussie to go in the shape of Sam, who had qualified faster than me, sat on my hopes like a lead weight on the wings of a butterfly. As Sam came down, thoughts of previous races came back. I tuned out of the noise of the crowd and the people around me. Here I was again, trying to make history, putting myself in the firing line. Adele was at home with George and Jake. There would be no Scott to celebrate with any more when I got back. Rob, Kathy and the team were all here making this possible. I thought about the worlds where I'd come second – to Myles Rockwell in 2000, to Nico in Vail in 2001 and Kaprun in 2002, and to Gee in Val di Sole in 2008 – and of course I thought of Les Gets in 2004.

I'd given up on the dream at the start of this season and here I was sitting in the hot seat again. It was impossible not to hope and dream. Keeping a lid on it was as likely as keeping the lid on a bottle of Coke full of Mentos. *Could I? Would I? Finally?* It would take ten more minutes of soul-churning anxiety before I found out.

I sat in a state of tortured bliss, half here and half there, with Sam on the course and me awaiting my fate. Sam was riding a short-travel bike with flat pedals, wearing shorts and no pads. I'm not sure if I was breathing or not,

FORGED BY SPEED

but I wore mirrored sunglasses to hide my eyes and any tears. Sam was down a second on my time at the first split so I felt confident it wouldn't be him that would unseat me. I couldn't see where he'd make up that time. He'd lost another half a second by the next split. By the end Sam would end up in fourth after losing more time on the bottom flattish section of the track.

Greg was next. *Here we go,* I thought. I had decided Greg would be my biggest threat. He's a skilful, technical rider, but also a machine when it comes to endurance. He was probably the world's best all-rounder on any track on any day. Greg had won the world cup round here in 2008. I hoped and prayed he wouldn't repeat that today. I would know in less than three minutes.

Against the odds, at the first split Greg was 1.15 seconds back on my time. If he had matched my time there, which I thought he might, it would have been game over for me and my crazy dream. I knew I was in with a chance now and felt the noose around my neck loosen a little. I took a breath and welled up – I realised I had been holding my breath. When I saw Greg was 1.22 seconds back at the second split the noose loosened a little more. Another breath. Now came the bottom part where I knew he was fast. This would be interesting as we were both using the same gear ratios. When Greg finally crossed the line, he was five-hundredths of a second down having pulled back almost all the time he had lost to me at the top. I gulped two deep chugs of air as I'd barely breathed for two and a half minutes. I couldn't stop my head from nearly popping. I wasn't staying cool. I was an emotional wreck.

Gee was next and I immediately flashed back to 2008, where it was me in the hot seat again having victory grabbed from me by the new kid on the block. Gee was also riding a special one-off bike for the worlds – different tubing, shorter travel, different suspension, the lot. All Greg and I really had that was different was our tyre choices. I don't mind admitting I nearly died of joy when I saw Gee was down two seconds at the first split. *Sixteen years, four times second* was all I heard in my head. By split two, Gee had lost another half a second. I knew then I'd won.

I started to flood with emotion and lay down in the back of the pick-up. I wanted the world to swallow me up and take me away to a place where I could be alone with my thoughts. At thirty-five years of age, I was finally a world champion. I could hear the crowd yelling as Gee crossed the line. They were chanting my name. I was sobbing my heart out. I got off the back of the pick-up to give Gee a hug. I remember Gee saying, 'Steve, you've done it, mate, you've done it.' I was surrounded by what felt like hundreds of cameras. I remember Josh giving me a huge hug. Brook Macdonald had won juniors earlier in the day and he came and grabbed me, saying 'We've done it, bro!' Although Greg was a bit deflated to have lost by so little, he gave me a huge hug too. He had had a tough weekend with bike problems and had lost his gran a few days before the race. I felt for him; he is one of my best mates on the circuit. I then grabbed a quart of whisky, chugged a load and made my way to the podium.

I still can't describe what it felt like to put that world champs jersey on. I guess it would be like being a fan of Spiderman as a little kid and then putting on your Spiderman outfit and all of a sudden you're Spiderman. It was so surreal, but pulling that jersey on changed everything. Every king needs a crown. I'd had to wait longer for mine than Sam, longer than Gee and longer than Greg. Now I could finally say, 'I am the downhill mountain bike world champion.' I can tell you how it felt getting that monkey off my back: it was like the feeling of being tied to the ground one minute and having no gravity the next. It felt like I was floating away from every single disappointment and upset in my life. I was free of it all.

The relief was there for all to see as the cameras focused on my face. If they hadn't been there, I would have responded very differently. When I knew I'd won, I had the immediate feeling that I wanted to be on my own, with my own thoughts and emotions. Unfortunately, that wasn't possible and that very intimate moment that I needed to have with myself was bottled up for another time. Fans were yelling and screaming, everyone was coming up to me and hugging me. My moment was there to be shared and I was swept away on a sea of joy and shock at finally winning. The tears were pouring out of me in buckets. Eric Carter told me after I crashed in Les Gets, 'Don't worry, mate, you will get it one day.' Eric wasn't in Canberra, but I could see the smile on his face from the other side of the world. After sixteen years of missing out, I had done it.

Later, I was relaxing a bit with Greg and the Santa Cruz team when I remembered something. At the start of the weekend, trail-building hero Glen Jacobs had given me an Aussie dollar coin that he said was lucky. I had put it in my race pants and forgotten about it. I got the coin out and told Greg the story. I also told him that the last time Glen had given someone a coin was Lopes when he also won the worlds. Greg looked at me. 'Glen Jacobs is a bastard. Why didn't he give it to me?' That made us laugh.

FORGED BY SPEED

Just before I got on the plane to fly home, I downloaded over 700 emails and during the flight I read every single one of them. I had got lucky with an exit row seat but was sandwiched between two burly looking blokes. I bet they wondered what was going on, this grown man next to them who kept bursting into tears.

Happy days.

EPILOGUE: NO FINAL CURTAIN

Now we're at the end, although there's been no such thing as retirement from mountain biking for me. In fact, I've just spent a week in Stoke hospital with three broken ribs, a collapsed lung, tubes draining fluid from all sorts of places, a broken collarbone, broken knuckles on my left hand to match the ones on the right, and a huge gash on my left calf that needed an operation to sort out. Those rollers at Dyfi Bike Park looked easy enough to jump. Or at least, I thought they did. The lick of the flame on the wings of desire has not waned for me. It's the first big off I've had for a while, so I've not done so badly. Most people spend their lives avoiding getting into dangerous situations on pushbikes. I've been lucky enough to get paid and have a career doing the exact opposite.

I haven't looked back with regret or through rose-tinted glasses. I raced my last world cup at Vallnord on 4 September 2016, aged forty-two. The send-off I got there was phenomenal. My race number for the day was 53 and I wasn't an automatic qualifier. So, the nerves were there. I didn't want to screw up qualification. I wanted to go out on the last run of my career by getting into the finals, which I did, finishing forty-fourth on the day. I had a ball, but the steep track in Andorra was always hard on me. My result showed I couldn't get off the brakes at the bottom and let the bike flow.

So many people came by during the weekend to wish me well. Legendary custom painters Fatcreations made a very special Spitfire-themed bike for me. A lot of tears were shed from close friends, teammates and competitors. The mountain bike family that I am part of made me feel loved. It was truly humbling. What a lucky bugger I have been.

The send-off at Vallnord was a happier vibe than my goodbye to the

EPILOGUE: NO FINAL CURTAIN

home fans earlier in the year at Fort William. That was a very different day. My speech at the end of the weekend was a difficult one. We'd only just lost our pal Stevie Smith in a dirt bike accident and I was pretty affected by that and not able to enjoy my home race farewell. I found it difficult to articulate what I wanted to say to all the fans that had supported me for so long. Stevie's passing affected the world of mountain biking in the same way Jason's had decades earlier. They were both family, our family. I was devastated when Stevie died.

You'll have gathered by now that I like to keep busy, so every single year since I've raced mountain bikes I've filled every day with something. There is no off switch. That part of me will never change and in the years I've been retired from racing it's still the same. I am lucky and blessed that I have a legacy to look back on. Only Greg and Aaron Gwin have won more world cup races than me. It's nice to have set a benchmark, both in results and also in having an approach to racing that some may say has no place in mountain biking any more. Maybe I'm the last of the old-time rock 'n' rollers, who, like my old pal Palmer, lived those words. Or like the motocross world champion Graham Noyce, whose fun but professional approach was a mirror in many ways to mine.

The sport is very different now in many ways and my boots are empty as far as I can see. I've left a legacy that took a hell of a lot of hard work and gallons to drink. Early on I made a pact with myself that I wouldn't sacrifice my happiness and the way I wanted to live my life for sport. It would have to work in a way where I could have my cake and eat it too. On the balance of things, I've done more than I ever thought I could.

I never would have achieved what I did without the help and support of good friends and the teams that gave me what I needed to compete at the highest level. It wasn't until I'd had that life-changing chat with Rob Roskopp that I really felt valued by a brand. It was a moment in time I will cherish for the rest of my life. I would not have been as successful as I was without being on Rob's team. I guess I was lucky. Led Zeppelin had their manager Peter Grant to guide them and look after them. At Santa Cruz we had Kathy Sessler. Kathy was a tour de force, and with her at every world cup, the Santa Cruz team – Rennie, Greg, Ratboy and me – were able to focus all our energies on racing. While I wouldn't be so presumptuous as to talk for the other Santa Cruz members, she was unreal for us guys. I never felt so supported. She helped make every day on the circuit better.

The media have been good to me and I to them. I said yes to just about everything they suggested, and for that I became one of the best-known cyclists in the world, even if at times I did some daft stuff that they thought

218

EPILOGUE: NO FINAL CURTAIN

was funny or cool, but which I thought was naff. I tried to keep everybody happy and due to my absolute love for mountain biking I'd do just about anything if it meant more people would get into the sport I love so passionately. If that makes me an ambassador for mountain biking then it's a badge I gladly wear, beside the pisshead one on the other lapel. I'm the open book of racers and I guess I've done okay by that. To be accepted and loved by the fans and other riders was an honour. It humbles me to acknowledge that I have a following. To be able to connect with so many people cannot be put into words, but the sense of community I feel as soon as I get on my bike takes my breath away even now. I owe mountain biking a career, a family, a home and a way of life. To be able to live as I do and be accepted by my peers is the greatest feeling ever.

I don't have any words of wisdom to offer. I am literally a near-qualified plumber who was handy on a bike. It's extraordinary, all the things I got asked to do and the people I got to meet. Life changes quickly when you succeed at sport. People see you as more than just a bloke on the street, but I am the bloke on the street. All the awards ceremonies, TV appearances, interviews and other activities that go on outside of race day were okay but I always took them with a pinch of salt. After the last race is won, those things slowly disappear like little paper boats down a stream. All the stars at Sports Personality of the Year have to wipe their own noses. No one is more or less special than anyone else. I've enjoyed those experiences but pay no thought to their value to me. After I retired, I suppose I could have walked away. That was never what I was going to do though. I loved riding too much and still love it, and so it continues.

One of the most enjoyable parts of my career has been helping other riders. The joy I felt when Josh won the junior world championships in 2008 at Val di Sole was just one highlight. I've been so lucky to get involved in helping to bring on Neil Donoghue, Rich Barlow, Stu Thomson, Brendan Fairclough and Marc Beaumont, to name a few, and all the Steve Peat Syndicate crew. I knew at the time that at some point they would be competing with me, but I always felt that bringing them on was more important than my ego. All of them have gone on to do great things on bikes and for our community. I get a lot of satisfaction out of that.

As an ambassador and team coach for Santa Cruz I go to world cup races to offer anything I can to our current team. Santa Cruz's European base is in Morzine and I don't need an excuse to get out there as often as I can because I love the mountains, summer or winter. Until recently I was still a shareholder in Royal Racing, the company I started with Nick Bayliss back in 1998. We put the cash to good use as a way of helping other downhill racers

EPILOGUE: NO FINAL CURTAIN

with sponsorship. I sold those shares in 2023 as my connection with Santa Cruz and their sponsors created an unnecessary conflict of interest. These days I'm head to tail in Fox gear, Monster logos and all our Syndicate partners' labels.

I've made some great friends on the circuit, people I'd never have met if it weren't for riding, and out of my normal circle of Sheffield drinking pals. I launched a new brand called Peaty's Products in 2017 with Bryn Morgan and Tom Makin, who I met through the Steve Peat Syndicate. We make useful functional products for mountain bikers. Tom is no longer working with us, but we brought BMX legend Martin Murray on board and things have really started to take off.

Being the dad of two teenage sons takes up a lot of time, as does riding the occasional trial and keeping an eye on my property portfolio. Racing also still plays a huge part in my life and I cherry-pick events I like to race in to keep the old bones from seizing up. The drinking has calmed down a little but the joy of socially necking a good few will never leave me. Due to my mountain bike career, Adele and I have always spent a lot of time apart. That's been hard at times. I still travel a lot now but try to make the most of our time together when I'm home.

Mountain biking was something I found for myself that I could do on my own. That came from necessity. I wasn't going to follow in the old man's footsteps and be a trials rider. I would love to have been, but the planets weren't aligned that way. I found something I enjoyed that wasn't Dad's. I did it without him because I had to, or nothing would have happened. Mountain biking became my world and my responsibility, where I could fix my own bike and get myself to the races, no one else needed. It was the making of me.

I didn't get a lot of acknowledgement from the old fella over the years. He came up to Fort William to watch me race and gave me a smile when I won. Mostly though he stayed in his own world. I'm not sure if that bothered me or not, but I'm guessing every kid wants their parents to be proud of them. Stepping out of his shadow and into the light of my own life is something I am eternally grateful for and something I have never taken for granted. And anyway, I always had support from Mum. I felt guided in some way by something – maybe you'd call it fate, others might call it luck, but I am eternally grateful for it. Everything I have came from a love of the outdoors, graft and playing hard. Oh, and bikes.

So why stop?

ACKNOWLEDGEMENTS

I have so many friends, teammates, fans, brands and sponsors to thank for making my mountain bike adventure so good over the years. Most of you know who you are and I want you to know how grateful I am for everything – every single race or championship I have won, you have all been a part of it. Thanks for all the rides, giggles, cheers and fun.

A few special mentions go to: Adele, Jake and George; Mum, Dad, Jonny and Andy; Rob Roskopp and Kathy Sessler for the belief and vision; and everyone past and present at Santa Cruz Bicycles. Also, a huge thank you to Tim March, who's gone above and beyond, scrolling through my diaries, recording our phone calls and turning these things into what's in your hands now.

Cheers, all.

BLACK & WHITE PHOTOGRAPHS

Photography and images © Steve Peat Collection unless otherwise credited.

Page ii: At the BMBF National Downhill Championships at Eastridge Woods in 1993. © Malcolm Fearon/blissimages.com

Page vi: Standing in the start gate at Mont-Sainte-Anne, Canada. © Sven Martin

Page x: A school portrait. What a handsome chap!

Page 12: Dad competing in the 1975 Scottish Six Days Trial.

Page 20: Pulling a wheelie on the campsite in Fort William.

Page 30: Primary school class portrait. I'm in the back row, in the middle.

Page 40: The Muddy Fox Roadrunner – I've still got it!

Page 50: The Langsett Cycles team – I'm on the right.

Page 60: Washing my first downhill bike in Mum and Dad's back garden.

Page 70: My first magazine appearance, *Mountain Biking UK*, January 1993.

Page 82: Racing the Grundig world cup in Plymouth in 1993.

Page 92: My first *Mountain Biking UK* cover. I was interviewed by Jim McRoy.

Page 106: Steve Behr's iconic photo of JMC looking cool as fuck, taken during the shoot for *Dirt*. © Steve Behr/Stockfile

Page 118: Andy Kyffin, Rob Roskopp and me at Vallnord in 2016. © Sven Martin

Page 126: Finally on top of the box after winning my first world cup at Snoqualmie Pass in 1996. © Malcolm Fearon/blissimages.com

Page 136: My diary entry from Christmas Day, 1999. I didn't drink too much!

BLACK & WHITE PHOTOGRAPHS

Page 148: Warner and me during a *Dirt* magazine shoot. © Paul Bliss
Page 160: Racing in Troy Lee's custom beer can helmet at Livigno in 2004 having already wrapped up the world cup series overall win. © Victor Lucas
Page 170: The Golden Princess. © Paul Bliss
Page 180: High-fiving the fans after finally winning at Fort William in 2005. © Steve Behr/Stockfile
Page 190: Me and a young Josh 'Ratboy' Bryceland! © Steve Behr/Stockfile
Page 202: No caption needed! © Sven Martin
Page 215: My world champs jersey and gold medal. © Sven Martin
Page 216: Cheers!
Page 221: Me, Jake and Uncle Greg riding back to our accommodation after I wrapped up the overall in 2006. © Victor Lucas